Imperial
Brain Trust

Imperial Brain Trust

The Council on Foreign Relations
and United States Foreign Policy

Laurence H. Shoup
and William Minter

Authors Choice Press

New York Lincoln Shanghai

Imperial Brain Trust
The Council on Foreign Relations and United States Foreign Policy

All Rights Reserved © 1977, 2004 by Laurence H. Shoup & William Minter

No part of this book may be reproduced or transmitted in any form or by any means, graphic, electronic, or mechanical, including photocopying, recording, taping, or by any information storage or retrieval system, without the written permission of the publisher.

Authors Choice Press
an imprint of iUniverse, Inc.

For information address:
iUniverse, Inc.
2021 Pine Lake Road, Suite 100
Lincoln, NE 68512
www.iuniverse.com

Originally published by Monthly Review Press

ISBN: 0-595-32426-6

Printed in the United States of America

Contents

Foreword by *G. William Domhoff*   vii

Preface   1

Introduction   3

I: A Portrait of the Council on Foreign Relations

1. A Brief History of the Council   11
2. The Council Network   57
3. The Council and the New York Financial Oligarchy   85

II: The Council on Foreign Relations and United States Foreign Policy, 1939-1975

4. Shaping a New World Order: The Council's Blueprint for Global Hegemony, 1939-1944   117

5. Implementing the Council's World View:
   Case Studies in United States Foreign Policy   188
6. The Council and American Policy in
   Southeast Asia, 1940-1975   223
7. Toward the 1980s: The Council's Plans
   for a New World Order   254

Postscript   285

Appendices
  1. Key Leaders of the Council, 1921-1972   289
  2. Trilateral Commission Membership, 1975   291
  3. Council Directors, 1921-1975   301

Bibliography   303

Index   327

Foreword
by G. William Domhoff

The book you are about to read is one of the most important works of Marxian historical sociology on the workings of twentieth-century United States capitalism since James Weinstein's *The Corporate Ideal in the Liberal State* appeared in 1968. Its painstakingly researched revelations about how monopoly capitalists in the Council on Foreign Relations carefully and secretively planned the policies of modern-day imperialism and then introduced them into government will come as a surprise even to those who have followed the ugly manifestations of these policies with great care.

Just as Weinstein's book showed us how the leading capitalists at the turn of the century created the National Civic Federation to discuss new ways to deflect their growing conflict with organized labor and socialists, so Laurence Shoup and William Minter in *Imperial Brain Trust* show us through close analysis of hitherto little-noticed position papers, memos, and personal letters how the most sophisticated corporate capitalists of the thirties and forties used the Council on Foreign Relations to develop an aggressive and expansion ist foreign policy for the post–World War II era, thereby helping to avert the possibility of another depression and renewed class struggle. Not only do they reconstruct the precise process by which this general strategy was developed, but they show how the Council leaders defended the strategy in the fifties and sixties by means of specific counterrevolutionary actions around the world. Although it may seem unlikely that further light could be shed on the origins of the much-studied war in Vietnam and the rest of Southeast Asia, they have managed to do that too, demonstrating how it was the outcome of the deliberations of various Council study groups which met during the forties and fifties.

In *Imperial Brain Trust* we learn in great detail about how leading capitalist planners think and act in relation to the American economy and the rest of the world. We learn that their thinking is exactly what we might expect on the basis of writings on the nature of American imperialism by Marxian political economists. This is not only a gratifying verification of theoretical expectations, but a highly useful book for educational purposes. Most Americans have a conception of power based in liberal ideology which refuses to believe that power can be known except by seeing it in action, that is, by seeing the process through which it operates. In *Imperial Brain Trust* we see major capitalists thinking and acting in their own interests to such an obvious and base degree that it will satisfy this process-oriented desire to know how "they" do it—and why they do it. Readers of this book will have a very vivid sense of what is meant by the seemingly abstract concept of "imperialism."

Before telling us how the ruling-class leaders created their imperial policies for the post–World War II era, however, the authors devote three chapters to the social, economic, and political connections of their primary object of study, the Council on Foreign Relations. They also trace the history and financing of this seldom-studied private organization. All this is intimately linked to the later chapters, for just as Marx wrote in a preface to the first volume of *Capital* that "here individuals are dealt with only insofar as they are the personifications of economic categories," so the authors of this study have traced the class and corporate connections of Council leaders and members to establish for even the most skeptical reader that the Council on Foreign Relations is the quintessential personification of United States imperialism.

Sociological information on the Council and its leaders is important not only to demonstrate this fact, but to remind us once again that capitalists do not easily and automatically deduce their policies and programs from a general reading of the laws of motion of capital. They too must labor to formulate new strategies and try to compromise conflicts among themselves, and in order to accomplish these tasks they have to develop institutional settings such as the Council on Foreign Relations. As the authors rightly and nicely emphasize, organizations like the Council on Foreign Relations are necessary in helping the capitalist class move from a class-in-itself to a class-for-itself.

The chapters at the heart of the book, four, five, and six, tell us how the Council on Foreign Relations led the American government into the policies that culminated in the murderous Vietnam war. This, as I said, is very revealing reading for even the most astute of foreign policy students, and it is a real contribution. But it should not allow us to overlook the more tentative information in the final chapter, where the authors turn to the ongoing projects of the Council on Foreign Relations, and provide insights that may help politically in dealing with the next phase of imperialism. This final chapter concerns the Council's so-called 1980s Project in conjunction with the now-famous Trilateral Commission, which had Jimmy Carter and Fritz Mondale among its early members. It tells us how the most internationally minded corporate capitalists and their political allies are striving to respond

x   *Foreword*

to the crises that their earlier policies created. This future-oriented chapter is important because leftist political strategy must take into account not only the nature of the present capitalist crisis (capitalists are always facing one crisis or another), but the capitalists' likely response to this crisis. The historical lesson can be found early in this century when the aforementioned National Civic Federation's new policies helped to slow the rise of the Socialist Party. Weinstein summarizes this dialectic as follows, after noting that fierce trade-union battles and the growth of the socialist movement had forced capitalists to move toward "humanizing" large-scale production.

> Ironically, these struggles finally led to the emergence of a unified socialist movement just as the more sophisticated corporations were beginning to organize to reduce overt class antagonism and the threat of class-conscious politics that a frustrated trade union movement was producing. . . . But precisely because the development of corporate liberalism was in large part a response to the long-term struggles in which the Socialists participated, it was difficult for them to understand the changes in the political economy then taking place. (*Ambiguous Legacy*, 1975, pp. 3-4)

In short, far-sighted capitalists, through the National Civic Federation, created reform policies that helped to outmaneuver a growing socialist movement. The message is clear: capitalists are not a standing target. They move, too, and they do so in part through organizations such as the Council on Foreign Relations. *Imperial Brain Trust* is not merely history, then, it is potentially prologue. As with all good Marxian scholarship, it can be an aid to political action as well as in political and scholarly education. It deserves a wide and careful reading inside and outside the classroom.

—*G. William Domhoff*

Preface

As part of our academic training, both of us had started research on the Council on Foreign Relations before we met. We were both convinced that such research could help understand how and why American foreign policy was really made. After our initial discussions and pooling of information, we reached the conclusion that we should try to put our results together in a book. Work on this project, from its first stages in early 1973 to the completion of the manuscript in December 1975, and final revisions in July 1976, was a joint effort. Both of us carried out research in archives, libraries, and manuscript collections. Both conducted interviews with individuals having first-hand knowledge of the Council on Foreign Relations and its activities. The introduction and first chapter were jointly written, but each of us had primary responsibility for certain of the other chapters: Bill for Chapters 2, 3, and 5; Larry for Chapters 4, 6, and 7. Even in these chapters there was an extensive interchange of ideas and drafts, however, so that we are jointly responsible for the whole book.

We would like to thank especially the following people for

their help in completion of the book: Suzanne Baker Shoup, who from start to finish served as an indispensable critic of both form and content, and who also typed the final manuscript; G. William Domhoff, who read over early drafts and made many helpful comments; and Harry Braverman, our editor at Monthly Review, who gave us an astute and useful critique at a key stage in the book's development. We also express our appreciation to several others who contributed to the book either as dissertation advisers or critics of all or part of the manuscript: Ruth Minter, Richard W. Leopold, Thomas A. Krueger, Robert H. Wiebe, Paul A. Hirning, David Wiley, Edward Silva, Robert Alford, Joseph Elder, and Thomas McCormick. Any errors which remain are, of course, our own.

W.M.   L.H.S.
July 1976

Introduction

Over fifty years ago, in the wake of the First World War, a group of wealthy and influential Americans decided to form an organization. The Council on Foreign Relations, as it was subsequently named, was designed to equip the United States of America for an imperial role on the world scene. Great Britain had dominated world politics during the nineteenth century, not only through its colonial empire, but also through an even wider informal sphere of influence. In a similar fashion, so felt these American leaders, would the United States play a dominant role in the years following the war.

But in 1919 the United States was not yet adequately prepared for world leadership, as was well illustrated by the confusion surrounding the issue of United States membership in the League of Nations. Even the leaders of opinion had been unable to arrive at a common understanding of the part the United States should take in world affairs. The Council on Foreign Relations would help remedy this defect. By keeping "its members in touch with the international situation"[1] and devoting itself to a continuous study of the "in-

4 Introduction

ternational aspects of America's political, economic and financial problems,"[2] it would develop a "reasoned American foreign policy."[3] As one early statement of aims ambitiously noted, the Council on Foreign Relations "plans to cooperate with the Government and all existing international agencies, and to bring all of them into constructive accord."[4]

The Council on Foreign Relations still exists today, more than half a century later. Yet it is hardly a household word. Even many of those Americans who are relatively well informed about foreign policy recognize it, if at all, only as the organization which publishes *Foreign Affairs* magazine. The Council is rarely mentioned in the press or on television. The number of articles, scholarly or otherwise, devoted to its activities is minuscule, even if one adds together the output of over fifty years. The lack of public attention might suggest that the Council's importance does not match its original ambitious goals. One might conclude that it had become simply another discussion group, or a specialized research organization, of little interest except to its own members, and not particularly important to the overall picture of United States foreign policy formation.

But such a conclusion would be profoundly mistaken. Reading the occasional references to the Council that do appear from time to time, one gets quite a different picture:

> *New York Times:* "The Council's membership includes some of the most influential men in government, business, education and the press."[5] The CFR "for nearly half a century has made substantial contributions to the basic concepts of American foreign policy."[6]
>
> *Newsweek:* The Council's leadership is the "foreign-policy establishment of the U.S."[7]
>
> Peter Schrag: The Council is "the ultimate organization of the Eastern Establishment."[8]
>
> Theodore White: "The Council counts among its members probably more important names in American life than any other private group in the country."[9]
>
> Marvin and Bernard Kalb: The Council is "an extremely influ-

ential private group that is sometimes called the *real* State Department."[10]

Richard Barnet: Membership in the Council is "a rite of passage for an aspiring national security manager."[11]

As several of the quotes imply, just the names of members give an impressive picture of Council importance. The current Council chairman is David Rockefeller of Chase Manhattan Bank, a man with incredible personal wealth and financial power. Wall Street lawyer Allen W. Dulles, a Council director for over forty years, helped establish the CIA and directed it while his brother John Foster (also a Council member) ran the Department of State. Diplomatic superstar Henry A. Kissinger was a Council protégé who began his career in foreign affairs as a rapporteur for a Council study group. Kissinger later told Council leader Hamilton Fish Armstrong, who had played a key role in Kissinger's rise to power, "You invented me."[12] The list could easily be prolonged with eminent financiers, Wall Street lawyers, Ivy League scholars, and high government officials—in short, a galaxy of "establishment" figures.[13]

It is such intriguing indications of the Council's significance that led us to a more detailed investigation of this little-known organization. Our results show that the Council on Foreign Relations, despite its relative public obscurity, plays a key part in molding United States foreign policy. In the Council, the leading sectors of big business get together with the corporate world's academic experts to work out a general framework for foreign policy.

Since the Second World War at the latest, the Council has had remarkable success in getting its point of view across to the government, regardless of the administration in office. As government officials, Council members have implemented policies. As "experts," they have generally succeeded in keeping public debate in line with "respectable" views. But they are by no means omnipotent. The decline of United States power faces them with new problems: defeat in Indochina, and the new independence shown by Japan, Western Europe, and the oil-producing countries. They are resourceful, however, and are presently busy thinking up new ways to maintain United States predominance and to convince the American people that such a role is best for everyone.

That the Council is little known is thus not a sign of insignificance, but rather points to its mode of operation. The men at the top meet and work out together the general direction of policy—the limits of respectable debate. Through a complex network of channels, the content and tone of their discussion reach the policymakers and the leaders of opinion. Eventually they may reach those of us who take an interest in what our country is doing in the world, but we may have little idea that what comes to be a natural "climate of opinion" was carefully fostered and guided. For the process is not public. Council members are selected by the Council's leadership and the meetings are confidential. As the *New York Times* expressed it, "Except for its annual public Elihu Root Lectures, the Council's talks and seminars are strictly off the record. An indiscretion can be grounds for termination or suspension of membership."[14]

Despite this conscious secrecy, it is possible to find out something about what the Council is and does. Putting together bits and pieces from many sources and searching out references to Council activities in government archives, we have put together a picture of the inner workings and significance of the Council. Our conclusions challenge the conventional interpretations of policy formation as dispersed among a wide variety of groups or elites. In contrast to this view, we will show, in the pages to follow, the leading role played by the Council on Foreign Relations and the sector of society it represents, the corporate upper class.

We believe that the process itself is not only undemocratic, but that the results have been and are against the interests of both the majority of the American people and of the people of the world.

Notes

1. Shepardson, 1960:3.
2. CFR, 1922:1.
3. Ibid.
4. CFR, 1919:5.
5. *New York Times,* January 14, 1975:18.
6. *New York Times,* May 15, 1966:34.
7. *Newsweek,* September 6, 1971:74.
8. Schrag, 1974:130.
9. White, 1965:87.
10. Kalb and Kalb, 1974:51.
11. Barnet, 1972:49. White, Marvin Kalb, and Barnet are all Council members.
12. *Newsweek,* October 2, 1972:40.
13. For journalistic commentaries on the Council and its prominent members, see Kraft (1958), Campbell (1971), and Lukas (1971). For the only previous systematic scholarly treatment of the Council and its membership, see Domhoff (1970), Chapter 5.
14. *New York Times,* May 15, 1966:34. Quoted in Domhoff, 1970:120.

I
A Portrait of the Council on Foreign Relations

The Council on Foreign Relations (CFR) is a key part of a network of people and institutions usually referred to by friendly observers as "the establishment." In the three chapters of this section we will sketch the Council's history and elaborate its links to the United States government, large foundations, mass media, elite universities, other private policy planning organizations, and the largest and most internationally oriented sector of the U.S. capitalist class.

1
A Brief History of the Council

Founding and Early History: 1918-1939

The Beginnings in Paris

The origins of the Council on Foreign Relations lie in the reactions of a small number of American "men of affairs" to the First World War. At the Versailles Conference a group of American and British participants began discussing the need for an organization which could engage in the continuous study of international relations. The official history of the Council's first fifteen years describes the problems faced at the conference in these terms:

> Under the pressure of a public opinion which was impatient to be done with war-making and peace-making, decisions had to be taken in haste; and the minds of diplomats, generals, admirals, financiers, lawyers and technical experts were not sufficiently well furnished to enable them to function satisfactorily on critical issues at top speed. Realizing their own shortcomings, some of these men found themselves talking with others about a way of providing against such a state of things in the future.[1]

11

12   Imperial Brain Trust

While the Versailles Conference revealed difficulties, it also showed some of those present a way of coping with them:

> In Paris were brought together leaders of thought and action from the same country and the same race, who had never before met for intercourse in their own land under one roof. More effective agencies for creating an opinion on international affairs at once charitable, sane, and well-informed have never been devised than these delegations so long as they existed.[2]

Thus on May 30, 1919, at the Majestic Hotel in Paris, a group of Americans and British agreed to form an Anglo-American organization. It was officially named the Institute of International Affairs and was to have branches in the United Kingdom and the United States.

While the idea for such an organization seems to have been "in the air" in Paris, the conception of the scheme was primarily that of British historian Lionel Curtis, formerly a colonial official in South Africa.[3] For the previous nine years Curtis had been in charge of setting up a network of semi-secret organizations in the British Dominions and the United States.[4] These bodies, called the Round Table Groups, were established by Lord Milner, a former British secretary of state for war, and his associates in 1908-1911. "The original purpose of the groups was to seek to federate the English-speaking world along lines laid down by Cecil Rhodes and William T. Stead, and the money for the organizational work came originally from the Rhodes Trust."[5]

Rhodes was an extremely wealthy imperialist whose will to power is illustrated by a statement he once made to a friend: "The world is nearly all parcelled out, and what there is left of it is being divided up, conquered, and colonized. To think of these stars that you see overhead at night, these vast worlds which we can never reach. I would annex the planets if I could; I often think of that."[6] Rhodes declared that his life ambition was "the furtherance of the British Empire, the bringing of the whole uncivilized world under its rule, the recovery of the United States of America, the making of the Anglo-Saxon race into one Empire."[7] To achieve this grandiose end in 1891 Rhodes proposed the founding of a worldwide organization for the preservation and extension of the British Empire. The original purpose of the Round Table was thus to establish an "organic union" for the entire British Empire with one imperial government, and to try to associate other nations with the empire. Curtis and Philip Kerr (later Lord Lothian) were the two full-time activists in this scheme, which was backed by money from Milner, who had access to large funds as a Rhodes trustee.

The Round Table Groups kept in touch by visits and correspondence, and published, beginning in 1910, the magazine *The Round Table*, with anonymous contributors and even an anonymous editorial board. During the First World War, Round Table leaders were important in the formulation of British war aims, and many came to Paris as part of the British delegation.[8]

American leaders were also concerned with war objectives. Shortly after American entry into the war, President Woodrow Wilson and his close adviser, Col. Edward M. House, established a special planning body, under House's direction, to develop United States war aims and its negotiating position at the peace conference. This organization, called the Inquiry, was composed chiefly of academic intellectuals whose efforts marked the first attempt to use teams of scholars to plan long-term foreign policy. Prominent among the Inquiry planners and Wilson-House advisers were a few Americans who had been members of the United States Round Table Group, including historian George Louis Beer, the United States correspondent for *The Round Table* during the war years, Thomas W. Lamont of the powerful J. P. Morgan banking house, and former Rhodes scholar Whitney H. Shepardson. Shepardson was to become one of the key figures in the Council on Foreign Relations, as well as a continuing *Round Table* correspondent. Beer met with Curtis in Paris and discussed the need for an additional joint Anglo-American organization to plan foreign policy and international relations.[9] Beer and Curtis then brought the Americans and British together at the Majestic Hotel meeting on May 30.

A committee of six was appointed to carry the proposal for the Institute of International Affairs forward. It consisted of international lawyer and State Department official James Brown Scott, Inquiry historians Archibald Cary Coolidge (Harvard) and James T. Shotwell (Columbia), all of the United States, and three British representatives. By June 17, a meeting was held to vote the new organization into existence, with its purpose "to keep its members in touch with the international situation and enable them to study the relation between national policies and the interests of society as a whole."[10] Lionel Curtis and Whitney H. Shepardson became the joint secretaries of the British and American branches respectively.

Organizational Beginnings in New York

While the British branch of the institute moved rapidly to establish itself, becoming known as the Royal Institute of International Affairs, or, more informally, Chatham House, the American section faltered, with no one taking the initiative to get a program and working organization started. At the same time, however, another fledgling group, the Council on Foreign Relations, was also suffering from inactivity. It had begun in 1918 as "a dinner club which gave those residents of New York City who were interested in international affairs—and who could afford expensive meals—an opportunity to hear speeches by distinguished foreign visitors."[11] The Council's handbook for 1919 relates its origin as follows:

In the late spring of 1918 a few gentlemen came together at a conference at the Metropolitan Club, New York, to discuss the most interesting and vital subjects concerned with the United States and its relations with the rest of the world. Two or three meetings were held, which showed that much could be learned and much good could be accomplished by such conferences, made up of people who were concerned in the world's affairs in a large way . . .

The object of the Council on Foreign Relations is to afford a continuous conference on foreign affairs, bringing together at each meeting international thinkers so that in the course of a year several hundred expert minds in finance, industry, education, statecraft and science will have been brought to bear on international problems.

It is a board of Initiation—a Board of Invention. It plans to cooperate with the Government and all existing international agencies and to bring all of them into constructive accord.[12]

Honorary chairman of the Council was Elihu Root, Wall Street lawyer and former secretary of state and secretary of war. The chairman was another New York lawyer, Lindsay Russell, and the chairman of the Finance Committee was Alexander Hemphill, chairman of the Guaranty Trust bank. The organization was composed almost entirely of "high-ranking officers of banking, manufacturing, trading and finance companies, together with many lawyers . . . concerned primarily with the effect that the war and the treaty of peace might have on post-war business."[13] Quite active in 1918 and 1919, the Council had fallen inactive by mid-1920. The officers of the Council suggested a merger with the American Institute of International Affairs.

Shortly thereafter, a new committee on policy was created to take responsibility for working out the merger. Shepardson became executive secretary of the committee, and George W. Wickersham its chairman. Wickersham was yet another Wall Street lawyer and had been President Taft's attorney general.[14] This committee set the directions for the new, merged organization, officially established in August 1921, which took the name of the Council on Foreign Relations, Inc.

The board, chosen by the committee on policy, was composed mainly of lawyers, bankers, and educators. It elected the new officers of the organization: Elihu Root, honorary president, John W. Davis, president, Paul D. Cravath, vice-president, and Edwin F. Gay, secretary and treasurer.[15] In its 1922 statement of purpose, the fifteen-man board reaffirmed the goals of the organization:

> The Council on Foreign Relations aims to provide a continuous conference on the international aspects of America's political, economic and financial problems ... It simply is a group of men concerned in spreading a knowledge of international relations, and, in particular, in developing a reasoned American foreign policy.[16]

The background of its officers also gives some clue as to the early direction of the Council. Elihu Root, the honorary president, was the prototype of the Wall Street lawyer and the elder statesman of the period. As one of his protégés and later secretary of state and secretary of war, Henry L. Stimson, observed: "He was the unchallenged leader of our bar, both in the state and in the nation."[17] Root was an early leader in America's imperial expansion, being responsible for organizing the administration of the overseas territories won by the United States in the Spanish-American War. He acted as counsel for several leading American corporations and banks of the time. In addition he advised Andrew Carnegie on his philanthropies, and served as first president of the Carnegie Endowment for International Peace.

While Elihu Root was one of the most prominent Republicans of his day, the president of the Council, John W. Davis, was almost as outstanding in Democratic politics. Davis had served as a congressman from West Virginia, and had then been chosen by President Wilson first as solicitor general and then as ambassador to Great Britain. Following the war and the peace conference, he set up a law practice in New York, became chief counsel for J. P. Morgan and Company, and was the Democratic presidential candidate in 1924. Vice-president Paul D. Cravath was also a New York lawyer, with a firm that had become one of Wall Street's largest and most prestigious, Cravath, Swaine and Moore.

Edwin F. Gay was the only "scholar" among the top officers. An economic historian and the first dean of the Harvard Business School, he had worked during the war as director of planning and statistics of the Shipping Board, which reported directly to President Wilson. At the end of the war he became editor of the *New York Evening Post,* owned by Thomas W. Lamont. Lamont had suggested to Shepardson that Gay would be a good member for the Institute of International Affairs. He was added to the membership in October 1920, subsequently joining the original committee on policy as well.

Foreign Affairs *Magazine and the Council's Goals*

It was Gay who seems to have taken the initiative to get the Council's first major program under way: publication of a magazine designed to be the "authoritative" source on foreign affairs. Gay suggested his Harvard colleague (and original institute member) Archibald Cary Coolidge as the first editor, and Hamilton Fish Armstrong, a reporter on the *Post,* as Coolidge's assistant and executive director of the Council. Another member of Gay's staff, Cass Canfield, later president and chairman of the board of Harper and Row, was assigned to raise the initial funds for the journal.

With $125,000 as his goal, Canfield found little difficulty in getting half that sum from members of the board and their friends. After some thought, he succeeded in obtaining the rest with a letter of solicitation to "the thousand richest Americans," signed by the Council directors. The second half of the $125,000 came in within ten days.[18] The first issue was published in September 1922. Gay had regarded the publication of a magazine as a crucial first step, and hoped it would become the most important magazine in the field. Evidently satisfied that this objective was being attained, the Council reported in 1924 that *"Foreign Affairs* has established itself as the most authoritative American review dealing with international relations."[19] By the time the Council wrote its fifteen-year history in 1937, the description of the journal's success was even more extravagant:

> In the fifteen years since its first number appeared, *Foreign Affairs* has won wide recognition because of the authoritative character of its contributed articles and the judicious temper of its editorial direction. Leading statesmen, economists, publicists and scholars of all nationalities representing a great variety of points of view are numbered among its contributors, and it is now regarded as the most authoritative publication of its character in any country.[20]

While Council claims may be somewhat inflated by pride, there is no doubt that the journal has been virtually unchallenged as the leading American periodical dealing with foreign affairs and practically the only one read regularly by decision-makers and "men of affairs" as well as academic scholars.

The intent of *Foreign Affairs,* as explained by an editorial note in the first issue, was "to guide American opinion," but to do so not by identifying itself with one school of opinion, but by keeping open to divergent ideas, "while keeping clear of mere vagaries."[21] The goal of "guiding public opinion" was felt at the time to be particularly crucial because of the failure of the United States to participate in the League of Nations. Many of those involved in forming the Council were, as has been seen, present at the Paris conference. A number were strong believers in the Wilsonian ideals embodied in the League charter. Gay, for example, with Lamont's approval, threw the editorial weight of the *New York Evening Post* behind the Democratic candidate for President, Cox, in 1920, primarily because of the failure of the Republicans to come out for ratification of the League. None of the Council leaders were among the die-hard opposition to the League, although some, such as Elihu Root and George W. Wickersham, were Republicans and leaders of the so-called mild reservationists. However, even those most enthusiastic in supporting Wilson's ideals tended to feel that he had made mistakes in not building the necessary support at home for the League, and, in particular, had erred in not including a man such as Elihu Root in the Paris delegation. The Council can be seen, in part, as an attempt to reestablish unity among the internationalist forces that were split by the League ratification controversy, and to organize a solid bipartisan base for educating American elite opinion as to the proper role the United States should play in the world.

There was general agreement among the Council members that the United States had to have a large, even dominant, global role. As early as 1898, Gay had written: "When I think of the British Empire as our inheritance I think simply of the natural right of succession. That ultimate succession is inevitable." He did add that "there is no hurry about it."[22] But within a few years it was clear that the time had come for greater involvement of the United States in the world. The sentiment of those in the Council is well summed up in the words of President Theodore Roosevelt, which Archibald Cary Coolidge used as "the moral for Americans" to conclude his 1908 book, *The United States as a World Power,* and which Shepardson repeated in 1942:

> We have no choice, we people of the United States, as to whether or not we shall play a great part in the world. That has been determined for us by fate, by the march of events. We have to play that part. All that we can decide is whether we shall play it well or ill.[23]

It was therefore important to educate wealthy Americans and the public at large to accept such a role.

Early Council Programs

The guiding of opinion through *Foreign Affairs* was only one aspect of the Council's goals. Another crucial feature from the beginning was a "continuous conference" on international affairs. General meetings and dinners for prominent statesmen, and several small study groups which met monthly were organized in the first years. The gatherings, held after 1929 in the house which the Council purchased as a headquarters on East Sixty-fifth Street in New York, brought to the Council foreign statesmen as well as American officials. For example, the Council sponsored a November 1922 appearance in New York by former prime minister Georges Clemenceau of France. His visit was the object of such great public attention that thereafter the Council opted for more private, less publicized appearances limited to Council members. Occasionally, however, such meetings might be used for the delivery of an important statement which would be released to the press. From 1921 to 1938, every secretary of state made an important foreign policy address at at least one such Council session.[24]

In 1927, with *Foreign Affairs* well established, more systematic attention was given to the study and research program of the Council. This aspect of the Council's work became its most important activity as the years went by. The goal of the study and research activities was, and still is, to provide advance planning to solve the long-range problems facing America's rulers. As such, the Council's work was often theoretical, putting scholarship at the service of corporate and financial interests. The program operated as follows:

The committee in charge of research and study, working

with other Council leaders, would choose a problem or region of the world on which a team of men with varied backgrounds would focus. Two kinds of groups existed: study groups, aiming at producing some kind of publication as a result of their work, and discussion groups, oriented toward helping inform Council leaders and members about a foreign-policy problem. Scholars, businessmen, government officials, journalists, military men, foundation officials, and Council staff members were the usual participants. This association of the business, governmental, and academic sectors of American society was what made the Council's study and discussion groups unique and extremely important. The Council provided a forum where leaders from these three key sectors of American life could meet and reach a consensus. Usually, more than twenty men met and discussed a problem approximately monthly for a year or more. Their conclusions about the direction of American foreign policy were often communicated to government officials, formally or informally. In the case of a study group, one member of the group took responsibility for writing an article or book, which was to represent personal views rather than a consensus, but which was understood to result largely from the work and thinking of the group. The number of inter-war publications in this category was quite small. Foster Bain's *Ores and Industry in the Far East,* published in 1927, was the first, and by 1938 only four more had appeared. Of the five, all but one dealt with economic questions.

Several important publications were stimulated by the CFR staff and published by the Council, but were not products of study groups. The aim of these books was to influence the thinking of the "attentive public." Three examples were Herbert Feis's *Europe: The World's Banker,* and accounts by Newton D. Baker of United States entry into World War I and by Henry L. Stimson about his role in the Far Eastern crisis of the early 1930s. A further set of Council publications stemmed from its role in a series of International Studies Conferences, held under the auspices of the League of Nations, for which the Council was designated the United States "National Center," with responsibility for coordinating American participation and for relations with other organizations involved. The reports prepared for these conferences again showed a heavy concentration on economic issues, with four of the six focused primarily on economic policy. During the 1920s, the Council began the publication of several reference books dealing with foreign relations, most of which are still being published.[25]

The Role of the Council Between the Wars

During the 1920s and 1930s, the majority of Americans seemed to want a withdrawal from the political, if not the economic, affairs of the world. The image of the period is one of "isolationism." While this picture has been exaggerated, there is a clear contrast with the period following the onset of the Second World War in 1939. Although most Americans wanted a restricted world role for the United States, Council leaders desired an expansionist foreign policy. The scope of *Foreign Affairs* was worldwide, the subject matter of many Council books was global, and Council leaders argued for an active United States foreign policy.

Geographer Isaiah Bowman, a Council board member and very active in the organization (he headed the Research Committee during much of the 1920s and 1930s), defined American interests in the late 1920s as worldwide and comparable to Britain's, embracing "a region whose extent is beyond the Arctic Circle in Alaska, southward to Samoa and east and west from China to the Philippines to Liberia and Tangier."[26] Bowman added that "if our territorial holdings are not so widely distributed as those of Great Britain, our total economic power and commercial relations are no less extensive."[27]

It is not difficult to find the reason for the Council's interest in the world and in an expansionist American foreign policy. The Council, dominated by corporate leaders, saw expansion of American trade, investment, and population as the solution to domestic problems. It thought in terms of preservation of the status quo at home, and this involved overseas expansion. As Bowman put it in 1928, foreign raw materials, imports, and exports were necessary "if we are to avoid crises in our constantly expanding industries."[28] Since the era of cheap land was over and population was increasing, "eastern social and industrial problems cannot be solved in the historical manner by a flow of population to another region."[29] Thus the United States had to increase its exports, "sell *something* abroad in greater degree—if not wheat or maize, then steel or copper."[30] Bowman and the CFR concluded that a more activist American foreign policy was necessary.

The Council, however, was not in a position to implement such a policy. There is little evidence that it was particularly close to the overall direction of foreign policy during the administrations of Harding and Coolidge, although, of course, Elihu Root maintained his role as elder statesman. Furthermore, Congress had vetoed an overtly activist foreign policy when it rejected unqualified American membership in the League of Nations.

The election of Herbert Hoover to the presidency in 1928 did increase the Council's influence on foreign-policy formulation. President Hoover had been a Paris member of the original Institute of International Affairs and his secretary of state, Henry L. Stimson, was a member of the Council on Foreign Relations. Stimson drew his economic adviser, Herbert Feis, from the CFR staff. But the promise of a greater American presence in the world faded when the depression hit in late 1929 and turned the country in a more nationalist direction. The political, economic, and social problems of the great depression reinforced the desire of local special-interest groups and the working class to eliminate foreign competition with a high protective tariff. As a result, Congress passed the high, restrictive Hawley-Smoot Tariff Act in 1930.

The trend toward economic nationalism in America initiated the "great debate" of the 1930s over national self-sufficiency. The dispute, in the words of *Foreign Affairs* editor Hamilton Fish Armstrong, "set the tone of American life for the next ten years and resulted in the sweeping political and economic reorientation of American foreign policy."[31]

The discussion concerned basic questions: Could the United States isolate itself economically and politically from the rest of the world, build a largely self-sufficient empire in the Western hemisphere, and thereby assure progress and peace? Or was it necessary to have totally free trade with the world, and therefore to be intimately involved in the political affairs of the world? The historian Charles A. Beard may be taken as representative of the first school of thought. In his 1934 book, *The Open Door at Home,* Beard argued that American foreign policy since the 1890s had been based on the mistaken assumption that United States agriculture and industry produced more than could be consumed at home and that the "surplus" had to be exported. Policymaking since the 1890s had revolved around the best way to assure the open door for overseas exports. Beard and others challenged this fundamental assumption, arguing that the "surpluses" could be consumed at home if a proper domestic policy were followed. An engineered, rational, planned economy at home with an efficient distribution of wealth and income could assure a high standard of living for all Americans. Economic decisions would be made collectively to assure full employment and prosperity. The government would control foreign trade and investment to prevent American dependence on and overinvolvement in unstable areas of the world.[32] This program, argued its sponsors, would assure a large degree of self-sufficiency and economic independence for the United States. While not a socialist program, it did propose to put an end to the monopoly of economic decisions by corporate and financial capitalists. For this reason the Council on Foreign Relations strongly opposed the self-sufficiency program.

The Council counterattack against high tariffs, possible government control of foreign trade, and central economic planning began with a 1932 *Foreign Affairs* article by Council secretary-treasurer Edwin F. Gay on "The Great Depression." Ignoring the shortcomings of laissez-faire capitalism as a cause of the depression, Gay focused on the international causes of the economic crisis and concluded that economic self-sufficiency was impossible:

> A time must come when the United States as a powerful world state and a great creditor nation, hence vitally interested in world trade and world prosperity, will face the realities of its new position. It will realize that a policy of self-sufficiency is not only impossible, but that a policy which presupposes it to be possible is stultifying and impoverishing. To say, as one frequently hears it said, that because the value of American exports is less than 10 percent of the total American production, we may therefore go our own way regardless of foreign trade or international responsibilities is to misinterpret the plain facts. The whole network of domestic prices and domestic credit in the United States is bound indissolubly with the system of world prices and with the stream of world credit. A dislocation anywhere in the fabric is now felt everywhere. The World War affirmed the international political responsibilities of the United States; the World Depression demonstrates the economic interdependence of the United States with other states. It cannot be a hermit nation.[33]

The Council followed the Gay article with a 1933 discussion group on the subject, aimed at influencing the newly elected administration of Franklin D. Roosevelt in an internationalist direction. It was during the Roosevelt administration that the ties between the Council and the government became exceedingly close. Norman H. Davis, a Wall Street banker who served first as a CFR vice-president (1933-1936) and then as president (1936-1944), was an intimate friend and adviser of both Secretary of State Cordell Hull and President Roosevelt himself, undertaking special overseas missions for both.[34]

The CFR Discussion Group on the Pros and Cons of National Self-Sufficiency met in New York on October 23 and 24, 1933, under the chairmanship of John Foster Dulles, a future secretary of state. In attendance were a number of government officials past and present: Henry L. Stimson, former secretary of state; Ogden L. Mills, former secretary of the treasury; Henry A. Wallace, Roosevelt's secretary of agriculture; Lewis W. Douglas, Roosevelt's director of the Bureau of the Budget; and Herbert Feis, economic adviser to the Department of State. Also present was the usual cross-section of corporate leaders, academic experts, journalists, and Council officers—a J. P. Morgan partner, a Harvard dean, a University of Chicago dean, economists from Columbia, Harvard, and the Chase Bank, as well as geographer Bowman and Walter Lippmann of the *New York Herald Tribune*.[35]

The conclusions of the discussions were communicated to government leaders in Washington, D.C., and were reflected in *Foreign Affairs* articles by two participants who were also CFR board members, Lippmann and Whitney H. Shepardson. Lippmann's article, "Self-Sufficiency: Some Random Reflections," appeared in January 1934. Lippmann identified two beliefs on self-sufficiency—nationalist and socialist—and argued that both were incompatible with freedom, because "to manage a whole social order according to a central plan, human behavior must be predictable."[36] He believed that the only way to assure predictability was rationing and, thus, regimentation. Therefore he rejected self-sufficiency as a viable alternative for America.[37] Since poor people with low purchasing power have always been rationed through the market, what Lippmann was really concerned about was that rationing might be applied equally to all.

Shepardson's article, which appeared in the April 1934

issue of *Foreign Affairs*, admitted that the United States could be self-sufficient at a price, but argued strongly that the cost would be so high as to make it impossible.[38] As a conclusion, Shepardson offered suggestions as to how the United States could increase exports.[39]

The Council's work stimulated a semiofficial Commission of Inquiry into American policy in international economic relations, which was established with President Roosevelt's approval in November 1933.[40] Three of the seven commissioners were Council members, two of whom—Bowman and Beardsley Ruml, a longtime aide to the Rockefeller family—had also been part of the Council's self-sufficiency discussion group. After several months work the commission recommended to the President that the United States reject even partial self-sufficiency and instead promote American exports and world trade as a solution to the depression.[41] This involved a downward revision of the tariff and the "speedy negotiation of reciprocal trade agreements."[42] The commission concluded that government restrictions on the foreign economic activities of private individuals and corporations should be kept to a minimum.[43]

The Roosevelt administration, prompted by the Council and allied bodies, dropped its initial nationalist stress on domestic reform as a solution to the depression. During 1934, the passage of the Export-Import Bank and Trade Agreements Act marked a return to traditional emphasis on foreign trade expansion as a solution to domestic problems.

The policy which the Roosevelt administration followed from 1934 on indicates that the Council's impact on long-range fundamental questions of foreign policy was substantial. In the 1937 Council history, there are references to several cases of Council impact on policymaking:

> In 1934 the Council brought together a group to consider the question of the role of minerals in international relations. It prepared a report, drafted by the Chairman, C. K. Leith, which was issued by the Mineral Inquiry under the title "Elements of a

28 *Imperial Brain Trust*

National Mineral Policy." Eventually the government decided to proceed further with investigation, and the Secretary of the Interior became head of a permanent committee of which Dr. Leith was named vice-chairman.

In the same year a group was formed to study American neutrality policy under the Chairmanship of former Secretary of State Henry L. Stimson, and with Charles Warren leading the discussion. Its work, which continued into 1935, was closely followed in Washington; indeed, Mr. Warren was soon invited to return to the State Department to aid in drafting the Neutrality legislation then impending.[44]

During its first fifteen years of existence the Council had established itself as a solid institution, with a large meetinghouse, a staff, a magazine, a study and research program, and a "continuing conference on international affairs." The function of the Council on Foreign Relations, stated the postscript to the 1937 history, was to "assist responsible men who are trying to inform themselves; to promote study and research in the field of international affairs; and to make the results of this work available to others."[45] Executive Director Walter H. Mallory, in a 1937 memorandum to the Council's board of directors, stated the case for moving to a deliberate further expansion of the Council's work, noting that "the Council is comprised of a group of the men in America best qualified to give counsel and assistance in the study of America's proper course in these trying days."[46]

The Council and the Postwar World, 1939-1952

War and Peace Studies

The Second World War and the subsequent cold war were decisive turning points in the history of American foreign policy. They marked a move on the part of the United States toward a full-blown imperialism—a largely successful attempt to organize a single, world-spanning political economy with the United States at the center.[47] Providing the intellectual rationale and leading this thrust toward global power was the Council on Foreign Relations.

Written in the midst of the Second World War, the Council's annual report for 1943 described the impact of the war on the Council's work in the following terms:

> For over twenty-five years the Council—one of a handful of such institutions in this country—has devoted itself to a study of the role of the United States in the world. Now, quite suddenly, almost every group, no matter what its normal purpose, is devoting prime attention to the problems of international affairs, and to America's postwar position. Naturally they depend upon the Council for light and guidance; and the Council, within the limits of a modest budget and an overburdened staff, is doing its best to meet its increased responsibilities.[48]

Among the groups depending on the Council for "light and guidance" was the United States Department of State. The department had just incorporated the top leadership of the Council's special War and Peace Studies Project into its own Advisory Committee on Postwar Foreign Policy, and the Council's research secretaries for the project into its own planning staff for half of each week.

The War and Peace Studies were a turning point in American history. They will be discussed in detail in Chapter 4 as an example of how the Council succeeded in defining the "national interest" for subsequent generations.

Other Council Programs

Although the War and Peace Studies Project was the Council's most important program during the 1940s, other activities continued, including regular study groups, the publication of *Foreign Affairs*, and meetings at the Council. Some newer projects were also initiated, particularly several oriented toward reaching somewhat broader constituencies. For example, in 1939 the Council organized a seminar for junior executives, to provide them "with some understanding of the broad implications of American foreign policy."[49] Among the twenty-six firms which participated were the Federal Reserve Bank, General Motors Overseas Corporation, Kuhn, Loeb and Company, J. P. Morgan and Company, Morgan, Stanley and Company, the National City Bank, Price, Waterhouse and Company, and Sullivan and Cromwell. This program, discontinued in 1941, was resumed in 1952.

Perhaps most important among the new programs were the committees on foreign relations, set up throughout the country with the aid of a grant from the Carnegie Corporation. The plan was to choose in a number of cities "men who occupy positions of leadership in their communities," bringing them together for regular discussions in their own localities and for an annual conference in New York.[50] The committees served a dual purpose for the Council—influencing the thinking of local leaders, and providing the Council and United States government with information about trends of thought on foreign affairs throughout the country.[51] Francis P. Miller, who organized the committees for the Council, observed that when they were first established during the 1938-1940 period,

> they were thought of primarily as a means of educating public opinion in their respective communities. But as it turned out, they became in time much more than that. In addition to being useful listening posts to sense the mood of the country, they played a unique role in preparing the nation for a bipartisan foreign policy in the fateful years that lay ahead.[52]

The committees on foreign relations thus had a major part in achieving one of the Council's principal goals: "To help in the education of American public opinion to understand and support ... the right kind of American foreign policy."[53]

How the Council conceives of the process is described in its 1951 report: "In speaking of public enlightenment, it is well to bear in mind that the Council has chosen as its function the enlightenment of the leaders of opinion. These, in turn, each in his own sphere, spread the knowledge gained here in ever-widening circles."[54] Through the committees the Council has been able to spread its ideas on policy to prestigious groups on the local level, such as businessmen, lawyers, educators, and journalists who disseminate these ideas to a larger public.

Just after the end of World War II, John W. Davis said:

> The Foreign Relations Committees have provided an avenue for extending the influence of the Council to every part of the country. Many of the men who have taken a leading part in the American war effort have been prominently associated with the work of these Committees and through them in no small measure have gained an appreciation of America's role in foreign relations.[55]

In talking about the committees, Henry M. Wriston, a former president of the Council, noted that they contrasted with the Foreign Policy Association in trying to attract more top management rather than the "League of Women Voters type."[56] The Department of State agreed, stating in a 1951 report that it regarded a Council report on these committee members' opinions—*The Containment of Soviet Expansion* by Joseph Barber—"as an amalgam of the considered views of men in positions of influence" around the country.[57]

The Council and the Cold War

During the war years, the Council and the government planners gave little attention to the Soviet Union in their plans for a new world order. What attention they did pay was of a negative kind, focusing especially on how to keep the Soviets from controlling Eastern and Central Europe. Leading Council theorists had long seen Eastern Europe as a possible bulwark against the expansion of Russian bolshevism. Isaiah Bowman, as early as 1922, had recommended that Poland and Romania be extended so as to give them a common border. They would thus be linked in a continuous belt from the Black to the Baltic Seas and jointly form a barrier to the expansion of communism.[58] Council planners during the Second World War had a similar approach. In postwar planning sessions at the Department of State in early March 1942, CFR leader Hamilton Fish Armstrong argued that Polish-Soviet relations involved a question of "what steps we would wish to take to keep these Eastern European states from becoming Communist."[59] Council president Norman H. Davis stated in May 1942 that the Eastern European area could serve as a buffer against the USSR.[60] To achieve this goal, the Council and the Department of State worked out plans for an Eastern European federation, with a customs union, one central bank, and a unified transportation system, eventually leading to political unification of the area from the Baltic states on the north to Greece on the south.[61] The Territorial Group of the War and Peace Studies Project produced a memorandum on the subject of an Eastern European federation in late October 1942, arguing that the United States and Britain could not "afford to see one hundred million Europeans added to the Soviet power."[62] The Council recommended that the British and Americans should therefore try to establish such a union over possible Russian opposition.[63]

The precipitating factor leading to the cold war lay in this desire to control Eastern Europe and establish a buffer against Soviet expansion, and in the USSR's equal determination to control the region, mainly for security reasons. Once the Soviets occupied the area at the close of the war, it became unrealistic, as events have since shown, to try to make them yield control. Nevertheless, during the key year 1945, Council members took the lead in working out tactics to try to force such a withdrawal. Council member W. Averell

Harriman, American ambassador to the Soviet Union, advised Washington policymakers to tie a January 1945 Russian request for a large loan to Moscow's behavior in international relations, so that diplomatic "leverage" could be gained in regard to Eastern Europe and other questions.[64]

Council members and leaders also had a key role in the tactical decision to use the atomic bomb on Japan. Secretary of War Henry L. Stimson was President Roosevelt's senior adviser on atomic questions, and headed the special Interim Committee which President Truman established in late April 1945 to recommend action on the bomb. The eight-man committee was dominated by five Council members, including Stimson, the chairman, who had been active in Council programs for over ten years.[65] One of the five Council men, scientist Karl T. Compton, president of M.I.T., stated at the time that the bomb should be used to "impress the world," giving credence to those who have argued that the bomb was used on Japan primarily to intimidate the Russians, and thereby reinforce the American position of world dominance.[66]

Decisions on the proper postwar political economy for Germany also occupied a key place in United States foreign policy between 1944 and 1946. The choices made by the Council and American officials played a central role in the development of the cold war. The basic question facing the policymakers was whether a moderate or harsh peace should be made with Germany. A corollary to this issue involved a decision as to which nation—Germany or the Soviet Union—was the main long-term threat to the United States, and thus which nation should be given preference in allocating resources to rebuild from the extensive devastation both countries suffered during the war.

Two positions on these interrelated questions emerged in the 1944-1946 period. One was the famous Morgenthau Plan proposed by Secretary of the Treasury Henry M. Morgenthau, which envisaged Germany as the main enemy and proposed a harsh peace. Such a settlement involved the creation of a deindustrialized, agrarian Germany incapable of conducting a modern war. The second American position on this question was put forward mainly by Council members and the War and Peace Studies groups. It involved a "moderate" peace for Germany—denazification, destruction of war potential, some reparation, but also the reintegration of Germany into the American-dominated postwar world economy, and the avoidance of measures which might cause political instability or unrest. The Council position implied that Germany was not a long-term threat to the United States and that Germany's economic reconstruction should be given precedence over the needs of the Soviet Union.[67] The conflict with the Soviet Union over reparations and the rebuilding of the German economy was the crucial reason for the break with the Soviets over Germany and the consequent partition of that nation.[68] The Council had laid the basis for American policy in spite of the opposing position represented by the Morgenthau Plan.

The popularization of the theoretical basis for a tough United States policy toward the Soviet Union can also be traced to the CFR. Council member George F. Kennan, who developed the famous "containment" doctrine, addressed the Council on the topic in January 1947 and published his celebrated article, "The Sources of Soviet Conduct," in *Foreign Affairs* (July 1947). At the time, Kennan was the head of the Department of State's Policy Planning Committee. The American government had recently adopted the containment doctrine, which held that the Soviets would try to pursue unlimited expansion, but that they could be stopped with a firm and vigilant American policy.[69]

Containment involved American aid for the economic reconstruction of Europe along lines favorable to America's largest corporations. This quickly became one of the most important focuses of the Council's study program between 1945 and 1951. One group's work had a direct impact on American foreign policy. In 1946-1947 lawyer Charles M. Spofford headed a group, with banker David Rockefeller as secretary, on Reconstruction in Western Europe; in 1947-1948 that body was retitled the Marshall Plan. The Council's annual report for 1948 explained that even before Secretary of State George C. Marshall had made his aid to Europe proposal in June 1947, the Spofford group had "uncovered" the necessity for aid to Europe and "helped explain the needs for the Marshall Plan and indicated some of the problems it would present for American policy. Moreover, a number of members of the 1947-1948 group, through their connections with . . . governmental bodies were in constant touch with the course of events."[70] In 1948 a new group was organized, led by General Dwight D. Eisenhower, on Aid to Europe, which continued its discussions through 1951, and resulted in a book by Howard Ellis. It was in reference to this study group that another member commented to journalist Joseph Kraft: "Whatever General Eisenhower knows about economics, he learned at the study group meetings."[71]

Council Expansion After the War

Early in 1945 the Council moved into its new headquarters, the Harold Pratt House, on East Sixty-eighth Street in New York. Immediately following the end of the war, the Council leaders began planning continued expansion of Council work along the lines established during the war. Goals remained the same—besides propagandizing the public, the Council stressed influencing the government. As its 1951 annual report expressed it:

> In placing emphasis on public enlightenment, however, it is not intended to suggest that the Council has no function in the evolution of foreign policies themselves, or indeed in assisting those

charged with implementing them to do their job better. The roster of Council members who now occupy high office is impressive. Many of them spent long hours in Council study and discussion groups in the years when they were private citizens, and some still participate actively in the work of the organization.[72]

Thus the study groups themselves were now seen as stepping stones to high government office. The Council's annual report of 1950 said: "Very often the groups serve ... as training ground for members called upon to serve the government in important positions. Such instances are too numerous to record here..."[73]

In September 1945 the Council held a special two-day conference in Princeton to consider its future program. The conference resulted in agreement on increasing the number of study groups organized on topical and regional lines and increasing the staff time allocated to them. The special relationship with the State Department would be maintained on an informal basis and ties with other agencies involved in formulating American foreign policy strengthened.

Two specific conferences followed closely on the planning meeting of 1945: one, on training for the foreign service, which the Council organized for the State Department, resulting in a proposal (later adopted) for the creation of a Foreign Service Institute; and another, on teaching and research in international relations. The second was followed up by regional conferences with university professors in different parts of the country.[74]

The study program was expanded to an average of nine study or discussion groups per year from 1946 through 1952. Out of these groups and from regular Council research between 1939 and 1952 came twenty books, as well as the continuing publication of reference books. Of those twenty, twelve dealt with economic subjects, and two others by the Harvard historian William L. Langer and government official S. Everett Gleason, *The Challenge to Isolation* and *The Un-*

A Brief History of the Council 37

declared War, were the establishment's version of American entry into World War II.[75] In 1951 the Council's capacity for research was enlarged by a grant from the Carnegie Corporation providing for three new research fellows each year.

The annual report for 1952, issued after the presidential nominating conventions of that summer but before the November election, indicated the continued importance of the Council in a somewhat understated comment about *Foreign Affairs* quarterly, saying that its "position is perhaps attested to by the fact that one of the Presidential candidates is a member of its Editorial Advisory Board, while the other, Governor Stevenson, outlined his views on our foreign policy in an article ... in the April issue."[76] In November 1952 Council member and *Foreign Affairs* editorial advisory board member Dwight D. Eisenhower was elected President of the United States. That same month, the Department of State began a reexamination of foreign economic policy in preparation for the new administration, and asked the Council to help. Three joint CFR-State Department meetings were held to stimulate new thinking on aspects of foreign economic relations.[77]

Also in 1952, the Council board appointed a committee on policy to consider the further extension of the Council's operations. Financiers David Rockefeller and Frank Altschul had just been selected as vice-presidents and Rockefeller in-law George S. Franklin, Jr. was shortly to take over as executive director. A new period in the Council's history was about to begin.

Council Expansion, 1953-1975

The Council's great influence over the overall, long-term direction of American foreign policy has continued into the present era. The correct mind-set for policymakers had been established and the "national interest" of global anticommunism conclusively defined. The stage was set for further American interventions in Asia and around the world in the guise of "containment." Examples of the CFR role in several of these interventions will be fully covered in Chapter 5.

In late 1952 the Committee on Policy brought in its suggestions for improvement and expansion of the Council's program. The committee, chaired by Council president Henry M. Wriston, included Council directors Hamilton Fish Armstrong, Devereux C. Josephs, and David Rockefeller, as well as retiring and incoming executive directors Mallory and Franklin and several other Council members. Some of its recommendations were:

> 1. Council study groups should concentrate primarily on problems of long-range importance, particularly emerging problems on which positions have not yet crystallized, in the hope that they may be able to identify opportunities for U.S. action early enough so that advantage may be taken of them....
> 2. The Council should organize at least several more study groups each year....
> 3. New Committees on Foreign Relations should be formed in at least ten additional cities.[78]

Thus the Council concentrated on extending the already established pattern of study and discussion groups. By this time the procedure was well institutionalized. A topic would be selected by the Council's Committee on Studies (formerly called the Research Committee), a chairman and rapporteur (or research secretary) appointed, and one of the Council's senior fellows assigned to participate. After consultation between the Council staff and the group chairman, Council members, particularly those knowledgeable in the field, from business, government, and academic life were invited to join. Meetings would then begin, and continue for a year or more.

On occasion, someone outside the Council with special knowledge to contribute would be asked to participate, often for only one or two meetings. Study groups that were successful resulted in a book by the research secretary or rapporteur. Occasionally a discussion group also resulted in a book or at least an article or two in *Foreign Affairs*. The topic of a discussion group one year might be chosen as a subject for a more focused study the following year.

The expanded program of study produced an average of four and one-half books per year between the early 1950s and the early 1970s. At times, as many as twenty study and discussion groups were functioning in any one year. Looking at the topics of the books published, one can notice some shift in emphasis as well as simple growth in numbers. In contrast to the earlier years of the Council's history, when a majority of books dealt primarily with economic subjects, slightly fewer than one-third of the ninety books published between 1953 and 1972 focused on economic issues. A much larger number (almost all the remainder) adopted a broader political focus, or concentrated on specific political or military matters. At the same time a greater proportion focused on a specific geographical area.

Some of the Council's studies had more influence on policy than others. Of particular significance during this period, because of the money and time allocated and the impact made, were four studies: on United States-Soviet relations, on nuclear weapons and foreign policy, and two major study projects from 1962 to 1965 on the Atlantic region and on China.

The study group on United States-Soviet relations, which Wall Street lawyer and banker John J. McCloy chaired and which had Henry L. Roberts, director of the Russian Institute at Columbia University as research director, enjoyed the services of a staff of six financed by a Ford Foundation grant. The Council's 1953 report noted that it was "one of the most ambitious projects the Council has ever undertaken."[79] The focus was "to examine Soviet capabilities, and the influence of developments in new weapons on the strategic assumptions underlying American foreign policy and, in the light of these discussions ... consider the problems of our relations with the Soviet Union in all the vital areas of the world as well as over-all."[80] The study group included, in addition to Council chairman McCloy, president Wriston, vice-president Altschul, John D. Rockefeller III, executive directors Mallory and Franklin, and four other Council directors, as well as two senior staff members of the Council, Philip E. Mosely and William Diebold, Jr. Observers were present from the CIA, the army, the State Department, and the air force. Three participants, Dean Rusk, McGeorge Bundy, and Walt W. Rostow were to play key foreign policy roles in the administration of President John F. Kennedy.

After two years of investigation and discussions, Roberts wrote a report, which was debated and criticized in a two-day conference, and finally prepared for publication as a book entitled *Russia and America: Danger and Prospects*. The contents could be characterized as a summation of the conventional wisdom on the proper cold war strategy for the United States. Although Roberts disclaims any intention of presenting the book as a "collective work," and some portions might meet with disagreement from some members of the group, it is clearly a collective product and may be taken as fairly representative of the thinking of the Council's own leadership in the mid-1950s. The book stated that the policy of the United States should be "preventing at whatever cost the world-wide imposition of Soviet Communism, and avoiding general war...."[81] At the same time America and its allies should build up all forms of strength—atomic, military, economic, political—and prevent any loss of territory to communism.[82]

The other major study group in the 1950s was on nuclear

weapons and foreign policy, chaired by Gordon E. Dean, with Carroll L. Wilson as secretary. Henry A. Kissinger, destined to play a key role in the foreign policy of the Nixon and Ford administrations, was study director from the second year of the project. A substantial number of the Council's leaders were involved.[83] The resulting book, *Nuclear Weapons and Foreign Policy,* which Kissinger wrote, ran for many weeks on the best-seller list and, commented the Council's 1956 report, "more important, it has been read and discussed by the highest officials in the legislative and executive branches of our Government.... This book is a prime example of the pioneering policy work that is now being done by the Council under its new study programs."[84] This book had an important impact on the prevailing climate of elite opinion on nuclear strategy, leading to a reconsideration of American policy. It will be discussed in more detail in Chapter 5.

No less crucial for the future was the immense impact the Council study group had on the life of Henry A. Kissinger. A Council member and old friend and colleague of Kissinger's later wrote that the appointment as study director "proved to be the most important event in Kissinger's adult life, second only to his decision to enroll at Harvard."[85] This was the "crucial" period of Kissinger's life; it brought him into contact with powerful men like the Rockefellers whom he would not otherwise have met.[86] Kissinger himself was touched deeply by the men of the Council. He "never forgot the moral support that these men gave him, and never underestimated its importance for his personal growth."[87]

Of the two major study programs of the Council in the 1960s financed by the Ford Foundation, one, on "The United States and China in World Affairs," will also be discussed in Chapter 5. The other project was the "Atlantic Policy Studies," which brought together, under the chairmanship of Council director Charles Spofford, a distinguished group of Council officers and directors. Henry A. Kissinger was a member of the steering committee and, within the scope of the project, wrote another book, this one dealing with the North Atlantic Treaty Organization. The studies in the Atlantic Policy series benefited from close collaboration with the Royal Institute of International Affairs in London and with other similar institutes on the European continent. The study groups produced ten books. The Atlantic Policy Studies made no clear impact on official policy, but were part of continuing reflection on an area long of primary importance to the Council and to United States government policy.

A continuing aspect of the Council's program was visits by prominent foreign leaders for speechmaking and discussion on present and future foreign relations. Although these meetings were secret and off-the-record, information is available on one, that illustrates well a major concern of Council leaders and members. Premier Fidel Castro of Cuba was invited to speak on "Cuba and the United States," and answer questions at the Council headquarters in New York during his visit to the United States in April 1959. Castro's reception by the large crowd present at the Pratt House was not a warm one. After his speech he was badgered with a series of questions expressing barely veiled hostility, many of them focusing on what he thought of communism. The antagonism of the Council members concerned civil liberties and the possible expropriation of Cuban properties owned by United States businessmen. After some artful dodging, the Cuban leader finally responded with a question of his own: If you took a poor man, which would he prefer to have—habeas corpus or a plate of beans? A Council man then asked: "How much does Cuba want?" Castro, insulted by this hint of bribery, drew himself up and replied: "We don't want your money. We want your respect." Since the unpleasant tone of the Council's questioning continued, Castro finally said, "I can see that I am not among friends," and walked out of the meeting.[88]

While Castro's visit with the Council was no doubt atypical because of the conflicting world views which it brought out, it is illustrative of a central concern of the Council: the worldwide preservation of existing property relations. It also suggests that world leaders and statesmen are aware of and respect the Council's power. Between June 1959 and August 1974, the Council hosted a truly amazing number of national and global leaders.[89] At the Council's invitation they gave speeches, answered questions, and became acquainted with Council members and leaders. The presidents, prime ministers, premiers, or foreign ministers of fifty-nine nations addressed the Council during these years.[90] Prominent individuals, such as Israel's Moshe Dayan, Britain's Edward Heath and Harold Wilson, West Germany's Ludwig Erhard, Willy Brandt, and Helmut Schmidt, all key leaders in their respective countries, also addressed the Council. Heads of such international agencies as the Council of Europe, the North Atlantic Treaty Organization, Southeast Asia Treaty Organization, the World Bank, the International Monetary Fund, International Labor Organization, and many others too numerous to mention here, spoke to the Council. The attendance of these notables shows the importance of the Council on Foreign Relations as a gathering place for world figures, a place where the ruling class of America can become acquainted with leaders of other nations.

Government leaders of the United States are also prominent in the list of speakers at the Council in 1959-1974. Dozens of officials from the Kennedy, Johnson, and Nixon administrations addressed the Council, including secretaries of state, special assistants to the President for national security, numerous other cabinet officers, State Department officials, ambassadors, White House advisers, agency heads, and military chiefs. In addition, there was a phalanx of senators

(Vance Hartke, Frank Church, J. William Fulbright, Jacob Javits, Henry Jackson, Edward Kennedy, Claiborne Pell), scholars, elder statesmen (Dean Acheson), ambassadors, journalists, media men (Walter Cronkite and Dan Rather of CBS), editors, heads of other policy planning organizations at home and abroad, and leaders of parliaments, parties, and movements in various countries.[91]

Along with the expansion of its meetings and research programs, the Council was able to move into other facets of work. One of the most important, both because of the money it brought in and because of the institutional ties established, has been the Corporation Service. Begun in 1953, it initially consisted of a series of seminars for younger business executives. From the 25 firms subscribing in 1953, the number had grown by 1972 to 157 companies. As could be expected, the largest multinational corporations subscribed to the service over the years, including such giants as General Motors, Exxon, Ford, Mobil, United States Steel, Texaco, Aramco, Gulf Oil, General Electric, Chase Manhattan Bank, First National City Bank, International Business Machines, and many others. In 1969 the Council's annual report described the benefits for subscribing companies as follows:

1. Invitations to name an executive to participate in the Council's Conferences for Business Executives, held twice yearly.
2. Annual off-the-record dinner limited to chairmen and presidents of member companies.
3. Free consultation with members of the Council's staff on international political and economic affairs relating to activities of the member company.
4. Use of the Council's outstanding specialized library on international affairs.
5. Subscriptions to *Foreign Affairs* for company executives and copies of all other Council publications.[92]

Other innovations after 1953 are worth mentioning, if only briefly. A special series of public lectures, the Elihu Root lectures, was inaugurated. A sequence of policy books, shorter and less technical than many other Council books, was initiated and authors recruited to write them, often with the benefit of a single review meeting of Council members. A variety of fellowships was institutionalized—military officers, journalists, senior research fellows, and, most recently, a large number of international affairs fellows were added to the Council staff for terms of one or two years.

The Vietnam War and Recent Changes in the Council

On the whole the Council's program during the last twenty years or so can be characterized as very similar to its earlier projects, but on a larger scale, involving more people, and better financed. At the end of the 1960s, however, it became apparent to the Council that certain adjustments were in order. These changes were, in the main, necessary due to the failure of American foreign policy in Southeast Asia. The second Indochina war was the central event of the late 1960s and early 1970s. The Council had played a key role in determining the United States response to the Vietnamese revolution, a topic covered in detail in Chapter 6. The failure of its policy, due to opposition at home and abroad, signaled a decline of American power in the world and a diminishing of the CFR-inspired cold war consensus at home. The Council leaders could not ignore these twin facts.

The sense of urgency for reforms was heightened in 1971 by unprecedented public controversy, which resulted in several substantial newspaper and magazine articles dealing with the Council and its affairs.[93] The controversy erupted over the appointment of William P. Bundy to replace Hamilton Fish Armstrong as the editor of *Foreign Affairs*. The appointment met with protest from a group of newer Council members, a small group of academic opponents of the Vietnam policy, headed by Richard Falk of Princeton, a leading legal scholar who had written on United States war crimes in

Vietnam. Falk and others protested the Bundy appointment because of his involvement in key decisions during the Vietnam war. They argued that Bundy shared moral and (at least hypothetical) legal responsibility for policies which many regard as criminal. His appointment to the editorship would be seen as approval of his role in carrying out those policies. Accordingly, he should not be appointed. Joining Falk in the initial protest were Richard Barnet of the Institute of Policy Studies in Washington, Richard H. Ullman, associate dean of the Woodrow Wilson School at Princeton, and Ronald Steel, a political scientist. The Council leadership immediately defended Bundy, who had been chosen for the editorship by chairman David Rockefeller. "Why, I know all the Bundys, they're a fine, upright family," Rockefeller is reported to have commented.[94] A Rockefeller memorandum of August 9, 1971, noted that

> having carefully considered and reconsidered the arguments advanced by the group [Falk et al.] the Board reaffirmed with confidence the decision to appoint Mr. Bundy.... Let me emphasize that this conclusion was reached despite the fact that many members of the Board, as well as many other members of the Council who support the appointment, have disagreed in varying degree with the wisdom of United States Vietnam policy.[95]

To many of the older Council members and leaders the very fact of public controversy was shocking. Particularly hard to take must have been the article in *New York* magazine by John Franklin Campbell, for Campbell had been one of their own fellows (his career was cut short later in the year by death from cancer). The article was not anti-Council, but did have some cutting comments on its style, revealing of what the Council itself was beginning to see as an "aging problem":

> If you can walk—or be carried—into the Pratt House, it usually means that you are a partner in an investment bank or law firm—

A Brief History of the Council 47

with occasional "trouble-shooting" assignments in government. You believe in foreign aid, NATO, and a bipartisan foreign policy. You've been pretty much running things in this country for the last 25 years, and you know it.

But today your favorite club is breaking up, just on the eve of its fiftieth anniversary. The same vulgar polarizations that have popped up elsewhere—young against old, men against women, hawks against doves—have at last invaded the secluded Pratt House sanctuary and citadel of the establishment itself.[96]

... The Council's leaders, and most of its members, are affluent New Yorkers from the financial and legal community—the establishment heartland.... Increasingly, they look and act like fossils.[97]

... The Council is stuffy and clubby and parochial and elitist, but it is a place where old moneybags and young scholars are able to sit down and learn something from each other. It is pompous and pretentious, but it still draws men of affairs out of their countinghouses and into dialogue with men of intellect. It is quaint, but not quite yet a museum-piece. It would be a pity, I thought, if it should die.[98]

Later in the year the Council received more unwelcome publicity. A seminar paper prepared by Council member Daniel Ellsberg was turned over to the FBI in 1971 without a protest, an action that provoked public criticism by Arthur Goldberg and other members.[99] While refusing to yield to the disapproval of some members on issues such as the Bundy appointment and the Ellsberg paper, the Council did move more rapidly toward an appearance, at least, of change and responsiveness in other cases.

Structural changes were deemed necessary to deal with this dissent and loss of consensus. New people and new ideas had to be brought into the Council. This required changes in the bylaws. Since directors and members tended to stay around indefinitely and the numbers of each were relatively fixed, the average age had increased from year to year. In 1971 the Council had changed its bylaws to specify that a director should serve no more than three consecutive three-year terms and that any director should retire at the age of seventy. Since enlarging the membership further was regarded as undesirable, similar measures were in order for members and a special effort is being made to lower the average age of Council members by recruiting younger people. In 1970 a comprehensive study of the Council membership was carried out under the chairmanship of director Carroll L. Wilson. The conclusions were disclosed in the 1970 report:

> Further emphasis will be given to electing members representing new and varying backgrounds and points of view, keeping in mind the special contributions that might come from younger people and minority groups. Their potential for participation will be an important factor in selecting new members, and a determined effort will be made to lower the average age of the total membership. The practice of not electing anyone over 60 as a new member was reaffirmed. Qualified women are now eligible for election to membership.[100]

The last sentence represented a further modification of policy for the organization which, for almost fifty years, had excluded women. By 1972 eighteen women had been elected as members. Council President Bayless Manning said in an interview on March 29, 1973, that diversification of the Council membership will continue with particular focus on attaining a desirable age distribution. Increased representation of women and minority groups could not be achieved rapidly, Manning asserted, because of their low representation among those interested in international affairs.[101]

A special committee on procedures was appointed in November 1971 to deal with changes in the Council's methods of governance. In April 1972 the Council modified its bylaws to provide for greater democracy in the election of the board of directors.[102] In the 1972 elections the nominating committee for the first time presented a list of names (eighteen) in excess of the vacancies to be filled. Eight more nominees were added by petition. Those elected included two women, the journalist Elizabeth Drew and economist Martha R. Wallace, who had been among the committee's nominees, and two of those who had been nominated by petition, scholars Zbigniew Brzezinski and Marshall D. Shulman. One of the nominees not elected was Professor Richard H. Ullman of Princeton, who had joined Falk in the Bundy protest. Although not elected to the board, he was shortly thereafter appointed as the Council's new director of studies. In 1973 only one new director was elected—the financier Peter G. Peterson.

In addition to attempting to foster a new consensus to replace the one destroyed by the Vietnam war, the Council has continued in its self-defined role of formulator of long-range foreign policy. In 1968 the Council started "an ambitious effort to help in the development of new guidelines for American foreign policy."[103] Thus the 1973 annual report stated the Council's objectives as follows:

> To enquire what action the United States, or elements in the United States, should take about particular problems and questions in the world ... the Council should hold firmly in view the objective of an intellectual product (whether written or otherwise) that is functionally relevant to the concerns of those who are, or will be, in operating positions, both public and private, in international affairs.[104]

To carry out this kind of study, the Council has planned to orient its work more around broad themes, rather than more specific regional or topical areas of study with which other organizations may be dealing in more detail. Beginning in 1971, three sets of problems were taken as a framework for the Council's studies:

> The cohesiveness of the non-Communist industrial world; the central issue of security, which, of course, includes our relations with the Soviet Union as well as conflict and security problems outside the direct U.S.-Soviet contest; and the economic and political development of the third world.[105]

The newest Council program, which will be by far its most ambitious and important during the second half of the 1970s, is called the "1980's Project." Initiated in the fall of 1973, the 1980's Project plans to make a systematic, overall examination of the entire international system, "its structure, key relationships, rules, processes and institutions."[106] The last such examination took place during the Second World War, when the Council's own War and Peace Studies Project planned a new world order to replace the defunct interwar system. The 1980's Project has a similar aim: to plan a new international order to replace one which has now become outdated due to the decline of American power, the rebellion of the Third World, the expansion and development of the Communist world, scientific and economic developments, the proliferation of new states, and other changes since the 1940s.[107]

Thus Council goals remain, as always, to influence the government and public opinion in favor of an imperial role for the United States. Since World War II, such a role has involved being the leading counterrevolutionary power, the policeman of the world. The Council on Foreign Relations has been extremely successful in achieving its goals in the past. How successful it will be in creating a new nationwide consensus to replace that destroyed by the Vietnam war and in imposing its policies on a world increasingly demanding of revolutionary change remains an open question.

Suggested Readings

For more details about the Council's history, the reader can check several publications of the Council, available in a number of major research libraries. Summary histories of the Council were published in 1937 and 1947. An account of the War and Peace Studies Project was published in 1946. The reports of the Council's executive director, published annually, have in the postwar years included quite a bit of information. Whitney H. Shepardson, one of the Council's founders, wrote in 1960 a privately published account of the early history of the organization.

For overviews of American expansionist foreign policy, the reader should see Williams (1972) and Gardner, LaFeber, and McCormick (1973). For specific time periods, the following are useful accounts:

First World War and aftermath: Levin (1968) and Mayer (1959, 1967).

Between the wars: Parrini (1969), Gardner (1964).

Second World War: Kolko (1968), Smith (1965).

Cold war: J. and G. Kolko (1972), LaFeber (1972), Paterson (1973).

Since 1945: Schurmann (1974).

United States intervention in the Third World: Horowitz (1965), Barnet (1968), Parenti (1971).

Few historians have paid attention to the social context of the policymakers. Among the exceptions are May (1968) and Divine (1967), who have interesting chapters on the group we have identified as the Council community. Although he refuses to go beyond description to analysis, Halberstam (1972) paints an unequaled social portrait of the same group. Other insights into the ambiance of this elite can be gleaned from biographies of several of the key figures: Jessup (1938) on Elihu Root; Stimson and Bundy (1947) on Stimson; Harbaugh (1973) on John W. Davis; Heaton (1952) on Gay. Hamilton Fish Armstrong's memoirs (1971) were left incomplete when he died, and are noticeably reticent on his involvement in the Council on Foreign Relations. For other Council leaders such as Russell C. Leffingwell, Whitney H. Shepardson, Frank Altschul, John J. McCloy, and David Rockefeller, there are as yet no substantial biographical accounts.

Notes

1. CFR, 1937:5.
2. Temperly, 1920:vi.
3. Toynbee, 1970:227; Nicolson, 1934:352.
4. Nimocks, 1968:158-168; Watt, 1970:425.
5. Quigley, 1966:950.
6. Huberman, 1936:268-269.
7. Marlowe, 1972:64.
8. Watt, 1970:425-426; Rothwell, 1971:9.

52 Imperial Brain Trust

9. Shepardson, 1960:3; Gelfand, 1963:xi-xii, 53-67, and 136-153.
10. Shepardson, 1960:3.
11. Heaton, 1952:203.
12. CFR, 1919:3, 5.
13. Shepardson, 1960:11.
14. Other members were: Wall Street lawyer and former undersecretary of state Frank L. Polk; Wall Street investment banker Paul M. Warburg; Columbia University professor William R. Shepherd; Edwin F. Gay, editor of the *New York Evening Post;* and Stephen P. Duggan, director of the International Education Board.
15. Besides John W. Davis, Cravath, and Gay, and the five men mentioned in footnote 14 above, the board consisted of the following men: Isaiah Bowman, director of the American Geographical Society; Archibald Cary Coolidge, Harvard historian; Norman H. Davis, New York banker and former undersecretary of state; John H. Finley of the *New York Times;* David F. Houston, former secretary of treasury; Otto H. Kahn, New York banker; Whitney H. Shepardson; and George W. Wickersham. In all, there were sixteen men (including Root). Eight—Cravath, both Davises, Finley, Kahn, Polk, Root, and Wickersham—were listed in the 1920 New York *Social Register* (Social Register Association, 1920:159, 175, 243, 379, 556, 604, 771). Warburg and Gay were corporate executives and Coolidge came from a wealthy Boston family, making, at minimum, eleven of the sixteen upper class.
16. CFR, 1922:1.
17. Century Association, 1937:21.
18. Canfield, 1971:63-64.
19. CFR, 1924:1.
20. CFR, 1937:17.
21. *Foreign Affairs*, 1922:1.
22. Heaton, 1952:51.
23. Coolidge, 1908:373-374; Shepardson, 1942:45.
24. "Mr. Hughes reviewed the foreign policy of the Harding Administration. Mr. Kellogg outlined his projected Pact of Paris. Mr. Stimson launched the 'non-recognition policy' in the face of Japanese aggression. Mr. Hull described the results and significance of the Inter-American Conference at Buenos Aires. These were general meetings of historic significance." (CFR, 1947[b]:9).
25. These reference books included a *Political Handbook of the World,* first edited by Walter H. Mallory and published annually

A Brief History of the Council 53

by the Council since 1927. In 1928 a *Survey of American Foreign Relations* was begun under the editorship of Yale professor Charles P. Howland. Published for four years, it was then replaced by the annual *United States in World Affairs*, edited for the next three years by Walter Lippmann and William O. Scroggs, and continued to the present by other Council authors. In 1931 Ruth Savord first published a directory of *American Agencies Interested in International Affairs*, which was to go through five editions by 1964.

26. Bowman, 1928:iii. Bowman was a member of the Council's research committee (he often served as chairman) and was on the editorial advisory board of *Foreign Affairs* during the entire 1921-1950 period as well as serving as a Council board member during those years. One of his biographers wrote that his connection with the Council "was always of the closest." (Wrigley, 1951:23).
27. Bowman, 1928:iii.
28. Ibid., 14.
29. Ibid., 690.
30. Ibid., 688.
31. Armstrong, 1947:132.
32. Beard, 1934b:212-214, 269-270.
33. Gay, 1932:540.
34. Shoup, 1974:29-32.
35. Lippmann, 1934:207.
36. Ibid., 209.
37. Ibid.
38. Shepardson, 1934:407-408.
39. Ibid., 417.
40. International Economic Relations, 1934:1-2.
41. Ibid., 5.
42. Ibid., 7.
43. Ibid., 8-9.
44. CFR, 1937:14-15.
45. CFR, 1937:43.
46. Memorandum, Mallory to Davis, March 1937, Davis Papers, Box 10, MDLC.
47. See the emphasis in Schurmann (1974). He argues that "imperialism as a vision and a doctrine has a total, world-wide quality. It envisages the organization of large parts of the world from the top down, in contrast to expansionism, which is accretion from the bottom up." Schurmann, 1974:6.
48. CFR, 1943:4.

54   Imperial Brain Trust

49. CFR, 1947(b):32.
50. Ibid., 48.
51. Ibid., 50; CFR, 1951:34-35.
52. Miller, 1971:87.
53. CFR, 1946(a):7.
54. CFR, 1951:2.
55. John W. Davis to Arthur Sweetser, November 21, 1946, Arthur Sweetser Papers, Box 45, MDLC.
56. Henry M. Wriston interview, March 28, 1973.
57. Department of State, "Special Report on American Opinion by Department of State," May 21, 1951, Philip C. Jessup Papers, Box 114, MDLC.
58. Bowman, 1922:294, cited in S. Cohen, 1963:219-220.
59. Shoup, 1974:241.
60. Ibid.
61. Ibid., 241-242.
62. Memorandum T-B55, October 26, 1942, CFR, *War-Peace Studies*, NUL.
63. Ibid., 5.
64. Paterson, 1974:71-72.
65. Stimson and Bundy, 1947:612-617.
66. Alperovitz, 1967:240.
67. This review of the German problem has been taken from several primary sources, including Acheson (1969), Byrnes (1947), Clay (1950), Hull (1948), Kennan (1967), Murphy (1964), Morgenthau (1945), Ratchford and Ross (1947), Stimson and Bundy (1947), and Truman (1955). More analytical and critical studies include Hammond (1963), Gimbel (1968), and Kuklick (1972). Among the Council's own publications dealing with Germany are Angell (1929), Viner (1945), and Price and Schorske (1947). Summary accounts are to be found in Royal Institute of International Affairs (1956), Campbell (1947, 1948), Feis (1960), and Zink (1957).
68. Kuklick, 1972:226-235.
69. Gardner, LaFeber, McCormick, 1973:456; CFR, 1947(a):29-31. For more details see LaFeber, 1972:43-56.
70. CFR, 1948:16.
71. Kraft, 1958:66. The Eisenhower study group, suggested by Paul Hoffman and Richard Bissell of the Economic Cooperation Administration, had its work facilitated by a special $50,000 grant from the Rockefeller Foundation.
72. CFR, 1951:2.

A Brief History of the Council   55

73. CFR, 1950:39.
74. Kirk, 1947; John W. Davis to Joseph C. Green, November 25, 1946, Joseph C. Green Papers, Carton 11, PUL.
75. Of the remaining books, four dealt with political concerns, one focused on the military of the United States, and one was the Kirk Conference Report.
76. CFR, 1952:4.
77. CFR, 1953:22.
78. Ibid., 7-8.
79. Ibid., 2.
80. Ibid., 9.
81. Roberts, 1956:81.
82. Ibid., 85-87.
83. The CFR leaders involved included vice-presidents Frank Altschul and David Rockefeller, executive director George S. Franklin, Jr. and four other Council directors.
84. CFR, 1956:2.
85. Graubard, 1974:60.
86. Ibid., xvii, 63, 106.
87. Ibid., 64.
88. Interview with a person who was present and who prefers to remain anonymous. CFR, 1959:33.
89. A partial list of the world notables who addressed the Council during this period (along with their office at the time) includes:

Chancellor Konrad Adenauer of West Germany
President Zulfikar Ali Bhutto of Pakistan
President Habib Bourguiba of Tunisia
President Nicolae Ceausescu of Romania
Anatoly F. Dobrynin, the Soviet Union's ambassador to the United States
King Faisal of Saudi Arabia
Finance Minister (elected president in 1974) Valéry Giscard d'Estaing of France
First Secretary of the Polish United Workers' Party Wladyslaw Gomulka
King Hussein I of Jordan
President Kenneth Kaunda of Zambia
President Ferdinand E. Marcos of the Philippines
Prime Minister Golda Meir of Israel
Prime Ministers Jawaharlal Nehru and Indira Gandhi of India
President Julius K. Nyerere of Tanzania
Prime Minister Olof Palme of Sweden

Prime Minister Lester B. Pearson of Canada
President Georges Pompidou of France
Emperor Haile Selassie I of Ethiopia
Shah of Iran
U.N. secretaries-general U Thant and Kurt Waldheim
President Josip Broz Tito of Yugoslavia

90. Besides those already mentioned in the text, the list of countries whose top leaders visited the CFR during the 1959-1974 period is as follows:

Afghanistan	Ecuador	Liberia	South Korea
Algeria	Egypt	Malaysia	South Vietnam
Australia	Great Britain	Morocco	Spain
Austria	Guinea	Netherlands	Taiwan
Belgium	Indonesia	New Zealand	Togo
Botswana	Ireland	Nicaragua	Turkey
British Guiana	Italy	Nigeria	Uganda
Cambodia	Ivory Coast	Peru	Zaïre
Colombia	Japan	Portugal	
Denmark	Laos	Singapore	

91. This list of speakers at Council meetings was drawn from CFR annual reports for: 1960:28-40; 1961:62-76; 1962:44-57; 1963:50-64; 1964:48-62; 1965: 44-59; 1966:46-59; 1967:41-55; 1969:47-62; 1970:54-66; 1971:43-62; 1972:21-38; 1973:24-40; 1974:14-36.
92. CFR, 1969:66.
93. Lukas, 1971; Campbell, 1971.
94. Lukas, 1971:138.
95. Memorandum, David Rockefeller to Council members, August 9, 1971.
96. Campbell, 1971:47.
97. Ibid., 48.
98. Ibid., 51.
99. See the *New York Times*, November 4, 1971:1, 15; November 5, 1971:5.
100. CFR, 1970:81.
101. Bayless Manning interview, March 29, 1973.
102. CFR, 1972:12.
103. CFR, 1971:18.
104. CFR, 1973:85.
105. CFR, 1971:19.
106. CFR, 1974:1.
107. Ibid., 1-2.

2
The Council Network

The Council on Foreign Relations set itself an ambitious goal—no less than to prescribe a course of world leadership for American foreign policy. It set out to educate public opinion and, thus, affect the evolution of policy within the government as well. The programs of the Council, from the initial emphasis on *Foreign Affairs* to a proliferation of meetings and studies covering the full range of foreign policy issues, carried out the initial mandate to establish "a continuous conference on foreign affairs."[1] But the Council's aims would have remained utopian, and its programs mere academic pastimes, were it not for another aspect missed by a purely formal description of the Council.

For the Council does not consist only of the activities officially carried out in its name, of the meetings in the Council house, or of the publications it sponsors. Of even greater importance is the fact that the Council is the center of a network of contacts linking together all those involved in the making of foreign policy, in or out of government. This network of contacts would exist even without the Council on Foreign Relations, but the Council helps to solidify and integrate the network, establishing itself as a visible focus. It consciously seeks out key men, or those it thinks should become key men, and puts them in contact with one another. The resulting network is systematically linked to every significant sector of the foreign policy community.

The existence of such a network, tied together by common organizational memberships, interlocking directorates, kinship, and other informal ties, facilitates contacts and the integration among foreign policy leaders. In many cases, without "inside" information the observer cannot know exactly when or how these contacts work, but it is beyond doubt that they promote the exchange of information and of opinions. They provide "access" and, thus, the possibility for influence. (As American folk wisdom puts it, "It's not what you know that counts, it's who you know.") As members move to and from government, private business, and the academic world, the network of contacts facilitates job hunting. As the interlocks multiply, so do the chances that those in the network form the key reference group for each other—those whose views are taken seriously. A community emerges and is solidified. This community shapes and reinforces a broad consensus on foreign policy aims.[2]

The Council in Government

The Council is, first of all, very well represented among those directly involved in making foreign policy on a day-to-day basis, the government officials. From 1945 to 1972, almost half (45 percent) of those who served as top foreign policy officials were also members of the Council on Foreign Relations.[3] It is not quite true, as one Council member wrote, that membership in the Council is a compulsory "rite of passage."[4] Not being a Council member does not automatically disqualify one from high office, but it is true that the Council serves as an important recruiting pool from which officials are chosen. This has been particularly important since the Second World War. During the war itself, Council member John J. McCloy was personnel chief under Secretary of War Stimson. He is quoted as saying, "Whenever we needed a man we thumbed through the roll of Council members and put through a call to New York."[5] In other cases the selection procedure may not be so blatantly related to Council membership, but given the network of contacts the result is the same. As a staff man for John Lindsay's presidential campaign once remarked, it was almost impossible for Lindsay to find alternatives (for advice on foreign policy) to "Cy Vance and those other people he knows from the Council."[6] More successful presidential candidates must have had similar experiences, for, as Council member Theodore White observed, the Council's "roster of members has for a generation, under Republican and Democratic administrations alike, been the chief recruiting ground for Cabinet-level officials in Washington."[7]

The recruitment process is not simply one-way, of course. Only one out of four of the top foreign policy officials were Council members at the time they took office. Others were recruited into the Council during or after their time in government. Council members in government keep their eyes open for other officials who might be good Council members and suggest them to the Membership Committee. Just as the career route to high office may include Council membership, so one of the routes to Council membership is through holding high office in the government. The result of these two processes is the establishment of close links between the Council and foreign policy officials.

When consulted for recruitment suggestions, Council members may well suggest other members. According to Hamilton Fish Armstrong, "Often a friend in Washington would call and say, 'Who do you know who knows anything about black Africa?' Usually the people I knew were Council members."[8] But nonmembers, such as Secretary of Defense Robert S. McNamara, might also be proposed. McNamara had worked under former CFR member Robert Lovett, who suggested his name to Kennedy. Also available are members of the foreign relations committees, local groups created by the Council. The Council's 1952-1953 annual report calls attention to government service by these men (in such posts as secretary of defense, director of mutual security, assistant secretary of state, adviser to the National Security Council). It goes on to note: "While there have been periodic calls upon the Committee membership in the past, it is gratifying to observe how well represented in the public service are the Council's affiliated groups at the present time."[9] The figures thus presented in this section refer only to *Council* membership, without taking into account committee membership or other ties to Council members, and are thus only minimum estimates of those officials with ties to the Council on Foreign Relations.

In some countries the top foreign policy officials are largely permanent government officials. In the United States, however, the majority (60 percent between 1945 and 1972) are men with other private establishment and corporate careers, recruited into government on a temporary basis. These "in-and-outers" are particularly likely to be members of the Council. Between 1945 and 1972, more than half of them were Council members, in contrast to the fact that only a little more than one-third of the career officials and only one-fifth of the small number of professional politicians were Council members. The Council is particularly useful for the in-and-outers. Whether they are in government at a particular moment, or back on Wall Street or at Harvard, they can conveniently maintain their contacts and keep in touch through the Council. As Council member James Thomson puts it, referring to the Council on Foreign Relations and the

Brookings Institution, "former insiders often look forward to a continued relationship with present and former policymakers—and a continued sense of involvement—through participation in such aspects of the extended Club."[10]

Focusing on the State Department, excluding for the moment foreign policy officials in other agencies, the ties with the Council are even closer. More than half of all top State Department officials were members of the Council. Among State Department in-and-outers the percentage climbs to 69 percent, more than two out of three. With such a substantial overlap, it is not surprising that the impression is created that everyone of importance in foreign policy must be a Council member. As J. Anthony Lukas observed, writing in the *New York Times Magazine,* "If you want to make foreign policy, there's no better fraternity to belong to than the Council."[11]

In the case of the CIA, the impression of close Council-government ties is further confirmed. Since its founding in 1947, the directorship of the CIA has been in the hands of a Council leader or member more often than not. CIA director Allen W. Dulles was also a CFR director, and John A. McCone, Richard Helms, William Colby, and George Bush were all Council members. This kind of tie has naturally resulted in Council members receiving the inside story first and most authoritatively. Colby, for example, spoke before the Council on December 16, 1974, revealing, almost a week before the *New York Times* broke the story, that the CIA had been involved in domestic spying.[12] The "investigations" of the CIA have also been dominated by Council members. Five of the eight members of the Rockefeller Commission, established early in 1975 to probe the illegal domestic activities of the CIA, were Council members. Vice-President Nelson Rockefeller, a Council member and brother of CFR chairman David Rockefeller, headed the commission, with a Council director, Douglas Dillon, serving as vice-chairman.[13]

Senator Frank Church, head of the Senate investigation of the agency, was a Council member for a number of years during the late 1960s and early 1970s.[14] It is clear that a close relationship between the CFR and the CIA has existed in the past and still exists today. As the authors of *The CIA and the Cult of Intelligence* put it:

> The influential but private Council, composed of several hundred of the country's top political, military, business, and academic leaders has long been the CIA's principal "constituency" in the American public. When the agency has needed prominent citizens to front for its proprietary (cover) companies or for other special assistance, it has often turned to Council members.[15]

This picture of close linkages between the Council and the government is confirmed in the case of every administration since the Second World War. Under Truman Council members filled 42 percent of the top foreign policy posts. For his successor, President Eisenhower, the figure was slightly lower—40 percent—but the relationship of the Council to the government was probably even closer. Eisenhower himself had been a Council member and a leader of one of its most important study groups. One incident, of relatively minor importance in itself, illustrates how the Council network functions. Eisenhower, appointed by Truman as United States representative to NATO, was disappointed with the initial terms of his appointment (for example, no direct access to foreign political leaders). When his dissatisfaction was expressed during a break at one of the Council meetings, the group helped him draft an alternative proposal. Allen W. Dulles (a member of the group) communicated the proposal to White House adviser and Council member Averell Harriman the next day, and this resulted in appropriate changes by President Truman.[16]

Those still impressed by the imagery of the "New Frontier" might expect to find that the Kennedy administration brought in a new breed of foreign policy officials. They would be mistaken, however. The recruitment of a number of top officials from the "Eastern establishment" was an important part of Kennedy's strategy for establishing confidence in his presidency. Council member Arthur Schlesinger's comments on the process of recruitment are quite revealing in this respect:

> Kennedy's acquaintance had, indeed, certain limitations... In particular, he was little acquainted in the New York financial and legal community—that arsenal of talent which had so long furnished a steady supply of always orthodox and often able people to Democratic as well as Republican administrations. This continuity was the heart of the American Establishment. Its household deities were Henry L. Stimson and Elihu Root; its present leaders, Robert A. Lovett and John J. McCloy; its front organizations, the Rockefeller, Ford and Carnegie Foundations and the Council on Foreign Relations; its organs, the *New York Times* and *Foreign Affairs*...
>
> The New York Establishment had looked on Kennedy with some suspicion... Now that he was President, however, they were prepared to rally round; and, now that he was President, he was prepared to receive them. This too was part of the strategy of reassurance.[17]

The key contact in this aspect of recruitment was Robert Lovett, to whom Kennedy first offered the choice of Defense, State, or Treasury. Lovett declined, because of health problems, but was willing to make suggestions. Because of his poor health, Lovett had participated relatively little in organizational activities for some years and had let his Council membership lapse. He remained, however, very much a part of the informal network of contacts with which the Council was associated, and had a number of names ready for Kennedy. For Defense Lovett suggested McNamara, who had worked under him in the Defense Department. For Treasury Kennedy chose Douglas Dillon, who had served under Eisenhower and was to become a Council director shortly after his term in office under Kennedy. Dean Rusk, whom Lovett proposed for secretary of state, had been active in the Council and, according to Council official MacEachron, was originally called to Kennedy's attention as a result of a 1960 article he wrote for *Foreign Affairs*.[18] It is an interesting commentary on the close relationships among the people in the establishment's "front organizations" that five of the men who were being mentioned for the position of secretary of state were at a meeting of the Rockefeller Foundation board when President Kennedy first contacted Rusk, the Rockefeller Foundation president. Others present at the meeting, according to Schlesinger, were Lovett, McCloy, Chester Bowles, and Ralph Bunche.[19] All except Lovett were Council members at the time.

Altogether, 51 percent of the top foreign policy officials under Kennedy were members of the Council on Foreign Relations. Among postwar administrations this percentage was only exceeded by Kennedy's successor, with 57 percent of the Johnson officials being Council members. It is logical that the Council ties should have continued under Johnson, in spite of the non-eastern Texas flavor of the administration, as the key foreign policy figures stayed on after Kennedy's assassination and into Johnson's second term. To these holdovers, such as McNamara, Rusk, and Bundy, were added other Council members, such as Walt W. Rostow and George W. Ball. Nevertheless, one Council official expressed the feeling that the Council had been somewhat more distant from the Johnson administration.[20] While this feeling may have been more a matter of style than of substance, it is interesting to note that, as if to remedy such a problem, several prominent people of the Johnson administration, not previously Council members, were brought into the Council and very shortly thereafter joined its board of directors. Bill Moyers became a director in 1967, Cyrus Vance in 1968, and Paul Warnke in 1972.

It is commonplace to note that in the Nixon and Ford

administrations there has been an unprecedented concentration of foreign policy leadership in the person of Henry A. Kissinger. As already noted, Kissinger's career has been molded to a great extent by his relationship with the Council on Foreign Relations. Kissinger himself wrote in 1961 that "the Council on Foreign Relations gave me my first opportunity to work systematically on problems of foreign policy. My relations with it have remained close and my admiration for it, if anything, increased."[21] In 1965 Kissinger wrote his second book for the Council in the Atlantic Policy Studies Series, and from 1965 to 1973 served on the editorial board of *Foreign Affairs*. While Kissinger's preeminence has recently exposed him to criticism from Council colleagues on both the style and substance of his policies, he is still part of that community. And one-third of his colleagues in the foreign policy bureaucracy in the first Nixon administration were also Council members.

The Congress also plays a role in foreign policy, although it is generally agreed that its role is secondary and reactive vis-à-vis the executive branch.[22] It has responsibility for legislation concerning foreign policy, which is important in some cases, although most key decisions are made by the executive branch without benefit of legislative consideration. Congress does have some importance since sentiment in Congress is often taken by officials as representative of public opinion.[23]

The Council on Foreign Relations has links with those committees in Congress which deal with foreign affairs, although in 1969 only 1 percent of Council members held elective government office. On the Senate Foreign Relations Committee in the Ninety-third Congress (1973-1974), eight of the seventeen senators were CFR members. The names of these senators are well known: Frank Church, Stuart Symington, Claiborne Pell, Gale W. McGee, George McGovern, Hubert Humphrey, Clifford Case, and Jacob Javits. Although some of those not in the Council are equally prominent, such as J. W. Fulbright and Hugh Scott, there can be no doubt that the Council has access to the Senate, as is also witnessed by the Council membership of Carl Marcy, the chief of staff for the committee since 1955. Among the forty congressmen on the House Foreign Affairs Committee, however, Council representation is more sparse, as befits the lesser role of the House in foreign policy. Only Congressmen Jonathan Bingham, Ogden Reid, and Peter Frelinghuysen were listed as Council members.

The Council and the Media

The importance of the media is not just that they are the primary sources of information about foreign policy for the "informed public." They are also primary sources of information for the government officials themselves, as well as instruments of intrabureaucratic warfare through open publicity and "leaks." Government officials also take the media as another important index to public opinion.[24]

At the top of the list is the *New York Times*, the newspaper most read by America's leaders and the only United States paper in Merrill's listing of the ten "primary elite" newspapers in the world.[25] In 1972, three out of ten directors of the New York Times Company and five out of nine editorial executives were Council members. In perusing the index of Gay Talese's book on the *New York Times*, one discovers at least twenty people associated with the *Times* who also belong to the Council on Foreign Relations.[26] Of particular note are the Sulzbergers, members of the owning family, and such well-known figures as James Reston, Max Frankel, and Harrison Salisbury. Among the original directors of the Council was John H. Finley, an associate editor of the *Times*. Hanson W. Baldwin, for years military correspondent for the *Times,* was one of the leaders of the Council's War and Peace Studies, as well as several subsequent studies focused on military affairs.

In terms of Council membership involvement, the *Washington Post* is also close to the Council, although somewhat less so than the *Times.* In 1972 one of its five editorial executives and four of its nine directors were Council members, including chairman Frederick S. Beebe (now deceased), president Katherine Graham, and vice-president Osborn Elliott. Elliott is editor-in-chief of *Newsweek,* which is owned by the same company.

Newsweek has had a number of other connections with the Council. One of its founders was Council director W. Averell Harriman, and either he or his brother Roland, also a Council member, was on the board of the magazine from the 1930s to the 1950s. Lewis W. Douglas, a Council director, was on *Newsweek's* board during the 1950s. Currently the links to the Council of *Newsweek's* rival, *Time,* appear to be stronger. *Time's* founder, Henry Luce, was a Council member for at least thirty years. Hedley Donovan, the present editor-in-chief, is on the Council's board, and an active participant in its leadership. Seven of sixteen directors are Council members. The third major news weekly, *U.S. News and World Report,* has few current ties, as judged by the absence of Council members among its executives and directors, but its founder and editor into the 1970s, David Lawrence, was a Council member for over twenty years. Of *Time's* and *Newsweek's* directors, in 1972 almost half were members of the Council.

Also linked with the Council through their directors are two of the three major radio and television networks. CBS is the closest in these terms, with seven of its directors in the Council, including W. A. M. Burden, also a director of the Council. NBC is also represented in the Council, with two of the directors of its parent corporation (RCA) as members.

Among prominent radio and television journalists in the Council are Richard C. Hottelet, Daniel L. Schorr, and Marvin Kalb of CBS, and John Chancellor of NBC. The Council has honored the memory of former member Edward R. Murrow with a fellowship for foreign correspondents, financed by a $300,000 endowment from the CBS Foundation.

While the Council's contacts in the general media are good, in the area of widely read foreign affairs magazines, it has virtually a monopoly. *Foreign Affairs,* for years the leading magazine in the field, is published by the Council itself. Now its preeminence is somewhat threatened by the new *Foreign Policy* magazine, which has a brighter, more readable format and is intended to be less stuffy than *Foreign Affairs.* It was initiated by John Franklin Campbell, the young foreign-service officer who died in 1971 at the age of 31. Following Campbell's death, the magazine obtained financing from the Carnegie Endowment for International Peace, under its energetic new president, Council member Thomas L. Hughes. The editors of *Foreign Policy* have all been Council members. Its eleven-man advisory board is composed exclusively of Council members, including two directors of the Council. *Foreign Policy* is somewhat more open to divergent views than *Foreign Affairs* and certainly projects a different image, but its direction is still solidly within the Council community.

Think-Tanks and Foreign Policy Organizations

In the foreign policy community external to the government, there are other organizations besides the Council with an interest in working out policy options to feed into the process of opinion and policy formation. One type is the nonprofit research organization, or think-tank, which gains its income from foundations or from government and business contracts. One of the most prominent is the Brookings Institution in Washington. Brookings deals with a wider range of issues than the Council and is best known for its studies of domestic and economic issues, especially government finance. It does, however, have a section dealing with foreign policy as well.

Brookings' ties with the Council are substantial. Over the years, at least eight Council directors have served as trustees on the board at Brookings. In 1966 this board included two Council directors and five other Council members among the twenty-two trustees. Henry D. Owen, the director of Brookings' Foreign Policy Studies Program, is a Council member. These ties at the top are often supplemented by working relationships, in which the same staff work on an issue at Brookings and at the Council, either at the same time or moving from one organization to the other. Thus Doak Barnett's studies of China policy and Fred Bergsten's work on international economic issues received backing from both organizations, and a recent book by Brookings staff member Seyom Brown was one of the products of a Council study group.[27]

Other important organizations similar to Brookings, with major ties to the Defense Department in particular, are the RAND Corporation, the Institute for Defense Analysis (IDA), and the Hudson Institute. RAND has worked particularly for the air force, the Institute for Defense Analysis organizes the work of several universities for the Defense Department, and the Hudson Institute is the place where Herman Kahn engages in his cosmic speculations for those who are willing to pay for them. Table 2-1 shows that in every case the interlocking with the Council is substantial. IDA's links are perhaps particularly close, as it is chaired by Council director William A. M. Burden.

There is another set of organizations dealing with foreign

Table 2-1

Number and Percentage of Trustees of Major Research Organizations Who Are Also Members or Directors of the Council

	Number of trustees	Number in Council	Percentage in Council	Number who are Council directors
Brookings Institution (1966 trustees)	22	7	32	2
RAND Corporation (1969 trustees)	20	9	45	2
Institute for Defense Analysis (1969 trustees)	22	9	41	4
Hudson Institute (1970 trustees)	14	8	57	0

policy, concerned with public education more than with research, the most prominent of which is the Foreign Policy Association (FPA). It is often confused with the Council on Foreign Relations, but they are really quite different in function, as is illustrated by the quip quoted by Joseph Kraft, that the difference is like that between the New York phone book and *Who's Who in America*.[28] With its Great Decisions programs and Headline Series pamphlets, the Foreign Policy Association seeks to define foreign policy issues for the "attentive public." Another of its wide range of activities consists in preparation of foreign policy briefs, which are sent to all incumbents and candidates for Congress. It is the FPA that will most often be in contact with local world affairs councils and which gets its material onto radio programs and into extension courses of universities around the country. The Council views it as a complementary rather than rival organization. Thus CFR director Isaiah Bowman wrote in 1935 that the FPA has "breadth of influence," and the CFR "depth." He commented that "anyone with the slightest experience in such matters knows that you must have policy-making individuals and groups working together closely in a government" (the Council's role) as well as "the support of an electorate," requiring bodies which act "as channel-ways of expression" (the FPA's role).[29]

Table 2-2 shows the extent of interlock between the Council and the FPA as well as a number of other organizations with similar functions, each with its own special focus. One of them, the American Assembly, is centered at Columbia University and was founded by Council president Henry Wriston on behalf of Dwight D. Eisenhower, who was then president of that university. As will be shown in Chapter 5, other organizations listed in the table, such as the United Nations Association and the National Planning Association, may also play a complementary and coordinated role with the Council when a particular issue is under debate.

Another kind of organization found in the external foreign policy community consists of special-purpose foundations, which both finance research and study projects and carry out some such projects with their own staffs. Particularly prominent is the Carnegie Endowment for International Peace, which carries on a number of programs, publications, and special projects. Fifteen of its twenty-one trustees (as of 1971) were members of the Council. Its president from 1950 to 1971, Joseph E. Johnson, also served as a director of the Council during the same period. The World Peace Foundation, in Boston, had nine of its nineteen trustees in the Coun-

Table 2-2
Number and Percentage of Leaders of
Major Foreign Policy Organizations Who Are
Also Members or Directors of the Council

	Number of directors	Number in Council	Percentage in Council	Number who are Council directors
Foreign Policy Association (1972 directors)	74	31	42	1
United Nations Association (1972 governors)	23	8	35	2
National Planning Association (1964 trustees)	39	8	21	1
American Universities field staff (1972 trustees and associates)	32	8	25	0
American Assembly (1969 trustees)	20	12	60	4

cil (also in 1971), including two Council directors, one of whom was World Peace Foundation's current chairman, Carroll Wilson. The series of Documents on American Foreign Relations, now published by the Council, was taken over from the World Peace Foundation in 1952.

Also of interest, although it ceased some years ago to involve itself in foreign policy to focus on publishing Woodrow Wilson's papers, is the Woodrow Wilson Foundation. It is indicative of the Council's ties to Wilsonian internationalism that eight of the twenty-two men who were Council directors for more than twenty years each also served as trustees of this foundation. When the Council acquired its present building after the Second World War, and abandoned its old offices, they were occupied by the Woodrow Wilson Foundation. In 1955, 60 percent of the Foundation's trustees were Council members.

A look at regionally focused foreign policy groups reveals the same pattern of extensive Council contacts. Included in Table 2-3 are seven groups, concerned with Europe, Asia, Latin America, and Africa. In each case more than one-third of the directors of the organization were members of the Council. In two cases, the Center for Inter-American Relations and the Atlantic Council, large numbers of the Council directors were involved. Yet these seven by no means exhaust the number of such groups with ties to the Council. One, the Asia Society, for which a list of directors was not available, was founded by Council member John D. Rockefeller III. Its president in 1971 was Philips Talbot, who, along with Rockefeller, has been active in Council studies dealing with Asia.

This list of foreign-policy organizations of all kinds is by no means complete. But the twenty considered certainly include most of the more prominent such groups in the United States. The striking conclusion is that not one of them has less than one-fifth of its leadership involved in the Council on

Table 2-3

Number and Percentage of Leaders of Regionally Focused Organizations Who Are Also Members or Directors of the Council

	Number of directors	Number in Council	Percentage in Council	Number who are Council directors
Center for Inter-American Relations (1972 directors)	23	17	74	3
Free Europe Committee (1960 directors)	17	10	59	1
Atlantic Council (1967 officers and directors	91	52	57	10
Council for Latin America (1970 executive committee)	20	10	50	1
Middle East Institute (1970 governors)	33	15	45	0
National Committee on U.S.-China Relations (1970 trustees)	27	12	44	1
African-American Institute (1971 trustees)	30	11	37	0

Foreign Relations. In some cases these men may have been selected for the Council because of their prominence in the other organization; in other cases their Council contacts may have led to the other involvement. But whatever the cause of the overlap, the result is the establishment of a solid network of contacts between the Council and a whole set of other organizations making up the external foreign policy community.

Elite Universities and the Council on Foreign Relations

It should be no surprise to anyone that the links between the Council and the private universities of the East Coast are quite close. While other large universities, such as Wisconsin and Michigan, may be tied to the federal government through contracts, grants, and advising, at the top policy levels it is the Ivy League schools that are in first place. There are a variety of ties between these universities and the Council.

To start with, 17 percent of the Council members with undergraduate degrees and 15 percent of the directors attended Harvard University. Yale is not far behind, with 13 percent of the members and 16 percent of the directors. If one adds Princeton and Columbia as well, 48 percent of the Council members (1969) and 42 percent of the Council directors (from 1922 to 1972) attended one of these four universities. At the graduate level the concentration is even more striking. Among those with graduate degrees (including law), 70 percent attended Harvard, Yale, Princeton, or Columbia, as did 58 percent of the directors. A high representation of graduates of these schools is not unusual in affluent sectors of American life. For Council members, however, the percentages are even greater than for such groups as the top executives of the 100 largest corporations, or the chief diplomatic officers from 1946 to 1964.[30] The high proportion is only comparable to that among Wall Street lawyers, 51 percent of whom attended the four schools as undergraduates and 73 percent as graduates.[31]

Council members are not just related to these universities as alumni. Twelve percent of the Council membership and 24 percent of the directors since 1922 could be identified as having some link, as an officer, director, or staff member,

Table 2-4

Number of Governing Board Members of Thirteen Major Universities Who Are Also Members or Directors of the Council (1973)

	Number of board members	Number in Council	Number of Council directors
Harvard	30	12	1
Yale	21	10	3
Princeton	58	10	1
MIT	71	8	0
Columbia	18	7	2
Johns Hopkins	50	7	2
Chicago	69	6	1
NYU	38	5	1
Cornell	61	5	1
Michigan	9	0	0
California	16	0	0
Illinois	15	0	0
Wisconsin	9	0	0

The Council Network 77

with Harvard University. That means that about 170 Council members (out of 1440) and 17 directors have been associated with Harvard. Six directors were associated with Yale, seven with Princeton, twelve with Columbia, and seven with MIT (although comparatively few Council members attended MIT). Approximately eighty Council members were connected with Columbia, the same number with Yale, almost sixty with Princeton, and more than forty with MIT.[32]

Looking at the same association from the other side, one finds similar results. Table 2-4 shows thirteen major universities (those whose graduates are most likely to make it into *Who's Who*, plus MIT and Johns Hopkins) with the number of governing board members who are also in the Council. Again these five universities are at the top, joined by Johns Hopkins. The state universities, at least judged by their boards of regents, are evidently not integrated into the Council's network. While scholars from these universities are included in the Council's membership, the institutional relationship is not nearly so intimate as in the case of the exclusive private universities.

The Financing of Foreign Affairs Research: The Council and the Foundations

Among the primary sources of funds both for university research and for other foreign policy organizations are the major foundations. As will be seen in the next chapter, the Council's own financing depends largely on these sources. But this part of the network is important for other reasons. A State Department publication reporting on 191 university-affiliated centers of foreign affairs research, notes the key role of three foundations, listing as most frequent sources of funds the Ford Foundation (107 centers), the federal govern ment (67 centers), the Rockefeller Foundation (18 centers), and the Carnegie Corporation (17 centers).[33] For eleven of the top twelve universities with institutes of international studies, Ford is the principal source of funding.[34] Rockefeller and Carnegie, with fewer assets than the gargantuan Ford Foundation, have concentrated their money on a smaller number of institutions, but these have been important ones, such as the Russian Institute at Columbia (Rockefeller) and the Russian Research Center at Harvard (Carnegie). These two centers have dominated the study of the Soviet Union in this country since their founding in the years following the Second World War. Similar domination by foundation-funded centers can be shown in the fields of African studies, Latin American studies, and China studies.[35]

It is logical, then, that the Council should have close ties with these three foundations, somewhat more distant relations with others, and no connection at all with most. Of the thirty-three foundations with assets exceeding $100 million in 1968, twenty had no trustees who were Council members.[36] In general these foundations were located outside New York, and concentrated on local affairs or on other nonforeign policy areas. Those with close ties to the Council included at most the seven foundations shown in Table 2-5. Topping the list is the Rockefeller Foundation, with fourteen of its nineteen trustees members of the Council, four of them as directors. The president of the Rockefeller Foundation, George Harrar, is a Council member and the chairman, Douglas Dillon, is a member of the Council's board. Not unexpectedly, the Rockefeller Brothers Fund also has substantial overlap with the Council, including three Rockefeller brothers David, Nelson, and John D. III, as well as Rodman Rockefeller in the next generation.

Also quite close is the Carnegie Corporation of New York. Among the ten Council members on its board are two Council directors. The Carnegie foundations have had no connec-

Table 2-5

Number of Council Members Among Trustees of Seven Leading Foundations (1971)

Rockefeller Foundation	14 out of 19
Carnegie Corporation	10 out of 17
Ford Foundation	7 out of 16
Rockefeller Brothers Fund	6 out of 11
A. P. Sloan Foundation	5 out of 17
Commonwealth Fund	4 out of 9
C. F. Kettering Foundation	3 out of 13

tions with a single family since they were established by Andrew Carnegie. But the Carnegie foundations themselves make up a kind of family which includes, in addition to the Carnegie Corporation, the Carnegie Institution of Washington, the Carnegie Endowment for International Peace, and the Carnegie Foundation for the Advancement of Teaching, as well as other smaller funds. These have been intimately associated with the Council. One-fourth (nineteen) of all the Council's directors up to 1972 have served as trustees or officers of at least one of the Carnegie foundations.

The interlocks between the Ford Foundation and the Council are also substantial, with seven of its sixteen board members in the Council. No Council directors were on the Ford Foundation board, according to data from 1971. In the 1950s, however, John J. McCloy was chairman of both the Council and the Ford Foundation. The current president of the Ford Foundation is Council member McGeorge Bundy.

80 *Imperial Brain Trust*

The Council's International Contacts

As an organization concerned with foreign policy, it is appropriate that the network of contacts in which the Council is involved should extend overseas as well. Since Council membership is limited to American citizens, however, such connections are not incorporated within the Council as such. Some contacts are made, of course, when foreign statesmen appear at the Council when in New York, but there are also institutionalized associations on a variety of levels.

A Council-connected organization which seems to play a role of promoting informal international communication, and which has a tradition of secretiveness, is the so-called Bilderberg group. It takes its name from its first session in 1954 at the Hotel de Bilderberg in Holland. The Bilderberg group is composed of leaders from Western Europe and North America, led by David Rockefeller and Prince Bernhard of the Netherlands. The Bilderberg meetings provide opportunities for informal off-the-cuff and off-the-record exchanges of ideas about world affairs. While these meetings are shielded from publicity, and no information on their content is available, the participants are known. Among the United States participants, 121 (71 percent) are members of the Council. The Steering Committee of fifteen and the Advisory Committee of seven are made up exclusively of members of the Council on Foreign Relations.[37]

Probably of greater importance, however, is the Trilateral Commission; of recent origin, it represents an attempt to establish a new level of cooperation among the leaders of the advanced capitalist countries. The commission's work will be covered in detail in Chapter 7.

Conclusion

While our analysis has not included every possible organization concerned with foreign policy, it is sufficient to show the existence of an extensive network, tied with the Council, reaching into sector after sector of the foreign policy community. The Council is thus able to acquire information and to communicate ideas—in short, to coordinate the formation of opinion on foreign policy. This by no means implies that the Council, as an organization, directs and organizes this whole web of formal and informal contacts, but it is the formal expression of an exclusive community. It reflects that community, it strengthens that community, and it helps guide its course. The Council, and the community it represents, are at the very center of the process through which opinion on foreign policy is formed.

Suggested Readings

For background on the concept of "elite," as applied to the United States, see Keller (1963), Prewitt and Stone (1973), Dye and Zeigler (1970), and Domhoff and Ballard (1968). Dye, DeClerq, and Pickering (1973) report an interesting study of interlocking elites, which incidentally identifies Council leaders as prominent among the "multiple interlockers." Kadushin (1974) focuses on the intellectual elite, and Hodgson (1973) on the foreign policy establishment.

On the social origin and background of government officials, there are a number of studies available. Matthews (1954) provides general background; Stanley, Mann, and Doig (1967) present the results of a detailed Brookings study; and Harr (1969) and Mennis (1971) have additional details on foreign policy officials in particular; Domhoff (1967, 1970) shows the overlap between top government officials and the social upper class. Kolko (1969) and Barnet (1972) note the importance of current ties of key officials to key sectors of finance and law. Cohen (1973) and Halperin (1974) are recent political science perspectives on how the foreign policy elite functions, although they pay little attention to identifying the elite as a social group. On members of Congress, see Green, Fallows, and Zwick (1972).

For further reading on the different kinds of organizations mentioned in this chapter, the following sources, incomplete and of varying quality, are suggested:

Media: Network Project (1973), Talese (1969), and B. Cohen (1963).

Think-tanks and other policy organizations: Domhoff (1970), Eakins (1966), Dickson (1971).

Universities: NACLA (1969), Smith (1974).

Foundations: Nielsen (1972), Goulden (1971), Horowitz (1969).

International organizations: Allen (1971), Quigley (1966), publications of the Trilateral Commission.

The readings suggested for this chapter are of widely varying perspectives and only a few put the information about elites in a context of class analysis, for which the reader should refer to the readings suggested for the next chapter.

Notes

1. CFR, 1919:5.
2. On the significance of social networks, see Mitchell (1969) for a general discussion. Perucci and Pilisuk (1970) and Laumann, Verbrugge, and Pappi (1974) apply the concept to the study of community elites. Kadushin (1974) has applied the concept to the study of the American intellectual elite, while Dye, DeClerq, and Pickering (1973) have examined interlocking among various national institutional elites in the United States. Granovetter (1973) has emphasized that even weak ties may be important in creating a network of relationships. Dooley (1969), Allen (1974), and Sondquist and Koenig (1975) have examined in particular interlocking directorates among American corporations. Domhoff (1975) has a useful network study of ruling-class cohesiveness.
3. See Minter, 1973a. The list was compiled from United States Government organization manuals, and included officials dealing with foreign policy from the assistant secretary level in the State

Department and from the undersecretary level in other agencies. There was a total of 513 names, including some repetitions for those who served in more than one administration.
4. Barnet, 1972:49.
5. Kraft, 1958:67.
6. Campbell, 1971:51.
7. White, 1965:87-88.
8. Lukas, 1971:126
9. CFR, 1953:42.
10. Thomson, 1974:67.
11. Lukas, 1971:125.
12. *New York Times*, December 22, 1974:26.
13. The CFR men on the Commission were Rockefeller, Dillon, Joseph Lane Kirkland, John T. Connor, and Lyman L. Lemnitzer.
14. CFR, 1967:79; CFR, 1973:103.
15. Marchetti and Marks, 1974:267.
16. Wriston interview, March 28, 1973.
17. Schlesinger, 1965:127-129.
18. Ibid., 141; MacEachron interview, September 26, 1972.
19. Schlesinger, 1965:141.
20. MacEachron interview, September 26, 1972.
21. Kissinger, 1961:xi.
22. See Cohen, 1973:113ff. and references.
23. Ibid.
24. Ibid., 106ff and references.
25. Merrill, 1968.
26. Talese, 1969.
27. Brown, 1974.
28. Kraft, 1958:64.
29. Bowman to Shepardson, November 1, 1935, Isaiah Bowman Papers, Shepardson File, JHUL.
30. Pierson, 1969:26-27, 112-113.
31. Ibid., 47-48.
32. These approximate figures are calculated from the percentages taken from a 1969 random sample of 200 Council members. See Minter, 1973a.
33. NACLA, 1969:35-41.
34. Horowitz, 1969:11.
35. On African studies see Africa Research Group, 1969, 1970; on Latin American studies see NACLA, 1970; on China studies see Horowitz, 1971.

36. The list of foundations is taken from Nielsen, 1972.
37. The list of Bilderberg participants is taken from Allen (1971, cloth ed.). For more information see Pasymowski and Gilbert (1971).

3
The Council and the New York Financial Oligarchy

We have located the Council on Foreign Relations at the center of a network linking both private and government sectors of the foreign policy community. The picture presented so far lacks an essential element, however, for neither the Council as an organization nor the Council network and community exist within an isolated world of foreign policy expertise. The Council is solidly based in the United States capitalist class and represents a conscious initiative of the dominant sector of that class, the New York financial oligarchy.[1] Unless this is taken into account, the content of the Council's views and the extent of its influence are largely inexplicable.

It is in this context that policy groups such as the Council on Foreign Relations take on particular significance. For they provide the opportunity, on the one hand, for the capitalist class to "get itself together"—in the particular case of the Council, to work out ideas on the broad lines of the correct foreign policy to adopt. On the other hand, they also provide the opportunity to incorporate into this consensus-building operation others outside the capitalist class whose roles are important in implementing the policy. In the case of the Council, these include particularly the government officials, scholars, and journalists involved in the Council's activities, and the broader "attentive public" that read the Council's publications. The Council seems ideally designed to maintain capitalist class consensus and hegemony in the area of foreign affairs.

Evidence that the Council is based in the United States capitalist class can be found in the membership, leadership, and financial backing of the Council, and in the links of the Council with specific sectors of the capitalist class.

The Capitalist Class in the Membership of the Council

Only scattered data on the assets held by Council members and on their ties to families involved in the control of the major corporations are available. It is, however, possible to get a bare minimum estimate of the proportion of Council members who are in the capitalist class by looking at what information is available. Seven percent of the members (from a 1969 random sample of the membership) fall into the category of prominent propertied rich.[2] That is, their names (or those of immediate family members) appear on lists of the prominent rich in books by Ferdinand Lundberg, S. Menshikov, and Don Villarejo, or in *Fortune* magazine.[3] Many of the names are familiar: the Rockefeller brothers, financiers John Hay Whitney, Clarence Dillon and his son Douglas, two members of the Corning Glass Works Houghton family, the Watson brothers of IBM. An additional 33 percent are top executives or directors of major corporations (those corporations appearing on the *Fortune* lists, plus leading investment banks and corporate law firms). Six percent more can be characterized as capitalists on the basis of a variety of such evidence as estate records and references in biographies. This gives a total of 46 percent of the Council membership as members of the capitalist class. This figure is of interest only as an extreme lower limit, since many in the sample may have wealth which has not come to public attention and may serve as executives or directors of large corporations not on the *Fortune* lists.

Social indicators of ruling-class membership give a somewhat similar picture. Again the estimate is a minimum one, because the criterion used is only one of those used by Domhoff in identifying this class sociologically. One-third of the Council members are listed in the *Social Register,* either of New York (24 percent) or of another city (9 percent). Combining the social indicator with the previous economic criteria, we find that at least 55 percent of the Council's members are included.

A look at club memberships of Council members is consistent with this picture. For the Century Association it was possible to locate a complete list of members, and the result was that one-fourth of all the Council members turned out to be in this one club. Membership in other clubs was determined by less complete information, such as listing of club membership in a *Who's Who* entry. Since many do not list club memberships and some Council members are not included in *Who's Who,* these are also low estimates. Even so, 13 percent were identified as members of the Metropolitan Club (Washington) and the same percentage as members of the University Club (New York). The Cosmos Club (Washington) and the Links Club (New York) followed with 8 percent and 5 percent respectively. This represents a substantial participation in the Council, since even 5 percent of the Council's membership is more than seventy people.

Since the capitalist class is composed of families and not just of individuals, it also makes sense to look at the family ties among Council members. If the Council were purely an organization of experts selected on "meritocratic" grounds, one would expect to find only occasional kinship ties among the members. However, a full 8 percent had a father, son, or brother who was also a member. At least 3 percent more had a father-in-law, son-in-law, or brother-in-law among the members. Adding in other relatives that it was possible to identify, a total of 11 percent of the Council members were found to have relatives among the other members. Since these results are based on very incomplete genealogical data, the actual proportion is undoubtedly much higher. It is not quite "one big family," but there are tendencies in that direction. Those who did have relatives in the Council were almost all among those identified earlier as belonging to the capitalist class.

What about the 45 percent of the Council members not so far identified as members of the "capitalist class"? They are uniformly of high status, suitable for assimilation into the class, and possessors of occupational skills needed for the Council's work. The occupations represented in the Council are shown in Table 3-1. The largest category—40 percent—is of business occupations. If one adds the media executives, who also run profit-oriented enterprises, the figure comes to almost 50 percent. Other large categories are academic and government officials. A small minority (less than 1 percent) are linked with the working class as labor leaders. They included in 1969 such figures as Jay Lovestone, Walter Reuther, and Irving Brown, prominent in the area of CIA subsidies to foreign labor leaders.[4] By 1973 this element of CFR membership also included Lane Kirkland, Leonard Woodcock, and Jerry Wurf.

The membership of these men, as well as of others whose particular skills or position are useful, indicates that the Council's base in the capitalist class does not automatically exclude those without wealth or the proper social standing. On the contrary, if they have needed skills and are "of the type which could understand and appreciate Elihu Root,"[5] they may be expected to be called upon by the Council to

Table 3-1

Primary Occupations of Council Members

	Percentage	
Business executive (other than financier)	22	
Financier	10	
Lawyer	8	
Total business		40
Scholars	21	
Academic administrators	7	
Media executives	8	
Reporters	2	
Organizational executives (foundations, labor, religious, other)	6	
Government official (including military)	16	

contribute to its deliberations. And, perhaps in compensation, in their contacts with the wealthy and distinguished they may have a chance to acquire those characteristics for themselves and their families.

Adequate evidence of assimilation into the capitalist class is not available, but a couple of examples may be indicative of the possibilities. Henry Kissinger probably did not have sufficient assets to be considered a member of the capitalist class when he began his career in foreign policy with a stint at the Council—none of the biographical references indicate a wealthy family background. But given gifts such as $50,000 from his patron Nelson A. Rockefeller, whom he met through the Council, a $60,000-a-year salary as secretary of state, a multimillionaire brother, and, in 1974, marriage into a socially prominent family, it is likely that he now has accumulated enough wealth to be considered a member of the class. One may also consider Henry M. Wriston, Council president from 1951 to 1964. Son of a clergyman, there is no evidence that his family had substantial assets, nor was he listed in the *Social Register*. But he became a member of the Century Association and a director of a number of financial institutions during his career as college president and Council executive. His son, Walter, also a Council member, became the chief executive of First National City Bank and in 1973 was reported as owning almost $2 million of stock in that bank alone.[6]

The fact that the Council and, one would suppose, other similar organizations of the capitalist class, are open to some people who are not already members of that class should not be regarded as a compromise of class dominance or as a sign of impending replacement of that class by "technocrats." Rather, it may more reasonably be taken as one of the mechanisms by which class dominance is implemented and new elements incorporated into the class.

Leadership of the Council

Of greater significance than the precise composition of Council membership is its leadership, because of the heavy concentration of power in the hands of the board of directors and a few senior staff members. The board of directors is responsible for the selection of new members for the Council on the recommendation of the Membership Committee, which is composed of the directors and a few other invited members. The board also has the authority "in its sole discretion" to terminate or suspend the membership of a member who violates, for example, the rule that Council proceedings must be kept confidential. The board also has the responsibility for directing the staff and the programs of the Council. Board members have taken their role seriously and have not been figureheads.

Table 3-2

Capitalist Class Representation in the CFR
(in percent)

Criteria used	Members (1969)	Directors (up to 1972)	Officers (up to 1972)
Economic	46 (n=200)	67 (n=72)	83 (n=30)
Social	33 (n=199)	57 (n=63)	63 (n=30)
Economic and/or social	55 (n=199)	84 (n=63)	93 (n=30)

This concentration of power in the hands of the board and senior staff has been equivalent to a concentration of power in a very small group of men, for their terms of service, in many cases, are of quite extraordinary length. Thus, Hamilton Fish Armstrong, originally assistant to Archibald Cary Coolidge as editor of *Foreign Affairs,* effectively continued the direction of that periodical for the first fifty years of its existence (he became full editor in 1928). Armstrong also served on the board of directors from 1928 through 1972. Walter Mallory was executive director for over thirty years from 1927 through 1959. John W. Davis, Whitney H. Shepardson, Allen W. Dulles, R. C. Leffingwell, and Frank Altschul all served as directors for more than thirty years. Of the total of seventy-two directors from the Council's founding to 1972, twenty-two had been on the board for twenty years or more.

Table 3-2 shows how capitalist representation increases dramatically when one considers, instead of the general membership, the set of directors, or the even smaller group of thirty men who have been officers of the Council.[7] The officers of the Council, if judged by both economic and social criteria, are almost exclusively members of the ruling capitalist class. Considering the two exceptions out of the thirty, the qualifying adverb "almost" is of little substantive significance. One of the two men is executive of a company which does not appear on the *Fortune* lists. The other is the president of the Committee for Economic Development, an organization of 200 leading businessmen which also includes a sprinkling of economists.

Council directors are also heavily involved in the social club and kinship networks observed among the Council members. Two-thirds of the directors were members of the Century Association. Over one-fifth were identified as members of the Links Club (New York), the Metropolitan Club (Washington), and the University Club (New York). Seventeen percent of the Council's directors had a father, son, or brother who was also a Council member; 7 percent had a father-in-law, son-in-law, or brother-in-law in the Council. In all, 22 percent of the Council directors had identifiable relatives who were also Council members.

The Financial Backing of the Council

The financing of Council activities confirms the picture of capitalist dominance indicated by the composition of the Council's leadership. The major sources of funds come through various channels from ruling-class members in the Council itself. These major sources have been dues, contributions from members, foundations, and corporations, income from investments, as well as subscriptions to *Foreign Affairs*. Only the subscriptions might be considered as widely based and as largely external to the Council.

Dues and contributions from members have been a substantial source of income from the start. In the early years they provided half of the Council's income, decreasing in the 1940s to about one-third, and then to only 18 percent from 1957 to 1972, as the Council's budget expanded dramatically. When the Council was founded, dues were set at $100 a year for resident members, $50 a year for nonresident members, and, as a special concession, $10 a year for academic members. By 1972 the dues for resident members had reached $425 a year, but there were a number of special concessions for academic members, government officials, journalists, or those under thirty-five years of age. Since the Council members in these exceptional categories are a minority of the membership, those able to pay the full regular dues were clearly providing most of the dues income.

Many Council members were willing and able to add to their dues substantial contributions to the Council programs. The $125,000 original underwriting fund for *Foreign Affairs* was typical. It was easily filled by Council members and a solicitation to the thousand richest Americans. Council member Howard Heinz of Pittsburgh contributed $25,000 of the total and, before the money was raised, Otto Kahn, a Council director, had promised to provide whatever portion of the first year's $25,000 was not raised from other sources.

At other crucial points in the expansion of the Council, there was similar generosity on the part of Council members. Elihu Root, honorary Council president during the 1920s and 1930s, donated a $25,000 award he received from the Woodrow Wilson Foundation to a sustaining fund for *Foreign Affairs*. When the Council moved to acquire its own building in 1929, Council director Paul Warburg contributed $25,000 toward the sum needed, and John D. Rockefeller II even more. When the Council expanded into a newer and larger building in 1945, the house was donated by Mrs. Harold I. Pratt, whose husband's fortune stemmed from Standard Oil.

John D. Rockefeller II contributed $150,000 toward the upkeep of the house and an equivalent sum was raised among other Council members.

Members continued their high level of support in the postwar period. In 1947 they raised among themselves a twenty-fifth anniversary fund of $225,000. In 1955 Frank Altschul, Council vice-president, contributed $200,000 for a new wing of the Harold Pratt House. Thomas W. Lamont left the Council a $100,000 bequest, and the deficit in the budget of *Foreign Affairs* which began to appear was taken care of regularly by a number of Council members, including directors Altschul, George O. May, David Rockefeller, and Russell C. Leffingwell.

In the 1960s there was an effort to raise a capital fund for the Council, so that a substantial proportion of future income would be insured from investments—the Council itself was to become an owner. David Rockefeller contributed $500,000 in 1964 to this fund. Mrs. Herbert Lehman gave $50,000 in memory of her husband, and eight permanent staff members pledged $102,750. A capital fund of $5 million was quickly raised in 1966 and 1967, boosted by a contribution of $1 million from the children of Thomas Watson of IBM.

It is not unusual in American society for an organization to be financed essentially by appeal to the rich. What is striking in the case of the Council is that the rich to whom the appeal is made are themselves Council members and leaders, including the people organizing the fund raising. The appeal is basically for self-reliance: let's support our own organization. But Council members are not limited to their own private pockets. They wear other hats and can address appeals to themselves as foundation trustees or as executives of corporations. As the financial needs of the Council grew and the programs expanded, increasing appeal was made to these sources in the 1940s and particularly after 1953.

Foundations began significant funding of the Council in

New York Financial Oligarchy

the late 1930s. Previously, foundation grants had averaged about $20,000 a year; from 1936 to 1946, the average jumped to about $90,000 annually. The foundations involved were primarily the Rockefeller Foundation and the Carnegie Corporation of New York. Both were from the start so closely related to the Council that going to them for funds can hardly be seen as going to "outside" sources. The Carnegie Corporation had been organized on the advice of Elihu Root, who continued on its board of trustees until his death in 1937. He was replaced on the board by his son, who was a Council member. In 1940 the Carnegie Corporation board of fourteen trustees included five Council members, including Carnegie Corporation president Frederick P. Keppel and Russell C. Leffingwell, shortly to become the Council's president. The links of the Rockefeller Foundation were even closer, with two-thirds of its twenty-one trustees in 1939 being members of the Council, including three Council directors. Raymond B. Fosdick, president of the Rockefeller Foundation, had been a Council member from the start, as had Jerome D. Green, a trustee of the Foundation and a member of the Council's Special Finance Committee. The Council's Budget Committee in 1940 included Lewis W. Douglas, a Rockefeller Foundation trustee, and Allen W. Dulles, whose brother John Foster was also a trustee of the Foundation.

Carnegie and Rockefeller continued their contributions into the fifties, sixties, and seventies. As was shown in the previous chapter, the interlocks are still substantial in the 1970s, but the biggest contribution to the post-1950 expansion of Council programs came from the newly organized Ford Foundation. In 1953 it made its first major contribution of $100,000 to finance the first year of a study of United States-Soviet relations under the chairmanship of John J. McCloy. Appropriately enough, in the same year McCloy became chairman of the Council, the Ford Foundation, and the Chase Bank. In 1954 the Ford Foundation made a ten-year grant of $1,500,000 to enable a sustained expansion of Council programs.

Another major new source of funds initiated in 1953 was the Council's Corporation Service, previously discussed in Chapter 1. It provides services to corporations which have paid a minimum of $1,000. This program brought in almost $10,000 by the end of the first year, and by 1956 it was bringing in $50,000 annually. Various Council members often took turns soliciting firms in their industries to join the Corporation Service. Particularly active was David Rockefeller, who helped initiate the service with appeals to the banking and oil industries. By the mid-1960s the Corporation Service was providing almost $200,000 a year to the Council.

The Council and the Multinational Corporations

The United States is a large country and its capitalist class, although a small percentage of the population, might number as many as 1.5 million adults, depending on where the borderline of the class is drawn. As such, it is quite large enough to have substantial internal differentiation: by region, by industry, into big business and small business, into financial groups tied to one or more of the major financial institutions. The Council's ties with these different sectors are not randomly distributed. Rather, they are concentrated on big business, which is at the same time that sector of business with the heaviest foreign involvement, the "multinational corporation."

Our previous account of capitalist class representation in the Council already focused on big business in that we paid special attention to those companies listed by *Fortune* magazine. The small businessman with a local clientele in Peoria, or even in New York City, is not likely to be found in the discussions taking place at the Council house. Even within this group of large corporations, the bigger the corporation the more likely it is to be represented in the Council. Twenty-two percent of our 1969 sample of the Council's membership and 29 percent of the Council's directors served on the board of at least one of *Fortune*'s top 500 industrial corporations. Only 5 percent of the sample and 7 percent of the directors were on the board of any of *Fortune*'s second 500 industrials. Even within the top fifty, the same trend was apparent. Companies ranked twenty-one through fifty had an average of one Council member each on their boards, while companies ranked eleven through twenty had an average of two. Among the top ten the average reached four Council members for every board of directors. The big business represented in the Council is really big business. Table 3-3 will give the reader an idea of the kind of companies closely tied to the Council. It represents all those companies we were able to identify with four or more Council members as directors or partners as of 1969.

The rankings in the table show that it is indeed the largest firms which are particularly intimate with the Council. This takes on added significance when one notes the pattern of concentration of foreign investment in the hands of a limited number of United States firms. As early as 1957, according to data quoted by Harry Magdoff, forty-five firms accounted

Table 3-3

Firms with Four or More Council Members as Directors or Partners (1969)

Industrials (with *Fortune* rank, 1970)
    8 members   U.S. Steel (12)
    7 members   Mobil Oil (6)
    6 members   Standard Oil (N.J.) (now Exxon) (2)
    6 members   IBM (5)
    5 members   ITT (8)

Industrials (with *Fortune* rank, 1970)
  5 members General Electric (4)
  4 members E. I. du Pont de Nemours (18)

Commercial banks (with rank by trust holdings, 1972)
  8 members Chase Manhattan Bank (2)
  8 members J. P. Morgan and Co. (1)
  7 members First National City Bank (5)
  7 members Chemical Bank (12)
  6 members Brown Brothers Harriman and Co. (private bank, not ranked)
  4 members Bank of New York (8)

Life insurance companies (with *Fortune* rank, 1970)
  9 members Equitable Life (3)
  8 members New York Life (4)
  4 members Metropolitan Life (2)
  4 members Mutual of New York (11)

Investment banks
  6 members Morgan Stanley
  4 members Kuhn, Loeb
  4 members Lehman Brothers

Law firms (with 1957 ranks from Smigel)
  8 members Sullivan and Cromwell (9)
  7 members Debevoise, Plimpton, Lyons and Gates (not in top twenty in 1957)
  7 members Davis, Polk, Wardwell, Sunderland and Kiendl (6)
  5 members Shearman and Sterling (1)
  4 members Milbank, Tweed, Hadley and McCloy (7)

Investment company
  7 members General American Investors

for almost three-fifths of all direct foreign investment.[8] For these firms, which also tend to be the largest firms, the combined importance of exports and foreign investment is often vital, not only because the profits from these activities may contribute substantially to total profits, but because overseas production and exports may provide the opportunity for growth lacking in a saturated home market. In the last two decades, the concentration of holdings and the importance of overseas investment have continued to grow.[9]

The firms listed in Table 3-3 are certainly included among the top "multinationals." Of the industrials and commercial banks, at least Mobil, IBM, and the First National City Bank earn more than 50 percent of their profits overseas.[10] Chase Manhattan Bank has subsidiaries in over 100 countries and obtains almost 35 percent of its earnings from foreign operations, while Exxon and ITT make 39 and 38 percents of their sales, respectively, overseas.[11] In 1974 DuPont made 28 percent of its total sales overseas and had over 100 plants in twenty-nine countries and territories outside the United States.[12] General Electric, which reported 18 percent foreign sales, is also a full-scale "multinational," with manufacturing facilities in twenty-four countries and an international orientation aimed at building the "GE World System."[13] J. P. Morgan does business in thirty-two different foreign countries and Chemical Bank in twenty-five.[14] Even U.S. Steel, which had only 5 percent of its sales overseas in 1973, is heavily involved abroad in other ways, owning a near majority of stock in a manganese mine in Gabon, a copper mine in South Africa, a nickel mine in Indonesia, iron mines in Canada, and manufacturing or steel making facilities in Spain, Nicaragua, Italy, France, Brazil, India, and Germany.[15] The other financial institutions and law firms listed, while not "multinationals," are intimately involved in the same world economic system as investors in and advisers to the industrial firms and commercial banks. It is thus clear that these corporations and their leaders, dominant in the Council on Foreign Relations, are most concerned with establishing and maintaining a foreign policy and world environment favorable to their very large economic interests overseas.

The Council and the New York Financial Oligarchy

Big business does not consist merely of a set of distinct, independent corporations, however large. A number of studies have shown a convincing, if not yet completely conclusive, picture of networks tying numbers of the major corporations together in cooperating financial interest groups. The ties consist of interlocking directorates, holding of stock, loans, and a wide variety of other links. Playing a prominent role in each group are generally one or more financial institutions, particularly the large commercial banks. One or more major law firms are likely to assist in coordinating affairs within each group.[16]

Certainly the internal power structure of the Council is consistent with the thesis of the prominence of financial groups. Among the Council members, 22 percent are business executives (other than financial), with 10 percent financial executives and 8 percent corporate lawyers. Among the Council directors, the percentage of nonfinancial business executives drops to 7 percent, while financiers and corporate lawyers are 35 percent of the directors. Among the thirty officers of the Council over the years, half have been financiers or corporate lawyers, and there have been no nonfinancial business executives at all. The highest officer of the Council has always been a leading Wall Street lawyer or banker. These facts point to a particular leadership role for the financial community.

While there is abundant evidence showing the existence of

financial groups, the borders between them are not always distinct, and a corporation may have ties with more than one group. This sometimes makes it difficult to determine with which group a corporation is most closely associated. Since much of the information on ties is confidential, inevitably there remains much uncertainty. There has been no fully adequate study of this topic as yet, but one of the better studies to date is by Menshikov.[17] Using his divisions based on historical study, interlocks, financial data, and interviews with many financial leaders, we can get a rough idea of the particular ties of the Council on Foreign Relations. Table 3-4 shows the companies already identified in Table 3-3 as especially tied with the Council, arranged in the financial groups as defined by Menshikov.

It is striking that all of these combinations, with the single exception of DuPont, are New York-based. Menshikov identifies two additional New York groups, in addition to the six listed in the table. Although they were not found in the list of corporations especially tied to the CFR, they are also represented among the Council's leadership. Gabriel Hauge of the Manufacturer's Hanover Trust combination, has been a director and the Council's treasurer since 1964. Douglas Dillon, of the Dillon, Reed group is also on the Council board. This should be contrasted with the minimal participation in Council membership of the nineteen smaller non-New York financial groups identified by Menshikov.[18] The Council is most clearly associated with the New York financial oligarchy.

This identification with New York City is already implicit in the Council's location and its structure as an organization. Membership is divided into resident and nonresident categories, residents being defined as those having their residence or place of business within fifty miles of City Hall, Manhattan. Even nonresident members (slightly more than half the membership) are heavily concentrated on the East Coast. In 1969,

Table 3-4

Companies with Close Council Interlocks

Rockefeller group
Chase Manhattan Bank
Chemical Bank
Bank of New York
Equitable Life
Metropolitan Life
Mobil Oil
Kuhn, Loeb
Debevoise, Plimpton, Lyons and Gates
Milbank, Tweed, Hadley and McCloy
Standard Oil (N.J.)

Morgan group
J. P. Morgan and Company
Morgan Stanley
New York Life
Mutual of New York
Davis, Polk
U.S. Steel
General Electric
IBM

First National City group
First National City Bank
Shearman and Sterling
ITT

Harriman group
Brown Brothers Harriman and Co.

Lehman-Goldman, Sachs group
Lehman Brothers
General American Investors

Sullivan and Cromwell group
Sullivan and Cromwell

Du Pont group
E. I. du Pont de Nemours

---

70 percent of the membership lived in the Northeast. An additional 14 percent were resident in the South, but almost all of these were actually in the Washington metropolitan

area (which counts as the South according to the Census division). Of the Council directors, 85 percent live in the Northeast, with an additional 10 percent in Washington. The representation in the Council from the Midwest, the Deep South, or the West is a mere sprinkling, and even those who are members are obviously less likely to participate in the frequent Council meetings than those located at a more convenient distance.

The subjective identification with New York is well illustrated by Hamilton Fish Armstrong. He was a member of an old "aristocratic" New York family, a descendant of Peter Stuyvesant, last Dutch governor of New Amsterdam, and related to Hamilton Fish, who was secretary of state under President Grant. He was proud of being the only person he knew in New York who was still living in the house he was born in. His father had been a member of the Century Association and he followed in the same tradition.

The pattern of New York concentration can also be observed if one focuses on corporations instead of individual members. Among *Fortune*'s top fifty industrial corporations, those with headquarters in New York had an average of three Council members on every board of directors. For the top ten banks and the top ten life insurance companies, those with headquarters in New York had an average of six Council members per board of directors. Companies included in the same lists, but with headquarters outside New York, averaged only one Council member for each board of directors.[19]

Morgan, Rockefeller, and the Council

While Menshikov and others have noted the division of the New York financial oligarchy into groups, there are ties existing between these combinations. The common participation in the leadership of the Council also points to a certain degree of unity transcending group divisions. Accounts of the New York financial community also indicate the leadership role played within the community by particular family groups, Morgan at the beginning of the century, and later Rockefeller. Thus it is interesting to note that within the Council the pattern of leadership has apparently reflected the changing position of these groups within the financial community. At the Council's origin and until the early 1950s, the most prominent place within the Council was held by men tied to Morgan interests. Since the 1950s the Rockefeller interests have taken the major role in directing Council affairs. But care has always been taken to involve participants associated with other centers of financial power in New York. These tendencies are well shown in the evolution of the Council's board of directors.

The identification with the House of Morgan was well apparent to knowledgeable observers from the composition of the Council's leadership. Thus, in 1933, the State Department was considering the appointment of a Bondholders Council, which would be officially related to the Council on Foreign Relations. But, on reflection, the officials concerned, including Dr. Herbert Feis (a former staff member of the Council) rejected the idea:

> [They] decided it would be inadvisable to ask them [the Council on Foreign Relations] to act in the matter. Unfortunately, among the present officials are two of the counsel for J. P. Morgan, to wit, John W. Davis and Frank Polk, Mr. Leffingwell, a partner of Morgan's, and among the other directors are Norman Davis and Paul Cravath. Not only would the organization appear to represent Wall Street, but above all, the House of Morgan.[20]

Four of the men mentioned here were on the Council's original board of directors in 1921. John W. Davis, who also served as the Council's first president from 1921 to 1933, was the senior partner in Davis, Polk, Wardwell, Gardiner and

Reed, the principal law firm in the Morgan group. As the Council on Foreign Relations is identified with the "liberal" establishment, it is interesting to note that Davis was instrumental in forming the right-wing American Liberty League to oppose the New Deal, and represented South Carolina in defending segregation before the United States Supreme Court. The Council perspective, popularly identified as "liberal internationalism," is, it should be clear, perfectly compatible with conservative views on the proper way to organize domestic society.

Davis served on the Council's board until 1955. His law partner Frank L. Polk, great-nephew of President Polk, was undersecretary of state in 1919 and 1920 before joining Davis in the Morgan law firm. Paul D. Cravath was a member of Cravath, Swaine and Moore, which has come to be one of Wall Street's leading firms. It had close but not exclusive relationships with J. P. Morgan and Company. Three other alumni of Cravath, Swaine and Moore—Thomas K. Finletter, Russell C. Leffingwell, and John J. McCloy—were also to be Council directors.

Norman H. Davis, banker and subsequent elder statesman, made his fortune in Cuba with the Trust Company of Cuba, a Morgan correspondent bank. In 1919 and 1920, after his return from Cuba, he held positions as assistant secretary of the treasury and undersecretary of state. Between the wars, he and others of his colleagues on the Council were members of an informal regular "luncheon group." Included were law partners John Davis and Polk, as well as Russell Leffingwell and George O. May, another Council director who headed the leading accounting firm Price, Waterhouse.

Also active in the early affairs of the Council, although not on its board, was Morgan partner Thomas W. Lamont. He was present at the initial meeting in Paris and took the initiative to recruit Edwin F. Gay for the Council's leadership.

These early leaders with Morgan ties continued to play

important roles in Council affairs into the 1940s and were joined by others. Russell Leffingwell, who moved from Cravath, Swaine and Moore to J. P. Morgan and Company, was added to the Council board in 1927, becoming president in 1944 and chairman of the board in 1946. Also joining the Council's leadership were Owen D. Young and Philip D. Reed of General Electric and Myron C. Taylor of U.S. Steel, both companies prominent in the Morgan group. When John W. Davis died, his law partner Charles M. Spofford filled one of the vacant directorships. The directors also included Devereux Josephs, a director of J. P. Morgan and Company.

Nevertheless, in the late 1940s the role of the Morgan interests declined. Strong leaders Norman Davis and Edwin Gay were no longer present by 1945. Leffingwell's chairmanship lasted until 1953. Then the leadership appears to have passed into Rockefeller hands. John D. Rockefeller II had not been a Council member, although his money had helped finance its activities and many of his associates had participated. His sons John D. III, Nelson, and David joined the Council in the late 1930s and early 1940s, and in 1949 David Rockefeller was chosen a director. In 1952 he became a member of the Committee on Policy which recommended expansion of the Council's programs. When the proposals met with some questioning due to the organization's financial deficit, Rockefeller commented that he thought the programs were essential, and that he, for one, would do his part to make them possible. According to George S. Franklin, Jr., Council executive director from 1953 through 1971, the tone of the discussion changed dramatically at that point.[21]

Franklin's own position is also indicative of the transition from Morgan to Rockefeller preeminence. One of David Rockefeller's college roommates, and a relative by marriage, Franklin was a law clerk in the Davis, Polk law firm, then became an assistant to Nelson A. Rockefeller. His father had been in the interwar "luncheon group" with both Davises and

Polk. With the Department of State during the war, he joined the Council on Foreign Relations staff in 1945. Also indicative of the same change were adjustments in the top leadership of the Council. David Rockefeller had become vice-president in 1950. John J. McCloy, formerly of Cravath, Swaine and Moore, replaced Leffingwell as Council chairman in 1953. While Leffingwell had started at Cravath, Swaine and Moore, moving subsequently to J. P. Morgan, McCloy assumed the chairmanship of Rockefeller's Chase Bank at the same time as taking over as Council chairman.

In the 1950s and 1960s a number of others joined the board who had some connection with Rockefeller, often as directors of a Rockefeller company or of the Rockefeller Foundation. Even John W. Davis, who continued on the board until 1955, had such ties—he had served on the board of the Rockefeller Foundation. Among others with similar connections are Robert V. Roosa and Bill D. Moyers (Rockefeller Foundation board), Elliott V. Bell, James A. Perkins, and Robert O. Anderson (Chase Manhattan Bank board), Grayson Kirk (Mobil Oil board), Najeeb Halaby (worked for L. S. Rockefeller and Associates), and Zbigniew Brzezinski, who is currently heading the Rockefeller-initiated Trilateral Commission. And in 1969-1970 David Rockefeller took over as chairman of both the Council on Foreign Relations and Chase Manhattan Bank.

The pattern of first Morgan and now Rockefeller predominance in the CFR should not be interpreted as a kind of dictatorship or command relationship vis-à-vis representatives of other financial groups. Rather, it appears to be more a pattern of informal leadership and coordination within a general framework of cooperation. As has already been noted, representatives of all the major New York financial groups have participated in the Council leadership, some with regularity and in important roles. Thus Allen Dulles, of Sullivan and Cromwell (as well as of the CIA), played an active role in the Council leadership for forty-two years, serving as secretary, vice-president, and president. His law partner Arthur H. Dean joined the board in 1955. The German-Jewish financial community was well represented on the Council's initial board with Otto H. Kahn and Paul M. Warburg, both of Kuhn, Loeb. When they departed in the early 1930s, Frank Altschul, associated with the Lehman-Goldman, Sachs group, joined the board, as if to fill the empty place. As Council secretary from 1944 and vice-president from 1951 to 1971, as well as a major benefactor, Altschul has played a major part in Council affairs and is one of the men most closely identified with the organization. Associated with First National City Bank was not only Henry Wriston's son, Walter, but also Council director Leon Fraser. Douglas Dillon (of Dillon, Read), Gabriel Hauge (of Manufacturers Hanover Trust), and Averell Harriman (of Brown Brothers Harriman) complete a broad spectrum of the New York financial groups. Another director, William A. M. Burden, an heir to Vanderbilt money, also serves on the board of Manufacturers Hanover Trust and was for a few years with Brown Brothers Harriman.

Other Business Links

The centrality of the New York financial oligarchy in the Council does not imply the complete exclusion of other financial groups, nor lack of contact with them. The Council's membership, if not its leadership, does include prominent capitalists as well as academics resident in Los Angeles, Chicago, San Francisco, Detroit, and other places in the United States outside the Northeast. Bayless Manning, appointed the new Council president in 1972, has a background as a lawyer in Cleveland and as dean of the Stanford

Law School, as well as having been a member of the faculty at Yale Law School. There are also a variety of channels which permit regular communication that can moderate a New York-Washington parochialism and lead to acceptance of the Council's leadership in other regions of the country.

First, the interlocks of the Council with top business magazines are substantial. These magazines speak for and to businessmen, and have nation-wide circulation. *Fortune* is most closely tied with nine of the nineteen executives and directors (1970) who are Council members. Hedley Donovan, editor-in-chief of *Time, Inc.*, which owns *Fortune,* was elected a Council director in 1969. In 1970 *Business Week* had only one executive who was a Council member, but the relationship has still been close. Elliott V. Bell, editor and publisher of that magazine from 1950 to 1967, also served on the board of the Council for many years. A third major magazine, *Forbes,* is apparently tied to the Council only through one of its directors. In the case of the *Wall Street Journal,* three of the fourteen directors of Dow Jones, the parent company, were members of the Council.

Secondly, the Council is interlocked with a number of leading business organizations. These are typically organizations representing the largest corporations, and have a national rather than purely New York or East Coast image. Most important, and most intimately linked, are the Business Council and the Committee for Economic Development (CED).[22] The CED is particularly close to the Council, with its president Alfred C. Neal a Council director, as well as trustees Altschul, Hauge, Dillon, William C. Foster, and Philip D. Reed. The CED plays a role similar to that of the Council in the formulation of policy options. The range of subjects is much wider, however, including both domestic and foreign policy issues. Also tied to the Council on Foreign Relations is the Business Council (which in turn has a substantial overlap with the CED). The Business Council rarely makes public statements. Originally an advisory body to the Department of Commerce, it regularly convenes top business leaders for discussion among themselves and with government leaders in an off-the-record informal context. Four Council directors are among its membership. The Business Council and the Committee for Economic Development each have 200 members and, in each case, 22 percent of these members are also members of the Council on Foreign Relations.

To these two major organizations should be added two more specialized organizations. The National Foreign Trade Council is composed of companies with a special interest in foreign trade, which are naturally the same large companies most prominent in the CFR, the Business Council, and the CED. Twenty-one percent of its directors are members of the Council on Foreign Relations. The National Bureau of Economic Research (NBER), centered at Columbia University, is a major center of establishment research on the American economy; 18 percent of its directors are CFR members. This is not surprising, since much of the initiative for its founding came from Edwin Gay, chairman of the Council's first Research Committee. Wesley Mitchell of the NBER was on the Council board from 1927 to 1934, and currently Robert Roosa, a Council director, is also on the board of the NBER.

There are several other major business organizations, however, whose current ties to the Council on Foreign Relations seem minimal. These include the National Association of Manufacturers, the National Industrial Conference Board, and the Chamber of Commerce of the United States. Among the leaders of these organizations, the proportion of Council members ranges from 2 to 10 percent. This still represents some linkage, of course, and it is possible that more detailed study would reveal other ties that are missed by just examining a list of directors. It seems safe to conclude that there are fewer ties than in the case of the organizations mentioned above. The stratum of the United States capitalist class represented by these bodies is apparently less close to the Council.

There is still another channel of contacts by which the Council reaches into smaller communities and touches a greater range of American leadership. The committees on foreign relations are specifically designed to relate to local leadership in cities around the country. By 1972 they were organized in thirty-five cities ranging from Albuquerque to Miami to Worcester. In cities where the Council does not have a committee, it is often because of the prior existence of a parallel organization, such as a World Affairs Council, or, in Chicago, the Council on Foreign Relations (a distinct organization in spite of the identical name). With these, as well as with the committees, the provision of speakers and other informal contacts bring about a nation-wide network in which the Council is a central point.

Thus the Council, primarily tied to the New York financial oligarchy, also has extensive ties in the rest of the country. One of the questions not yet answered by our research is which sectors of the United States capitalist class are definitely not tied to, or may even be hostile to, the Council and its perspectives. Certainly the extreme right-wing attacks on the Council are well financed by certain sectors of the capitalist class, and the more generalized right-wing opposition to the "Eastern establishment" may be a reflection of certain intraclass divergencies. But the extent and basis of these divergencies is not clear. The challenge to the New York financial oligarchy from other sectors of the capitalist class is by no means strong and consistent. It does warrant further study and justifies a reminder that, important as the Council is, one organization does not speak for the whole class. But the main conclusion should still be clear: the Council on Foreign Relations and the New York financial oligarchy, which it primarily represents, have a leading position in molding United States foreign policy.

Suggested Readings

Basic general sources on the concept of class include the article on social stratification in *International Encyclopedia of the Social Sciences* (1968), Bottomore (1966), Ossowski (1963), and Bukharin (1925). In spite of the absence of a focused discussion of class as such, Marx's *Capital* (1967), *Eighteenth Brumaire* (1963), and *Class Struggles in France* (1964) are indispensable sources.

The class structure of the United States is discussed clearly in Zeitlin (1970), Hamilton (1972), and Braverman (1974). On the United States capitalist class, basic sources are Menshikov (1969), Lundberg (1938, 1968), and the recent article by Zeitlin (1974). On the overseas role of United States capitalism, one should refer to Lenin's classic *Imperialism* (1939), and Magdoff (1969). Data on "multinational companies" can be found in Vernon (1971), Barnet and Muller (1974), and Wilkins (1974).

Basic sources for the Marxist theory of the ruling class are the works of Marx and Bukharin already mentioned, Lenin (1932), and Gramsci (1971). Useful summaries are Sanderson (1969) and Moore (1957). Domhoff's several works provide extensive data on the social and political role of the United States capitalist class. More general and theoretical reflections on the ruling class in advanced capitalist societies can be found in Miliband (1969), Poulantzas (1970), O'Connor (1973), and *Politics and Society* (1974).

Notes

1. We have not discussed here the theoretical or empirical background to the conception of the United States capitalist class made use of in this chapter. The interested reader should see the readings suggested above.

    Note on terminology: We have used three terms to refer to the group of families at the highest level of American society—those who make up roughly 2 percent of all American families. "Capitalist class" and "corporate upper class" refer explicitly to the most important defining characteristic of this class: possession of enough capital to live without working. "Ruling class" is used when the focus is on the political role of the capitalist class.

2. Data in this section are drawn from Minter (1973a). The information collected on the sample of CFR members and all directors during the 1921-1972 period is coded and stored on data cards, and is available at the DPLS, Social Science Building, University of Wisconsin, Madison, Wisconsin 53706. Those making use of the data are requested to inform William Minter, the original researcher. Information on the members and directors was collected from public sources available in libraries and references recorded in the researcher's files. Not all are recorded in the bibliography. Standard sources checked included *Poor's Register of Corporations and Directors*, *Who's Who in America*, the *Social Register* for various cities, *Biography Index* (and articles and books listed there), *Dictionary of American Biography*, *National Cyclopedia of American Biography*, and *Encyclopedia of American Biography*.
3. Menshikov (1969), Lundberg (1938, 1968), Villarejo (1962).
4. For more information on the role of labor leaders and the CIA in United States foreign policy, see Agee (1975), Marchetti and Marks (1974), Morris (1967), Radosh (1969), as well as NACLA (1974).
5. Century Association, 1937:21. The Century Association seems to represent quite graphically what Baltzell terms the "aristocratic" as opposed to "caste" tendency within the upper class, i.e., the willingness to incorporate new blood into the class, not making judgements purely on the basis of birth.
6. *Forbes*, 1973:231.
7. The thirty Council officers were: presidents John W. Davis, George W. Wickersham, Norman H. Davis, R. C. Leffingwell, Allen W. Dulles, Henry M. Wriston, Grayson Kirk, Bayless Manning; honorary president Elihu Root; chairmen of the board John J. McCloy, David Rockefeller; vice-presidents Paul D. Cravath, Edwin F. Gay, Frank L. Polk, Isaiah Bowman, Frank Altschul, Devereux C. Josephs; treasurers Whitney H. Shepardson, Clarence E. Hunter, Elliott V. Bell, Gabriel Hauge; committee chairmen George O. May, Arthur H. Dean, Carroll L. Wilson, Alfred C. Neal, Hedley Donovan; *Foreign Affairs* editors A. C. Coolidge, Hamilton Fish Armstrong; executive directors Walter H. Mallory and George S. Franklin, Jr. (some of the above held other posts in addition to the one listed). See Appendix 1 for details about each of these men.
8. Magdoff (1969) is an important summary analysis of capitalist class interests as they affect U.S. foreign policy, which builds on and updates the basic Leninist analysis of imperialism (Lenin, 1939). The data quoted are found on page 192. See also Zeitlin, 1970: 43-45.

114 Imperial Brain Trust

9. See Vernon (1971), Tugendhat (1971), and Barnet and Müller (1974) for recent accounts of the "multinational" phenomenon. Particularly focused on Latin America is NACLA (1971).
10. Barnet and Müller, 1974:26.
11. National Council of Churches, 1973:145, 148, 154.
12. DuPont, 1974:17, 27.
13. National Council of Churches, 1973:145, 148, 154.
14. *Moody's*, 1975a:60, 191.
15. *Moody's*, 1975b:2421; U.S. Steel, 1973:6, 9-11.
16. See, in addition to sources mentioned earlier, a computer analysis of cliques defined by interlocking directorates carried out by Sondquist and Koenig (1975). The results in general correspond with the groups identified by Menshikov (1969). See also Perlo (1957).
17. Menshikov, 1969:200-317.
18. Ibid., 284, 301-317. These include the Ford companies and institutions and eighteen regional financial groups.
19. The *Fortune* lists used are from 1970.
20. Nixon, 1969:417.
21. Interview with George S. Franklin, Jr., October 2, 1972.
22. A forthcoming dissertation at Tufts University, by William Wolff, should throw much new light on the CED and the Business Council. At present, the most detailed information is in two books by Schriftgiesser (1960, 1967).

II
The Council on Foreign Relations and United States Foreign Policy 1939-1975

Since the beginning of the Second World War, the Council on Foreign Relations has had a decisive impact on the history of American foreign policy. Part Two contains a number of detailed case studies, which collectively illustrate that the Council is an "imperial brain trust." These case studies show the great influence the CFR has had on the American government, by setting an imperial policy on such key issues as American entry into the Second World War, the shape of the post-1945 world order, the Cuban missile crisis, the Vietnam war, and relations with important nations in Europe, Latin America, Africa, and Asia. The final chapter focuses on the Council's current efforts, through the 1980's Project, to plan out and implement a new world order to replace the one presently disintegrating.

4
Shaping a New World Order: The Council's Blueprint for World Hegemony, 1939-1975

Near the end of the Second World War, two of the Council's senior directors wrote that the CFR had "served an increasingly useful function in the period of the twenties and thirties; but it was only on the outbreak of World War II that it was proved to have come of age."[1] They were referring to the Council's successful efforts, through its special War and Peace Studies Project, to plan out a new global order for the postwar world, an order in which the United States would be the dominant power. The War and Peace Studies groups, in collaboration with the American government, worked out an imperialistic conception of the national interest and war aims of the United States. The imperialism involved a conscious attempt to organize and control a global empire. The ultimate success of this attempt made the United States for a time the number one world power, exercising domination over large sections of the world—the American empire.

The process of planning a new international system was decision-making of the most important kind. Such blueprinting was by its very nature determining the "national interest" of the United States. Those having this crucial

117

function were the most powerful of the society. The Council and government planners began with certain assumptions, excluding other alternatives. These assumptions became intentions and were ultimately implemented by government actions.

Unlike other private groups, which focused with restricted scope and vision on local, regional, and national domestic problems, the Council saw the purpose of postwar planning as the creation of an international economic and political order dominated by the United States. In its planning the Council had the cooperation and assistance of President Roosevelt, the Department of State, and numerous Council members in the government.

The main issue for consideration was whether America could be self-sufficient and do without the markets and raw materials of the British Empire, Western hemisphere, and Asia. The Council thought that the answer was no and that, therefore, the United States had to enter the war and organize a new world order satisfactory to the United States. This chapter will trace how the Council saw the problem, the government's acceptance of its imperialistic perspective, and the resulting new international structure which was developed from this planning.

The War and Peace Studies Project

The fast-paced events of the first two years of the Second World War set the context for the early period of postwar planning. With the outbreak of war in September 1939, Council leaders immediately began considering the need for advanced planning to deal with the difficulties which the United States would face during the war and the eventual peace. Council director Isaiah Bowman, who had been a key figure in the

"Inquiry"—the postwar planning done during the First World War—was particularly adamant about the need for adequate preparation this time, so that previous mistakes would not be repeated.[2] Council leaders believed that blueprints for a new world order were necessary and, furthermore, that this was exactly the kind of activity the Council had been created to undertake.

Less than two weeks after the outbreak of the war, Hamilton Fish Armstrong, editor of *Foreign Affairs,* and Walter H. Mallory, the executive director of the Council, traveled to Washington, D.C., meeting with assistant secretary of state and Council member George S. Messersmith on September 12, 1939. They outlined a long-range planning project which would assure close Council-Department of State collaboration in the critical period which had just begun. The Council would form several study groups of experts to focus on the long-term problems of the war and to plan for the peace. Research and discussion would result in recommendations to the department and President Franklin D. Roosevelt, and would not be made public.[3] Messersmith approved of the Armstrong-Mallory suggestions and met with Secretary of State Cordell Hull and undersecretary and Council member Sumner Welles later that same day to outline the Council's proposition. Both Hull and Welles expressed interest. Council president Norman H. Davis, Hull's close friend and adviser, spoke with the secretary soon afterward, receiving verbal approval for the proposal and securing Hull's agreement to have "representative people" from the department meet regularly with Council leaders.[4] Welles and Messersmith concurred, and communicated their positive feelings to Joseph H. Willets of the Rockefeller Foundation, to which the Council had applied for funding. On December 6, 1939, the Foundation granted the Council $44,500 to finance the War and Peace Studies Project for the following year.[5]

By mid-December 1939, details of the organization, purpose, scope, and procedure of the Council project had been worked out. A meeting between representatives of the Council and the department was held at Messersmith's home to bring these plans to completion. It was agreed that the Council would set up several special groups to "engage in a continuous study of the course of the war, to ascertain how the hostilities affect the United States and to elaborate concrete proposals designed to safeguard American interests in the settlement which will be undertaken when hostilities cease."[6] A central Steering Committee was established to unify and guide the work of the groups. Norman H. Davis, President Roosevelt's ambassador-at-large, was chairman of this committee, with Armstrong as vice-chairman, Mallory as secretary, and Alvin H. Hansen, Jacob Viner, Whitney H. Shepardson, Allen W. Dulles, Hanson W. Baldwin, and Bowman as the other members. These last six men, together with vice-chairman Armstrong, headed the five study groups which were established—Economic and Financial, Political, Armaments, Territorial, and Peace Aims. Hansen, professor of political economy at Harvard University, and Viner, professor of economics at the University of Chicago, led the Economic and Financial Group. Shepardson, a corporate executive who had been secretary to Edward M. House in 1919 at the Versailles Peace Conference, did the same for the Political Group. Dulles, an international corporate lawyer who had worked closely with Davis in disarmament negotiations during the 1930s, was co-rapporteur of the Armaments Group along with Baldwin, military correspondent for the *New York Times*. The Territorial Group's leader was Bowman, America's leading geographer and president of Johns Hopkins University. Armstrong later headed the Peace Aims Group, established in 1941.[7] The Steering Committee was to meet only infrequently to map out the studies in broad outline.

Each group leader received an honorarium and had the help of a full-time paid research secretary.[8] The Steering Committee assigned topics to each group and a member or the research secretary produced a draft statement of the problem. The group then discussed it thoroughly, sometimes at several meetings, and put the consensus into a recommendation to be forwarded with a digest of discussion to the President and State Department.[9]

The study groups averaged about ten to fifteen men each between 1940 and 1945. Almost 100 individuals were involved in this work during these six years:[10] academic experts, particularly economists such as Alvin H. Hansen and Jacob Viner, Eugene Staley of the Fletcher School of Law and Diplomacy, and Winfield W. Riefler of Princeton's Institute for Advanced Study; historians William L. Langer and Crane Brinton of Harvard, A. Whitney Griswold of Yale, and James T. Shotwell of Columbia; government policymakers, such as Ambassador-at-Large Norman H. Davis, State Department officers Lauchlin Currie and Benjamin V. Cohen; military leaders such as Maj. Gen. George V. Strong, chief of army intelligence, retired chief of naval operations Adm. William V. Pratt, and retired Maj. Gen. Frank L. McCoy. Corporation lawyers, such as Allen W. Dulles, John Foster Dulles, and Thomas K. Finletter, and newspaper correspondents such as Hansen W. Baldwin of the *New York Times,* George Fielding Eliot of the *New York Herald Tribune,* and John Gunther were also active in the project. The business community was directly represented by banker Davis, industrialist Ralph E. Flanders, financiers Leon Fraser of the First National Bank of New York and Frank Altschul of General American Investors Company. Isaiah Bowman, a territorial expert and Roosevelt adviser, played an important role, as did Owen Lattimore, an expert on the Far East. During 1940, two of the Council's planners, former governor of New Hampshire John G. Winant and retired chief of naval operations Adm. William H.

Standley, were tapped to become United States ambassadors in the two most important overseas diplomatic posts—London and Moscow. All these men and almost seventy more contributed to the success of the Council's War and Peace Studies Project.[11] Through these individuals, at least five cabinet-level departments and fourteen separate government agencies, bureaus, and offices were interlocked with the War and Peace Studies Project at one time or another.[12] They collectively attended 362 meetings and prepared 682 separate documents for the Department of State and the President. Up to twenty-five copies of each recommendation were distributed to the appropriate desks of the department, and two to the President.[13]

The aim of this vast undertaking, to which the Rockefeller Foundation alone gave over $300,000 in a six-year period, was to directly influence the government.[14] The Council's own official report, published after the war, stated that the "real touchstone" of the War and Peace Studies Project was "the usefulness of the studies to the Government. This was the criterion which the Steering Committee and the Rapporteurs of the groups had to keep in mind at all times, and especially in reviewing work done and in planning new work for the future."[15] The desire for influence began to be fulfilled immediately after the first meetings of the groups in March 1940. The Territorial Group, headed by Bowman, considered the strategic importance of Greenland to the United States during that month, and sent a recommendation on the subject to President Roosevelt and the Department of State in mid-March. This memorandum discussed the possibility that Germany might conquer Denmark and thus be in a position to claim Danish colonies, including Greenland, a development which could be dangerous to the United States. It suggested that applying the Monroe Doctrine to Greenland could deter Germany.[16] Early in April 1940 the German army overran Denmark. Bowman was summoned to the

White House to talk with the President, who, with a copy of the Council's recommendation in hand, questioned Bowman concerning what the American government should do about Greenland. At his press conference on April 18, Roosevelt stated that he was satisfied that Greenland belonged to the American continent, and later that year he "carried the memorandum to a Cabinet meeting and cited it as the basis for some conclusions he had reached."[17]

During mid-1940, key members of the Council exerted their influence in yet another way by creating an ad hoc pressure organization. This body was called the "Century Group" because it met at the Century Association, an upper-class club in New York. Its small group of founders included Francis P. Miller, the organizational director of the Council and a member of the Political Group of the War and Peace Studies Project; Lewis W. Douglas, a Council member who joined the Council's board in 1940; Whitney H. Shepardson, a Council director and leader of the War and Peace Studies Project; and Stacy May, Edward Warner, and Winfield W. Riefler, all members of at least one of the War and Peace Study groups.[18] The Council community clearly controlled this new pressure group.

At a July 25, 1940, meeting, the Century Group decided that something had to be done to aid Britain, specifically the transfer of fifty destroyers to Great Britain in exchange for bases on British possessions in the Western hemisphere and a pledge never to surrender its fleet to Germany.[19] Miller took the lead in approaching the government with this suggestion. He and four others traveled to Washington on August 1, 1940. Some met with President Roosevelt, others with various cabinet members. The next day the President discussed the Century Group's idea with the cabinet. At this meeting it was decided to explore the suggestion with the British. In this way the negotiations began which culminated in the Destroyers for Bases agreement in early September 1940.[20] The

Century Group, in the words of historian Robert A. Divine, "had broken the logjam on the destroyer issue."[21] The Destroyers for Bases agreement marked the end of any pretense of American neutrality during World War II; the United States government had definitely taken sides.[22] A statement of long-time Council director Edwin F. Gay further illustrates the importance of the Council role. He reported in a September 1940 letter to his wife that he had just sat in on a meeting with a handful of Council men who had "put across the fifty destroyer deal against the opposition of the Navy and the reluctance of the President, who, they tell me, is playing politics with the whole movement."[23]

The Council leaders also met regularly with the State Department's postwar planners once the department had established its own structures for such long-term thinking. In so doing, they formalized long-standing personal relationships with many of the top policymakers. For example, the economist Leo Pasvolsky, special assistant to the secretary of state in charge of postwar planning during the war years, was familiar with most Council leaders. He had joined the Council on Foreign Relations by 1940 and was quite close to it during the war years; some Council men affectionately called him "Pazzy" for short.[24] Pasvolsky became, along with Davis, the main liaison between the Council and the State Department. He met frequently with the War and Peace planners during 1940 and handled the distribution within the department of the War and Peace Studies recommendations beginning in late 1940.[25] Pasvolsky also traveled regularly to New York City to attend the Economic and Financial Group's meetings. He was present at a majority of the ten meetings held by this group during the February-October 1940 period, and at the special plenary session for the members of all the study groups held in late June of the same year.[26] He also sometimes joined Council leaders when they gathered in Washington, D.C. On May 1, 1940, for example, Pasvolsky met there with Davis, Hansen, Mallory, and Arthur R. Upgren, the research secretary of the Economic and Financial Group, "in order to coordinate the project's studies still more closely with the State Department's needs and to discuss the Economic and Financial Group's study program."[27] Pasvolsky attended the Council's special plenary session of June 28, 1940, stating his desire for a close relationship between the Council group and the department, and his own willingness to aid the Council. Other top State Department officers strongly supported the Council's project.[28] Both Secretary of State Hull and Undersecretary Welles wrote letters of appreciation at various times praising the Council's work, calling it "excellent," "extremely useful," and "valuable."[29]

Beginnings of Grand-Scale Planning: Summer and Fall 1940

The German army's sweep across the French countryside to victory in May and June 1940 shocked the Council and government planners. They were suddenly faced with an entirely new situation. Germany might expand farther and defeat Britain, capturing its fleet and empire. Led by the Council, American policymakers began grand-scale contingency planning to deal with this and other eventualities.

The key questions which had concerned American leaders for almost ten years centered on the problems of self-sufficiency and economic warfare. Was the Western hemisphere self-sufficient, or did it require trade with other world areas to maintain its prosperity? How self-contained was the Western hemisphere compared to German-controlled Europe? How much of the world's resources and territory did the United States require to maintain power and prosperity? The importance of this Council concern should be emphasized because these are questions that have been debated for some years by Marxists and liberals. Marxists have argued that these things were and are essential to United States capitalism as presently organized, and that American foreign policy is largely based on these needs. The CFR's conclusions, as we shall see, effectively support the Marxist position and shaped American policy accordingly.

In the summer of 1940, the Council, led by the Economic and Financial Group, began a large-scale study to answer these questions. The world was divided into blocs and the location, production, and trade of all important commodities and manufactured goods were compiled for each area. About 95 percent of all world trade in every commodity and product was included.[30] The self-sufficiency of each major region —the Western hemisphere, the British Empire, Continental Europe, and the Pacific area—was then measured, using net export and import trade figures.[31] These were determined by assuming that the countries within a bloc would buy and sell to each other first, thus maximizing internal trade within each area. To give a hypothetical example, if all the Western hemisphere nations together exported 100 tons of tin to Europe during the normal trade year of 1937, while at the same time different countries within the hemisphere imported the same amount of tin from the Far East, the area would be self-sufficient in tin, since the amount going to Europe could, if necessary, be rechanneled within the hemisphere. Using this type of analysis, the self-sufficiency of the German-dominated Continental European bloc was found to be much higher than that of the Western hemisphere as a whole.[32] To match this economic strength the Western hemisphere had to be united with another bloc.

The effects of integrating the Pacific area with the Western hemisphere were considered first. Trade was divided into two types: complementary—the exchange of commodities and manufactures which one region has and the other needs—and competitive—raw materials and products which both areas have surpluses of and wish to export. In the first case, the Pacific area required the machinery, vehicles, cotton, petroleum products, chemicals, iron, and steel which the Western hemisphere desired to export; and the Western hemisphere wanted to import the rubber, jute, tin, cotton, textiles, silk, and sugar that the Pacific area had to sell. The integration of the two zones, at least as far as these products were concerned, would very substantially help both areas reduce export-market dependence on the "outside" world.[33] The competitive aspects of production and the difficulty of finding export markets for their similar surplus commodities grains, lead, zinc, coffee, oilseeds, and hides—were, however, disadvantageous. After applying the principle of purchase first from within one's own sphere and then integrating the hemisphere with the Pacific area, the export dependence on the outside world was decreased by $1,800 million because of the great amount of complementary trade. This, compared to an increased export surplus of only $700 million, indicated that joining the two regions into one bloc would aid, but not solve, the problem of self-sufficiency.

The United States would be the biggest beneficiary of such a union because the Pacific area was a significant market for United States manufactured products and the "foremost source of many of the most important raw material imports of the United States."[34] The rest of the Western hemisphere, especially the southernmost countries of South America, would not profit much from this union, however, because of the large export competition between them and Australia and New Zealand.[35] Since the surplus commodities in question were primarily agricultural, the addition of the United Kingdom, a large consumer of imported farm products, to the proposed "Western hemisphere, Pacific area" bloc would provide the needed market for these exports, solving the greater part of the surplus difficulty and resulting in an integrated whole. The degree of self-sufficiency of the new region, initially called the "Western hemisphere, British Empire and Far East" bloc, was substantially greater than that of any other feasible union. For the new and larger bloc, the intra-area trade was 79 percent of total trade in the case of imports and 86 percent for exports. This self-sufficiency was greater than that of Continental Europe, whose intra-area trade figures were 69 percent and 79 percent respectively.[36] The Council planners thus concluded that, as a minimum, the American "national interest" involved free access to markets and raw materials in the British Empire, the Far East, and the entire Western hemisphere. They now turned their attention to making sure that the government and the nation at large defined the "national interest" in the same way.

Policy Recommendations: Mid-October 1940

Out of the conceptualization of the national interest developed during the summer and early fall of 1940 ensued the type of military, territorial, and political policy necessary to ensure a satisfactory functioning of the American economic system. In mid-October 1940, the Economic and Financial Group drafted a comprehensive concluding memorandum (number E-B19) summarizing its work and drawing out all possible implications for United States policy. The purpose of this recommendation to President Roosevelt and the Department of State was "to set forth the political, military, territorial and economic requirements of the United States in its potential leadership of the non-German world area including the United Kingdom itself as well as the Western Hemisphere and Far East."[37]

The Council group saw two features of the war as central to the situation facing the United States—German domination of Continental Europe and Britain's continued resistance, which limited Germany's territorial expansion. Up to this time, United States military policy had been designed around the Western hemisphere. Now Britain was protecting most of the world from German penetration, leaving the entire world outside of Continental Europe open to the United States. There was therefore "a great residual area potentially available to us and *upon the basis of which United States foreign policy may be framed.*"[38] The freedom of action thus presented forced choices about how to protect this area for American foreign trade. The Council planners pointed out that decisions looking toward such preservation "necessarily will involve increased military expenditures and other risks."[39] They argued that, since the loss of outside markets and raw materials would force serious economic readjustments within the smaller region of the Western hemisphere, such an enlargement of the United States economic domain, with the attendant increase of necessary military commitments and costs, would be essential over the course of time.[40] The British blockade of Europe was thus protecting the United States while at the same time allowing the United States to cultivate a new economic order in the non-German world. Britain itself was an indispensable market for the agricultural surpluses of the Western hemisphere and Pacific area:

> Some form of integration of the Western Hemisphere serves very well indeed the needs of the United States, but it does not serve the needs of other economies. It appears this can be done only by the preservation for them of *their* vital market—the United Kingdom.[41]

The next section of this revealing memorandum dealt with the requisites of the United States, illustrating the imperial expansion which the Council advocated: "The foremost requirement of the United States *in a world in which it proposes to hold unquestioned power* is the rapid fulfillment of a program of complete re-armament"[42] (emphasis added). Japanese expansion possibly endangered the United States preponderance of power in the non-German world. This threat *"will have to be dissipated through peaceable means if possible, or through force"*[43] (emphasis added). Council planners were thus ready to go to war with Japan if that nation threatened American control of the world outside of Continental Europe, an area which they later called the "Grand Area."

Memorandum E-B19 concluded with a statement on the essentials for United States foreign policy, summarizing the "component parts of an integrated policy to achieve *military and economic supremacy for the United States within the non-German world"*[44] (emphasis added). The first part was a prerequisite: the maintenance of the present resistance of Britain. Another major element was the "coordination and cooperation of the United States with other countries to secure the limitation of any exercise of sovereignty by foreign nations that constitutes a threat to the minimum world area essential for the security and economic prosperity of the United States and the Western Hemisphere."[45] An American-led group authority was needed to settle disputes, a non-German world political organization of some kind. In addition, this approach required appropriate measures in the fields of trade, investment, and monetary arrangements, so that each friendly country could live peacefully. Finally, since the German-controlled world was expected to exist side by side with this proposed new non-German world order, the organization of the Western hemisphere, the British Empire, and the Far East bloc would have to be strong enough to bargain with the German-controlled world. Ultimately, perhaps, this structural form could become a complete world organization.[46]

On October 19, 1940, members of all War and Peace Studies groups attended an Economic and Financial Group meeting to consider this memorandum before submitting it to the authorities in Washington. Leo Pasvolsky, the Department of State's chief postwar planner, was also in attendance. Pasvolsky agreed with the Council's initial blueprint for world power. His belief that the United States had to have more than just the Western hemisphere as living space is indicated in his statement that "if you take the Western Hemisphere as the complete bloc you are assuming preparation for war."[47] Pasvolsky thus felt that the United States would have to go to war to gain more living space if limited to the Western hemisphere, a conclusion clearly following from the Council's work.

The Problem of Japan

The major impediment to integrating the non-German world was Japan's refusal to play the subordinate role which the United States had assigned it. All War and Peace Studies groups recognized that Japan was an expanding power and a threat to Council plans. On November 23, 1940, the Economic and Financial Group discussed possible actions against Japan to prevent that country's takeover of Southeast Asia and destruction of American access to that part of the non German world. Aid to China to entangle Japan's military machine there and economic sanctions were considered.[48] This raised two questions: how much would Japan be hurt by such sanctions, and what would Japan do politically, economically, and militarily if it were hurt?

Having pressed their discussion to the limits of economic analysis, a special meeting of all War and Peace Studies groups and government representatives was called on December 14, 1940, to explore the broader aspects of these important questions and to search for solutions.[49] Outside guests included Maxwell Hamilton, chief of the Far Eastern division of the Department of State and historian Tyler Dennett, an expert on United States-Far Eastern relations. At least one leader from each of the Council groups was present.

The meeting discussed a memorandum, "Japan's Vulnerability to American Sanctions." It had been compiled by using the Economic and Financial Group's world trade research to discover what major imports Japan normally received from the United States, the British Empire, and the Dutch East Indies. It was evident that Japan, poor in raw materials, depended on these nations for iron, petroleum, copper, aluminum, ferroalloys, many iron and steel products, machine tools, autos, tin, rubber, zinc, nickel, lead, mica, asbestos, and manganese.[50] Thus a trade embargo by the United States would seriously undermine the Japanese economy and, according to CFR reasoning, hamper any military drive by Tokyo. The memorandum concluded by suggesting that Japan was "peculiarly vulnerable to blockade."[51] A supplement to this study considered the possibility that the Japanese could obtain necessary raw materials from Latin America and the possible effects of a Japanese trade embargo of the United States. Neither of these appeared to offer serious difficulties. Preclusive purchasing of Latin American supplies could be implemented, and American imports from Japan were not important enough to cause serious effects on the American economy.[52]

At the same meeting, Territorial Group member and Far Eastern expert Owen Lattimore linked a trade embargo to aid to China. He argued that the more raw and finished war materials Japan expended in China, the easier it would be to constrict Japan's total supply. If the Chinese could take the offensive, Japan could not release troops for a movement toward Southeast Asia. Lattimore concluded that taken together, aid to China and a step-by-step embargo on Japan offered an "excellent means" to implement United States foreign policy.[53] A program of graduated pressure on Japan was best because total sanctions "would undoubtedly force her to move into the Dutch East Indies and Malaya to secure the oil and iron necessary to the life of a modern nation."[54] While one member present argued for a policy of economic concessions in exchange for Japan's withdrawal from China and from its advanced positions to the south, another member thought this viewpoint was entirely mistaken. He felt that Japan either had to have lebensraum—economic living space— or be totally defeated.[55] Finally, the Council men considered the connection between Japanese expansion and the survival of Britain. They concluded that if Japan drove the British out of the Far East, the results would be very serious, both for Britain's raw-material situation and political control.[56]

Despite some disagreement, there were enough areas of consensus to issue a summarizing memorandum to President Roosevelt and the Department of State suggesting what policy the nation should pursue in the Far East. This memorandum is very important for an understanding of the role of the Council in the process of postwar planning. It was the initial recommendation to the government aimed at the implementation of the Council's proposals for a worldwide non-German bloc dominated by the United States. In addition, as a policy suggestion concerned with the means rather than the ends of policy, it can be used as a test case to determine whether there was a correspondence—and likely a cause and effect relationship—between the Council recommendations and governmental actions.

The aide-mémoire, numbered E-B26, which came out of the December 14 meeting, was issued on January 15, 1941, under the title of "American Far Eastern Policy." It began by stating that it was in the national interest of the United States to check a Japanese advance into Southeast Asia, and that this could best be done by taking the initiative rather than waiting for Japanese action. The main interests of the United States in Southeast Asia were twofold. The first was economic: "The Philippine Islands, the Dutch East Indies, and British Malaya are prime sources of raw materials very important to the United States in peace and war; control of these lands by a potentially hostile power would greatly limit our freedom of action."[57] Secondly, strategic considerations demanded prevention of Japanese occupation of Southeast Asia, since Japanese control would impair the British war effort against Hitler, threatening sources of supply and weakening the whole British position in Asia. Many would view it as the beginning of the disintegration of the British Empire, and Australia and New Zealand might decide to concentrate on home defense.[58]

The program which the Council proposed to stop the Japanese move southward had three aspects. First was to give all possible aid to China, especially war materials, in order to pin down Japanese troops in that country. Second, the defenses of Southeast Asia should be strengthened by sending naval and air forces and by making an agreement with the British and Dutch for defense of the area. Finally, Japan should be weakened by cutting off some of its supplies of war material.[59] Since Japan was largely dependent on the United States for many vital necessities, a refusal to export such materials could "seriously embarrass the Japanese war effort."[60] Because these were the same materials America needed for its own defense program, there could be a rapid tightening of such exports without giving Japanese extremists an excuse for war. Preclusive purchasing by the United States in Latin America and Southeast Asia could prevent Japan from getting alternative supplies of these strategic goods.[61] Memorandum E-B26 concluded by stating:

> These three steps should serve to check Japan in the Far East without involving the United States in war, curtailing Britain, or leaving this country powerless in the Atlantic should Britain fall.

There are risks of course, just as there are risks in doing nothing. The expectation of gain is greater from a coordinated, active policy than from a piecemeal, passive one.[62]

On January 28, 1941, Pasvolsky gave Secretary of State Cordell Hull a copy of this Council recommendation.[63] The two most important aspects of these suggestions—aid to China and embargo of Japan—were implemented by government action within seven months.[64] These policies, which the Council proposed and the government adopted, had extremely important ramifications, leading to American entry into World War II.

The Grand Area

The Grand Area, as the United States-led non-German bloc was called during 1941, was only an interim measure to deal with the emergency situation of 1940 and early 1941. The preferred ideal was even more grandiose—one world economy dominated by the United States. The Economic and Financial Group said in June 1941, "the Grand Area is not regarded by the Group as more desirable than a world economy, nor as an entirely satisfactory substitute."[65] Because the group thought it unrealistic to plan at that time for a British or Anglo-American victory, it suggested that blueprints for integrating the existing Grand Area under American leadership should be worked on as a short-range war or defense measure. This area would then be an organized nucleus for building an integrated world economy after the war. Deciding the means to economically unify this existing area was the next necessary step.[66]

A July 24, 1941, memorandum to the President and Department of State outlined the Council's view of the national interest, describing the role of the Grand Area in American economic, political, and military policy. The memorandum, numbered E-B34, summarized the Grand Area concept, its "meaning for American policy, its function in the present war, and its possible role in the postwar period."[67] It began by stressing the basic fact that the "economy of the United States is geared to the export of certain manufactured and agricultural products, and the import of numerous raw materials and foodstuffs."[68] The Economic and Financial Group had found a self-contained United States-Western hemisphere economy impossible without great changes in the American economic system.

To prevent alterations in the United States economy, the Council had, in the words of group member Winfield W. Riefler, "gone on to discover what 'elbow room' the American economy needed in order to survive without major readjustments."[69] This living space had to have the basic raw materials needed for the nation's industry as well as the "fewest possible stresses making for its own disintegration, such as unwieldy export surpluses or severe shortages of consumer goods."[70] The extensive studies and discussions of the Council groups determined that, as a minimum, most of the non-German world, the "Grand Area," was needed for "elbow room." In its final form, it consisted of the Western hemisphere, the United Kingdom, the remainder of the British Commonwealth and Empire, the Dutch East Indies, China, and Japan itself.[71] The recommendation stated that failure to militarily defend and economically integrate this area would seriously strain the American economy by cutting off vital imports like rubber, tin, jute, and vegetable oils and by restricting the normal export of surpluses.[72] The loss of Britain, for example, would "greatly intensify" the problem of surplus production and thus unemployment, since, as Riefler expressed it, it "was difficult for a fairly liberal area to cope with the surpluses by transferring factors of production."[73]

Military defense of the Grand Area involved facing the

twin German-Japanese dangers. Because the German-controlled world had a high degree of self-sufficiency and could not be reduced by blockade, it was considered the foremost long-term threat to the Anglo-American region. Recommendation E-B34 advised that Germany be prevented from gaining control of North Africa, the Near East, and the Soviet Union, and hindered from consolidating its economic gains in Europe. The Economic and Financial Group's studies had shown how dangerous a unified Europe, with or without Nazi domination, would be to the United States. Hamilton Fish Armstrong pointed out in mid-June 1941 that a unified Europe could not be allowed to develop because it would be so strong that it would seriously threaten the American Grand Area.[74] Europe, organized as a single entity, was considered fundamentally incompatible with the American economic system.[75] Japan posed a more immediate difficulty, threatening the Grand Area's integrity by its expansionism, especially into the important region of Southeast Asia.[76]

In E-B34 the Economic and Financial Group stressed the significance of the economic integration of the Grand Area. All member countries had to be able to prosper within the region, or instability would inevitably result. Since the Grand Area could provide a broad economic base for either war or defense, as well as for consolidation of the new postwar world order, studies should begin to develop means for unifying the area. Memorandum E-B34 stated:

> In the event of an American-British victory, much would have to be done toward reshaping the world, particularly Europe. In this the Grand Area organization should prove useful. During an interim period of readjustment and reconstruction, the Grand Area might be an important stabilizing factor in the world's economy. Very likely the institutions developed for the integration of the Grand Area would yield useful experience in meeting European problems, and perhaps it would be possible simply to interweave the economies of European countries into that of the Grand Area.[77]

The Grand Area was thus considered a core region, which could always be extended to include more countries. As Jacob Viner, Treasury Department adviser and co-rapporteur of the Economic and Financial Group, said in May 1941: "It would be the aim of American policy to spread the organization of the Grand Area."[78] Group member Winfield W. Riefler also stressed the "dynamic character of the area, and the help it would be as an organized nucleus in building a postwar world economy."[79]

Integration of the various world regions into the Grand Area was a problem which involved discovering ways to achieve economic unity among disparate countries and areas. Council theorists stressed economic means in their study of the problem during 1941. An initial memorandum on the subject, dated March 7, 1941, identified two historical types of economic integration. The first was a customs union, a horizontal consolidation. This consisted of joining, mainly by preferential tariffs, nations or areas with similar economies. The second historical variety was the empire form, a vertical consolidation. This was a combination of countries with complementary economies—raw material-producing areas at one extreme and industrial manufacturing areas at the other. The British Empire was an outstanding example of such a combination. Integration in this case could be achieved by preferential tariffs, investment, colonization, and outright political control.[80]

The Council's planning had shown that three separate geographical areas—the Western hemisphere, the Far East, and the British Empire—had to be consolidated to allow the United States economy, as presently organized, to function efficiently. The key problem was that territories were included in the Grand Area which were economically competitive as well as complementary to the United States. Climatically temperate countries, such as Canada, Argentina, Australia, and the British Isles, were competitive. The tropical regions of the Western hemisphere and Southeast Asia (including the Dutch East Indies, British Malaya, and India) were complementary. Indeed, the tropical part of Asia was described as probably more complementary to the United States economy than any other important area of the entire globe, a conclusion having great future implications.[81]

Council planners concluded that both traditional integrating methods—customs unions and empire—had to be used to merge these two different types of regions within the Grand Area. The countries of the competitive bloc could be included in a system of preferential trade agreements, a customs union. In regard to the complementary areas, however, trade barriers normally did not exist, so a greater dependency had to be created in other ways, such as guaranteed markets for the raw material-production of unindustrialized nations.[82] Should the guaranteed-markets arrangement fail, control of the resources of these territories through investment and political-military dominance might be used.

At the end of recommendation E-B34, the Economic and Financial Group outlined the key topics for future study on integrating the Grand Area. Leading the list were financial measures—the creation of international financial institutions to stabilize currencies, and of international banking institutions to aid in investment and development of backward areas.[83] They had thus identified at a very early date the need for the International Monetary Fund and the World Bank, which they were to specifically suggest in February 1942.

This analysis of the Grand Area's requirements implied certain political, economic, and military policies. One was the necessity for preserving Britain and establishing solid Anglo-American collaboration. Another was the need to maintain access to Asia. Lastly, Britain and the United States required more shipping capacity. The Grand Area and any worldwide postwar organizations would depend on sea communication and transportation for much of their unity. The endangered position of Britain and its losses to submarines made the need even greater.[84] The government, in close touch with the Council, accepted this perspective. It took measures during 1940 and 1941 to maintain Britain and the Grand Area— including Lend-Lease, naval assistance in the Atlantic, and an economic embargo to try and prevent Japan from moving into Southeast Asia. It is clear that the Council and the government had an identical worldview and that patterns of influence flowed between them. The story only begins there, however. Evidence for the Council's key role in setting and implementing American war aims from mid-1941 to mid-1944 is even greater than for the earlier period. It is to these events that we now turn.

The International Setting, 1941-1944

Internationally, the period between mid-1941 and mid-1944 was marked by intensified warfare and stepped-up planning for the postwar world. Germany attacked the Soviet Union in June 1941. Three months later, the United States began an undeclared naval war against Germany in the Atlantic. During the second half of 1941, the danger of conflict in the Pacific heightened as Japan prepared to push south and west from its bases in Indochina. In the year following the December 7, 1941, attack on Pearl Harbor and American entry into full belligerency, the nadir of Allied fortunes was reached. During 1943 and 1944, however, the Axis powers suffered sharp and increasingly disastrous reverses as their complete defeat and the end of the war approached.

After mid-1941, both the Council and the government

assumed that the defeat of the Axis was both necessary and inevitable. American plans, as had been suggested in the final formulation of the Grand Area, expanded to include the entire globe. A new world order with international political and economic institutions was projected, which would join and integrate all of the earth's nations under the leadership of the United States. The unification of the whole world was now the aim of the Council and government planners.

The Council and American Entry into the Second World War

The assumptions, perspectives, and framework for the policymaking which led to United States entry into World War II were based on the Council's Grand Area planning. Council memoranda to the Department of State during 1940 and 1941 often emphasized that Southeast Asia, including the Netherlands Indies, was a key world area of great strategic and economic importance. Owen Lattimore, a member of the Territorial Group of the War and Peace Studies Project, argued as early as May 20, 1940, for example, that the interest of America would be "gravely prejudiced" should Southeast Asia be controlled by an "unfriendly or monopolistic nation, because of the need for access to rubber, tin and other resources and because of the strategic importance of converging sea and air routes."[85] The Economic and Financial Group stated that the area was highly complementary to the United States economy because "we secure from it huge amounts of raw materials and sell to it huge amounts of finished goods."[86] This group also emphasized the fact that there were only two great raw material-producing regions within the Grand Area--the Western hemisphere and the Far East. If one of these fell to the Axis, the "position of the free world would then be fraught with the greatest danger."[87] The Far Eastern area was the one most likely to become subject to the control of alien powers, resulting in the United States being "hemmed in, economically as well as militarily, by a unified totalitarian world."[88]

The Council groups, meeting jointly in mid-January 1941, produced memorandum E-B26, which recommended to the State Department that it was in the national interest of the United States to check Japan's advance into Southeast Asia. Not only were the raw materials of that area very important to the United States in peace and war, but a Japanese takeover would greatly weaken the whole British position in Asia.[89] This concept of the national interest prevailed among the government policymakers in Washington. Undersecretary of State Sumner Welles pointed out in July 1941, for example, that Japanese expansion tended to "jeopardize the procurement by the United States of essential materials, such as tin and rubber, which are necessary for the normal economy of this country and the consummation of our defense program."[90] Secretary of State Hull also felt that the country's national interests were directly involved in Southeast Asia. He stressed in August 1941 that a successful strike against the British colonies in the Far East would cut off supplies to Britain from that region and therefore would "be more damaging to British defense in Europe perhaps than any other step short of a German crossing of the channel."[91]

President Roosevelt agreed with the State Department-Council on Foreign Relations view, stressing the danger to British and American raw material supplies which Japanese expansion posed. The President stated during the second half of 1941 that a Japanese attack on British and Dutch possessions in the Far East would immediately threaten the vital interests of the nation and "should result in war with Japan."[92] In off-the-cuff remarks in late July 1941, the President bluntly explained that the United States "had to

Shaping a New World Order 143

get a lot of things—rubber, tin, and so forth and so on, down in the Dutch Indies, the Straits Settlements and Indo-China."[93] Japanese seizure of these areas would deprive both the United States and Britain of these essential sources of raw materials and so had to be prevented.[94] Prime Minister Churchill also emphasized the need to prevent Japanese movement south, which would cut the lifelines between the Dominions and England. Such a blow to the British government, he argued, "might be almost decisive."[95] Thus the top governmental policymakers on both sides of the Atlantic agreed that their joint interests demanded that Japan be prevented from capturing Southeast Asia.

Japan also saw its essential national interests joined with the fate of Southeast Asia. Japan had its own equivalent of the Grand Area, called the Greater East Asia Co-Prosperity Sphere. Japan's new order involved control over the Dutch East Indies (which it coveted as the "finest pearl" in the prospective colonial booty), China, Indochina, Thailand, Burma, Malaya, the Philippines, and certain Pacific Islands.[96] The Japanese felt that control of these areas was necessary to attain economic self-sufficiency, especially in raw materials. They planned to eventually create a self-contained empire from Manchuria on the north to the Dutch East Indies on the south, for the same economic reasons the United States and Britain wanted to dominate the region.[97]

The three great European colonial powers—Britain, France, and the Netherlands—controlled Southeast Asia in 1941. Since only Britain, much weakened by its struggle with Germany, was still an independent power, Japan recognized a prime opportunity to secure present and future economic needs. In late July 1941 Japanese leaders decided to move into southern Indochina as a first step toward control of Southeast Asia. The American reaction was forceful. Japanese assets in the United States were frozen and a total economic embargo, including oil, was imposed. Britain and the Netherlands government-in-exile followed suit.[98] The Council had recommended this policy in January 1941. The seriousness of this action was well known at the time. Many people had previously warned that it would provoke Japan into war, since it cut off many raw and finished materials, including oil, which that country had to have to survive as a great power.[99] Japanese leaders now had to either compromise with the United States or go to war to obtain oil and other raw materials available in the East Indies and Southeast Asia.

After the institution of an embargo, Japanese leaders seemed more willing to strike a deal with the United States. Therefore negotiations between the United States and Japan became more serious during August–late November 1941. While Japanese leaders were willing to make some short-range concessions—including at least a postponement of their planned move south—in exchange for renewed trade, the United States raised the question of Japanese evacuation from Chinese territory, something Japan would not accept.[100] The Japanese were informed that there would be no relaxation of the embargo until Japan gave up the territory it had fought for years to gain in China.[101]

The American stand weakened the moderates in Tokyo and, joined with the previously mentioned factors, made war inevitable. There were several reasons for the American position. First, America's minimum living space, the Grand Area, included China. The Council felt that China's economic development could lay the basis for a peaceful Far East during the postwar period, since its industrialization would create a large demand for Japanese and American production, giving great aid to both countries in solving surplus and unemployment problems. This meant that Japan had to restore the territorial integrity of China.[102] In addition, as we shall see in more detail shortly, the long-range war aims of the United States, which became fixed during this time, involved a single

Shaping a New World Order 145

world economy, an "open door" world, the maximum possible American living space. In November 1941, Leo Pasvolsky wrote a draft of a projected declaration on economic policy between Japan and the United States with which State Department trade adviser Harry C. Hawkins concurred. It stated that Japan should withdraw from China, restore complete control over economic, financial, and monetary affairs to that country, end monopoly rights given to the subsidiaries of Japanese companies in China, and urge, together with the United States, a program of economic development for China with equal opportunity to participate given to all.[103] This fundamental aspect of American postwar plans —elimination of all forms of discrimination in international commercial relations—meant a worldwide open door and an end to the spheres of influence and bloc division of the world prevalent during the 1930s.

Short-range issues were also important. If United States leaders made a deal with Japan at the expense of China, this would cause distrust among the other anti-Axis powers, who might fear similar treatment. Chinese resistance might collapse and there was no assurance Japan would not again begin its push to the south once the China "incident" was settled. China's opposition was weakening Japan's potential and actual military power. The fall of China would free Tokyo for renewed aggression, since Japan had not necessarily given up its drive for hegemony over Asia. Thus the mutual trust needed to make a binding agreement was lacking. In addition, many felt the time had come to stand up to Japan even if this meant war. As Assistant Secretary of State Adolf A. Berle wrote Hull a week after the Pearl Harbor attack, since the possibility of war in the Pacific depended almost entirely on the attitude of Washington after 1940, the secretary had been wise not to force the matter until the fall of 1941, when it became clear that Soviet Russia could survive the Nazi attack. Only then, said Berle, did it "become even remotely feasible to meet the issue which the Japanese were tendering as they extended their southward advance."[104]

Final negotiations took place during November, culminating in the ten-point plan from the United States to Japan on November 26, 1941. This memorandum took a hard line, visualizing a return to the status quo of 1931 by demanding a Japanese withdrawal from China and Indochina in return for resumption of trade relations.[105] With its oil supplies getting low because of the trade embargo, Japan had to choose between submission and war.

Roosevelt and his advisers, expecting Japan to advance south, had concluded that this movement would endanger the American national interest and had to be stopped, by a United States declaration of war and armed intervention if necessary. Roosevelt told Harry Hopkins that a Japanese attack on the Netherlands East Indies should result in war between the United States and Japan.[106] On November 28, the War Council made up of Hull, Secretary of War (and longtime Council member) Henry L. Stimson, and Secretary of the Navy Frank Knox, decided that Roosevelt should inform Congress and the American people that if Japan attacked Singapore or the East Indies, the security of the United States would be endangered and war might result.[107] It was agreed that Hull, Stimson, and Knox should draft this projected message to Congress. The idea behind the message was to persuade Congress and the public that Japanese expansion constituted such a threat to the national interest of the United States that military counteraction was necessary.[108]

These drafts illustrate how the top policymakers defined the national interest of the United States in Southeast Asia as of late November 1941, and show that this definition was identical to that which the Council on Foreign Relations put forward. Hull used Stimson's and Knox's drafts as a basis for his own final draft for the President. Hull and Roosevelt agreed that the message would not be sent to Congress until

Shaping a New World Order 147

"the last stage of our relations, relating to actual hostility, has been reached."[109] This draft message, which the secretary of state and the President discussed during the final days of peace, stressed, as the Council had concluded, that American national interests in Southeast Asia were primarily strategic and economic, and that Japanese expansion threatened these interests. Hull stated in his draft for the President's message that the situation created by Japan

> holds unmistakable threats to our interests, especially our interest in peace and in peaceful trade, and to our responsibility for the security of the Philippine Archipelago. The successful defense of the United States, in a military sense, is dependent upon supplies of vital materials which we import in large quantities from this region of the world. To permit Japanese domination and control of the major sources of world supplies of tin and rubber and tungsten would jeopardize our safety in a manner and to an extent that cannot be tolerated.[110]

The secretary of state further concluded that

> If the Japanese should carry out their now threatened attacks upon and were to succeed in conquering the regions which they are menacing in the southwestern Pacific, our commerce with the Netherlands East Indies and Malaya would be at their mercy and probably be cut off. Our imports from those regions are of vital importance to us. We need those imports in time of peace. With the spirit of exploitation and destruction of commerce which prevails among the partners in the Axis Alliance, and with our needs what they are now in this period of emergency, an interruption of our trade with that area would be catastrophic.[111]

Secretaries Stimson and Knox had taken the same position in their drafts for the President's message.[112] Their view clearly corresponded to that of the CFR during 1941. Roosevelt himself felt the same way, but faced the difficult task of persuading Congress and the American people that war for these ends was justified. How to convince the American people that an attack on British and Dutch colonies in the South Pacific "was tantamount to an attack upon our own frontiers," was a tremendous difficulty for the President.[113] Nevertheless, during the last week of peace, Roosevelt gave Britain assurances of armed support in case of Japanese aggression.[114] The assault on Pearl Harbor on December 7, 1941, which came because the Japanese had correctly calculated that the United States was likely to declare war when they moved further into Southeast Asia, made the whole problem moot.

Merger of Council and State Department Planning in 1941-1942

In late December 1941 the Department of State created a special committee to carry out postwar planning. The Advisory Committee on Postwar Foreign Policy was, Undersecretary Welles wrote, a "new approach to a problem that the Department had previously handled in a wholly desultory fashion."[115] The Council had a central role in establishing the Advisory Committee, in which its leading planners filled key positions.

The immediate origins of the Advisory Committee on Postwar Foreign Policy can be traced to a September 12, 1941, memorandum drafted by Leo Pasvolsky in consultation with Norman H. Davis. Pasvolsky, acting on directions from Secretary Hull, proposed an Advisory Committee structure, noting that this suggestion was "the result of a recent conversation between Mr. Norman Davis and myself, arranged in accordance with your desires in the matter. It has been read and approved by Mr. Davis."[116]

The Pasvolsky-Davis memorandum favored the establishment of three subcommittees on each of the main postwar questions: armament, political-territorial, and trade-financial. This corresponded almost directly to the structural setup of

Shaping a New World Order 149

the Council's own work. Actual research and memoranda-drafting would be done by the "appropriate divisions of the Department of State, by similar divisions of other departments and agencies of the Government, and by such nongovernmental agencies as the Council on Foreign Relations."[117] The memorandum noted that the Council's past cooperation had been "very useful."[118] Pasvolsky and Davis concluded that in this way the recommendations which the secretary of state would give the President would be the result of input from the entire government and the best brains outside of the government.[119]

The entry of the nation into a state of full belligerency in early December 1941 gave strong incentive to both the Council and State Department efforts to set up a postwar planning committee. Both Davis and Hamilton Fish Armstrong, the vice-chairman of the War and Peace Studies Project, pushed for the establishment of the committee and a large Council role in it. On December 12 Armstrong informed members of the Council groups that

> with the approval of Mr. Norman Davis, I went to Washington and had a talk yesterday morning with Mr. Sumner Welles, Undersecretary of State. He expressed generous appreciation of the work which our groups have done so far and said that it must continue at all costs. He agreed that in the circumstances a more intimate liaison between the Department and our project was desirable, and he expressed the hope that he would be able to work out the terms of this liaison within the coming week.[120]

Over the next four months the Council and State Department agreed on several forms of contact. The most important was direct representation of the Council on the Advisory Committee on Postwar Foreign Policy, which President Roosevelt approved on December 28, 1941. The Advisory Committee's mandate gave the Department of State control over postwar planning, since all recommendations on international postwar problems from all departments and agencies of the government were to be submitted to the President through the secretary of state. The historian Theodore Wilson has verified this fact, stating "On many matters FDR bypassed his Department of State; in regard to postwar planning he gave the inhabitants of 'foggy bottom' great if not sole responsibility."[121]

The Advisory Committee set the value framework for all key decisions on the postwar world made during 1942, 1943, and 1944. It dealt with fundamental issues of national policy, such as the needs of American economy and society, the relationship of these requirements to the rest of the world, and the role of international organizaions. The makeup of the fourteen-member committee therefore merits a detailed description. Secretary Hull, Undersecretary Welles, and Davis were first in importance. Myron C. Taylor, retired board chairman of United States Steel and formerly President Roosevelt's personal representative at the Vatican, was next. He joined the Council's board of directors in 1943. Dean Acheson, assistant secretary of state specializing in economic matters, Armstrong, Assistant Secretary of State Adolf A. Berle, Jr., and Isaiah Bowman, Territorial Group leader, followed these four. Rounding out the committee were Benjamin V. Cohen, simultaneously a New York corporate lawyer, Roosevelt adviser, and member of the Economic and Financial Group; Council member and former employee Herbert Feis, who was an adviser on international economic affairs for the State Department; Green H. Hackworth, a legal adviser for the department; Harry C. Hawkins, chief of State's division of commercial policy; Anne O'Hare McCormick, a member of the editorial board of the *New York Times;* and Pasvolsky himself. As chief of the division of special research, and special assistant to the secretary of state in charge of postwar planning, Pasvolsky had great impact on every phase of the work.[122]

The fourteen planners of the Advisory Committee may be

grouped in various ways for purposes of generalization and analysis. Harley A. Notter, in his official State Department history of postwar planning, recognized two groups—private citizens and government officials. The five private citizens—Davis, Taylor, Armstrong, Bowman, and McCormick—were chosen, according to Notter, "because of their high personal qualifications for policy consideration and because of their capacity to represent informed public opinion and interests."[123] Of the nine government officials, all but Cohen were from the State Department. This group was composed of generalists—Hull, Welles, Berle, Cohen, and Pasvolsky—who worked on the broader aspects of postwar planning, and specialists—Acheson, Hawkins, Feis, and Hackworth—who concentrated on one field.

Four leading members of the Council on Foreign Relations were among the five representing "informed public opinion and interests." Davis, Armstrong, and Bowman were principal directors of the Council's postwar planning efforts, and Taylor was a member who joined the Council's board of directors in 1943. McCormick had no direct relationship to the Council since women were then barred from that body. The addition in mid-1942 of James T. Shotwell as another general member representing the "public" strengthened Council dominance. A founder of the Council, Shotwell also belonged to the Political Group from February 1940 until June 1943.[124]

It is thus clear that the "public opinion and interests" being represented on the Advisory Committee were overwhelmingly those of the Council and of the section of society it spoke for. Obviously, the reference group the government had in mind when it talked of "public opinion" was the upper class, not the mass of Americans.

Four of the "government" members of the Advisory Committee also had Council ties. Cohen was active in the Economic and Financial Group. Feis had long experience in

Table 4-1
Members of the Advisory Committee on Postwar Foreign Policy

Member	Primary occupation	Importance in official post-war planning	Council member during WWII	Known level of CFR involvement	Involved in War and Peace Studies?
Cordell Hull	Politician	Great	No	—	No
Sumner Welles	Career government official	Great	Yes	Slight	No
Norman H. Davis	Banker	Great	Yes	Great	Yes
Myron C. Taylor	Corporation executive	Great	Yes	Great	No
Isaiah Bowman	University president	Great	Yes	Great	Yes
Leo Pasvolsky	Economist	Great	Yes	Moderate	Yes
Dean Acheson	Lawyer	Great	No, but had joined by 1948	—	No
Hamilton Fish Armstrong	Editor	Great	Yes	Great	Yes
Adolf A. Berle	Lawyer	Great	No, but had joined by 1946	Slight	No
Benjamin V. Cohen	Lawyer	Moderate	Yes	Moderate	Yes
Herbert Feis	Economist	Moderate	Yes	Moderate	No
Green H. Hackworth	Lawyer	Moderate	No	—	No
Harry C. Hawkins	Economist	Moderate	No	—	No
Anne O'Hare McCormick	Journalist	Moderate	No	—	No

152

Shaping a New World Order 153

Council affairs, and Pasvolsky and Welles were members. The original Advisory Committee was thus an amalgam of people with close ties to New York (10), the Council on Foreign Relations (8), and to the Department of State (9). The East Coast was in control, with other sections of the country unrepresented. White, Anglo-Saxon upper-class businessmen, lawyers, and technocrats dominated the committee. The working class generally—labor, consumers, small business, minorities, and ethnic groups—had virtually no representation. Table 4-1 summarizes information about the original Advisory Committee.[125]

Those at the top of the department and those from the Council made up the core of the Advisory Committee decision-makers who decided the fate of the postwar world. The core group consisted of Hull, Welles, Davis, Taylor, Bowman, and Pasvolsky. They were the people, who, beginning in early 1943, became known as the Informal Political Agenda Group, which President Roosevelt called "my postwar advisers."[126] They were the senior men, who selected, planned, and guided the agenda for the entire Advisory Committee and also drafted the United Nations Charter.[127] Of these top six, only Hull was not a Council member, and four out of the six were active in Council affairs, with Davis and Bowman filling key roles in the War and Peace Studies Project. Only Pasvolsky was not a member of the upper class.

Between February and June 1942, eleven special members —officials from other sections of the government who would work on only one aspect of the postwar program—were invited to join the committee. In no way did they threaten control over postwar planning by the Council and State Department. The new men represented the White House staff, the Department of Agriculture, the Board of Economic Warfare, the secretaries of the navy, war, and treasury, the Department of State, and Congress.[128] The two men from the legislative branch of government—Senators Tom Connally and Warren R. Austin of the Senate Foreign Relations Committee—were asked to join in May 1942, but were never active participants. The only new people who appear to have made an important contribution during 1942 were Maj. Gen. George V. Strong, representing Secretary of War Stimson, and Harry Dexter White, from the Treasury Department. Strong, head of the military intelligence section and former chief of the war plans division, served in the special area of security questions. He was also an active member of the Council's Security and Armaments Group during 1940 and again in 1944-1945.[129] White worked on economic problems, drafting a plan for a monetary stabilization fund and international development bank. He had no known ties with the Council.

Although the three main leaders of the Council, along with several others who were active in its postwar planning, were brought in as part of the Advisory Committee structure at the very beginning, Armstrong and Davis desired an even closer liaison. In a letter to Davis in January 1942, Armstrong made the concrete suggestion that the Council should "loan" its War and Peace Studies research secretaries to the department for part of each week. This way the secretaries would be free to develop the work of the study groups in New York, still have inside information about what the Advisory Committee was doing, and bring ideas and suggestions for policy both to and from the Department of State. This close two-way communication would become a main form of liaison between the Council's and the Department of State's postwar planning efforts. This objective, Armstrong wrote, "is one more reason for giving our groups some sort of semi-official standing, perhaps in an advisory capacity, because without that the regular staff of the Department might feel some inhibitions about dealing with us as frankly as I know Welles is prepared to have them do."[130]

Armstrong also reported to Davis that he had talked with

Shaping a New World Order 155

Pasvolsky by phone, extracting from him the promise not to let the final plans for the organization of the Advisory Committee solidify without notifying Armstrong, so that he could talk it over with Davis, Pasvolsky, and Hull. Armstrong closed by stating that everyone at Council headquarters was relying heavily on Davis to see that this new advisory function would be achieved.[131]

By February 1942, the leaders of the Advisory Committee projected six subcommittees—three political, two economic, and one for coordination. The last included the function of providing "contact with private organizations actively discussing postwar problems."[132] Davis was named as head of this subcommittee, indicating that the Council on Foreign Relations was the primary private organization with which to be kept in contact. Pasvolsky's division of special research, located in the State Department, was to be the principal research agency for the Advisory Committee. The members of the division drafted memoranda for the subcommittees' consideration. They labored at the "working level" of postwar planning, while the members of the Advisory Committee worked at the higher "policy level."[133]

The initial organizational meeting of the subcommittees on political problems, territorial problems, and security problems took place on February 21, 1942, with Welles presiding. There the patient background work of Armstrong and Davis paid off. Davis was chosen to head the security subcommittee, Bowman the territorial, and Welles the political.

Early in this crucial meeting Armstrong proposed that the research secretaries of the Council should work in the department for two or three days each week, attending the subcommittee meetings. The Council would thus be in "close relation to the actual functioning of the Advisory Committee."[134] Welles agreed, stating that he "wished to have the most effective liaison that could be devised."[135] Armstrong then described the details of his plan. The Council's discussions could be scheduled early each week, leaving the research secretaries free to come to Washington during the last half, when the department's subcommittees would meet. In this manner the Council's research secretaries could keep in touch with the department's efforts and also "carry back to the Council the exact research needs of the Advisory Committee."[136] Bowman added that the Council was in a position to work with private individuals in New York, to coordinate their research, and obtain their cooperation. The State Department's Advisory Committee could not do this officially and therefore it had great need for the Council as an unofficial body.[137]

At this point in the discussion Pasvolsky proposed that Armstrong's plan be adopted.[138] After further deliberation without dissent, Welles concluded that formal liaison should be maintained through the research secretaries of the Council. The undersecretary suggested that Davis, Bowman, and Armstrong work out the specifics with Pasvolsky.[139]

The final arrangements for effective Council-Department contact were made in late March 1942. Each subcommittee would have a research secretary to prepare memoranda and circulate them to the members.[140] As Armstrong and the other Council leaders had suggested on February 21, the CFR research secretaries were brought into the department to aid in this task. They were given the title of "consultants." William P. Maddox, research secretary for the Council's Territorial Group, became consultant for the Advisory Committee's territorial subcommittee. William Diebold, Jr., research secretary for the Economic and Financial Group, served the same function for the economic subcommittee. Walter R. Sharp of the Political Group did likewise for the political subcommittee, and Grayson L. Kirk from the Armaments Group became a consultant for the Advisory Committee's security subcommittee.[141] Philip E. Mosely, who served as research secretary for the Council's Territorial Group from March 1940 to September 1941, and from August 1942 until

February 1945, became research secretary for the territorial subcommittee and then assistant chief of the division of special research in November 1942.[142] As had been planned, the "consultants" continued their work with the Council while meeting with the division of special research and the Advisory Committee. Davis, Armstrong, Bowman, and Cohen also maintained their active roles within the War and Peace Studies Project, providing additional liaison between the committee and the Council.

The Advisory Committee held its last general meeting, chaired by Secretary Hull, on May 2, 1942, after which the work went ahead on the subcommittee level. The secretary thanked the members for their contribution to the planning efforts and expressed his special thanks to the Council on Foreign Relations, which had devoted the last two years to examining postwar problems and "whose spirit and activity were cordially appreciated by the Department."[143]

After this gathering, the subcommittees met separately in order to insure secrecy.[144] Pasvolsky sent a memorandum to the staff of the division of special research on July 20, 1942, which reemphasized the "extremely confidential nature" of the division's work, stressing that members of the staff must refrain from discussing their tasks with "anyone outside the Division, whether in or out of the Government."[145] As we have seen, however, the Council had its leading postwar planners in key positions and knew every detail of this work. In his official State Department history of postwar planning, Notter makes the point that secrecy was especially important on the territorial subcommittee, since the territorial problems of countries and peoples were explosive.[146] Yet Bowman, the Council's leading territorial specialist, headed this subcommittee, and Mosely, the CFR's research secretary on these questions from August 1942 until February 1945, was also research secretary for the Advisory Committee's subcommittee on territorial problems starting in August 1942.[147]

The CFR Controls Postwar Planning

The position of the Council on Foreign Relations within the Department of State had become so powerful by mid-1942 that a few of the lower-level planners in the department's division of special research, who were doing the basic studies necessary for postwar planning, began to feel some resentment and discontent. These men had little or no previous contact with the Council. As the Council took over more and more of the planning work, the assistant chief of the division of special research, Harley A. Notter, launched a counterattack. In mid-July 1942 he complained to Pasvolsky, his immediate superior, that Walter R. Sharp, a Council consultant to the department's political subcommittee, was attending the meetings of Bowman's territorial subcommittee. Barely concealing his anger, Notter recounted the close collaboration among the Council men to maximize their influence in the Advisory Committee's work. Sharp was still only a consultant and had, according to Notter, produced nothing for the department, yet had been able to prepare materials for the Council. That he could be invited to conferences of the territorial subcommittee, which were, in addition, on topics outside the area of his special competence, rankled Notter.[148]

Notter went on to raise another issue concerning the Council and the Department of State's planning. When Bowman came to Washington for meetings of his subcommittee, he would phone Philip E. Mosely and discuss the session's topics in advance. Mosely had been the research secretary for the Council's Territorial Group prior to joining the department and was soon to serve the Council again in that capacity. Notter said that he could not escape the feeling that these conversations resulted in a prior plan. This was his suspicion, he added, because during the last such meeting chairman

Bowman had suddenly broken the line of the subcommittee's conversation, something which was "completely artificial, albeit deliberate and planned."[149] Notter continued:

> The variety and number of surprises constantly arising in the territorial meetings owing to discussions between the chairman and Mr. Mosely, of which I am not informed, and other discussions about which I may have no right to be informed, are, regardless of other considerations, productive of embarrassed confusion on my part during these meetings. Perhaps because of your absence in recent meetings for a considerable part of each, Mr. Bowman and Mr. Armstrong have shown unmistakably that they wish to build up Mr. Mosely and the other Council men. Their successful effort in regard to the Committee, and secondly the Division, most unfairly disregards the contributions actually made by other members of our staff. In *their* name a protest must be laid against that sort of treatment.[150]

Notter added that he felt that there was a "limit to patient endurance—in our case of the slights and rudeness inflicted upon the staff in order to put forward the members of the Council. There is bound to be trouble in the staff, and I feel obliged to report that it exists and will increase."[151]

Notter's irritation continued during August 1942, when Sharp was appointed a high-level officer of the division. In a letter to Assistant Secretary of State Howland Shaw, Notter wrote that Sharp would continue his work at both the Council and the College of the City of New York. While Notter felt that "an officer—particularly one of senior grade—should give undivided attention to his work in the Department, amicable relations between Department and the Council demonstrably seem to require favorable consideration of Dr. Sharp for an appointment."[152]

By mid-September 1942 things had reached a crisis, and Notter drafted a letter of resignation to Pasvolsky, saying that his position in the division was no longer tenable.[153] He cited two reasons for his decision. First, he was receiving one set of instructions from Pasvolsky and contradictory ones from Welles, due to a power struggle within the department. Notter's second reason concerned

> relations with the Council on Foreign Relations. I have consistently opposed every move tending to give it increasing control of the research of this Division, and, though you have also consistently stated that such a policy was far from your objectives, the actual facts already visibly show that Departmental control is fast losing ground. Control by the Council has developed, in my judgment, to the point where, through Mr. Bowman's close cooperation with you, and his other methods and those of Mr. Armstrong on the Committee which proceed unchanged in their main theme, the outcome is clear. The moves have been so piecemeal that no one of them offered decisive objection; that is still so, but I now take my stand on the cumulative trend.[154]

Notter went on to say that he did not want to carry out policies that he believed harmful to both the division of special research and relations between the division and the Advisory Committee. He feared that the committee might be operating under the direction of the Council, not the State Department. Consequently, he wanted to be relieved of his post at the earliest possible time.[155] To hasten that date, Notter suggested—somewhat sarcastically—that Mosely of the Council should take over the territorial work within a few weeks, and that the remainder of the present political section of the division's endeavors be placed under Sharp as his successor, with Kirk as second in command. "These three Council men at present head the major units and are already so well put forward through the tactics of their sponsors that they doubtless can assume the responsibilities in stride, so to speak."[156]

Notter's letter of resignation was never sent, according to a note attached in his handwriting.[157] No concrete steps were taken, however, against any of the Council men on the Advisory Committee or in the division of special research during this whole period, so the existing situation did not change.

Shaping a New World Order 161

The Council men remained in their positions of power in the department and continued their own work concurrently but independently of the government.

The last two sections have shown that Council planners were very loyal to their organization. They were extraordinarily successful in increasing its influence. The Council was the only private organization in the United States with such great representation on and control over the Advisory Committee and, by extension, the Department of State and the postwar national-interest decision-making process. Through the active participation of Davis, Bowman, Armstrong, Cohen, and the research secretaries in both the Council's and the committee's work, the Council was in the unique position of being privy to the national secrets concerning plans for the shape of the postwar world.

Since its leaders and research secretaries had access to the most sensitive and highly confidential state secrets, it is clear that the CFR was an extremely important private body. Only an organization which shared with the government fundamentally identical goals and means could be trusted with such secrets. This congruity on postwar plans points out not only the Council's great power vis-à-vis the government, but also indicates that the Council's strength was so overwhelming as to amount to de facto control over the state. This issue can be answered partly by analyzing the means which the Council advocated to carry out American war aims and ascertaining if the government seemed to follow its wishes. The Council had maneuvered itself into key positions in the postwar decision-making process. How did it envisage implementing the postwar goals laid down in the Grand Area concept? The remaining sections of this chapter confront this question.

The Grand Area and United States War Aims

Military conflicts are fought to determine who will shape the peace following victory, and on what basis. Therefore the complex of assumptions and goals, labeled for the sake of convenience as "war aims," are most crucial for understanding long-range foreign policy. Analysis and description of these aims throw light on both the origin and consequences of the conflict.

The Grand Area concept and the means which the Council proposed to integrate this territory became the initial basis for United States war aims. Two problems faced the Council and government planners in regard to these goals. First, the American people had to be inspired and mobilized to enter the war and win it. This involved issuing plausible propaganda. Secondly, the detailed and specific means for integration of an expanded Grand Area into a United States-dominated world order had to be devised. This involved working out the mechanics for new international institutions.

The CFR's War and Peace Studies groups recognized at an early date the difference between these two types of problems. The Economic and Financial Group pointed out in July 1941 that "formulation of a statement of war aims for propaganda purposes is very different from formulation of one defining the true national interest."[158] While this group's main concern was with the latter function, it did give the government ideas on how to deal with the former. In April 1941 the group suggested to the government that a statement of American war aims should now be prepared, coldly warning:

> If war aims are stated which seem to be concerned solely with Anglo-American imperialism, they will offer little to people in the rest of the world, and will be vulnerable to Nazi counter-promises. Such aims would also strengthen the most reactionary elements in the United States and the British Empire. The inter-

ests of other peoples should be stressed, not only those of Europe, but also of Asia, Africa and Latin America. This would have a better propaganda effect.[159]

Since such propaganda statements had to be at least close to actual American interests, the war aims declaration had to be vague and abstract, not specific. The statement which resulted was the Atlantic Charter of August 1941. It was the public war aims statement of the United States, and its reason for being was propaganda.[160] The generalized aims it advocated were those which people everywhere would agree were laudable: freedom, equality, prosperity, and peace. The Council had made suggestions about what should be in such a public statement, and a member of the Council—Undersecretary of State Sumner Welles—was President Roosevelt's chief adviser on the Atlantic Charter.

With the entry of the United States into World War II, American planners were virtually unanimous in the belief that the nation should claim a dominant position in the postwar world. As usual, however, the leaders of the Council on Foreign Relations were stating this view most clearly. Council director and Territorial Group leader Isaiah Bowman wrote Hamilton Fish Armstrong, a week after the entry of the United States into the war, that the Council and the American government now had to "think of world-organization in a fresh way. To the degree that the United States is the arsenal of the Democracies it will be the final arsenal at the moment of victory. It cannot throw the contents of that arsenal away. *It must accept world responsibility.* . . . The measure of our victory will be the measure of our domination after victory."[161] The next month, in January 1942, Bowman further asserted that at minimum, an enlarged conception of American security interests would be necessary after the war in order to deal with areas "strategically necessary for world control."[162]

Council president Norman Davis, now chairman of the

Department of State's security subcommittee of the Advisory Committee on Postwar Foreign Policy, asserted in early May 1942 that it was probable "the British Empire as it existed in the past will never reappear and that the United States may have to take its place."[163] Gen. George V. Strong, a member of Davis's subcommittee who had worked on the War and Peace Studies Project during 1940, used even stronger language during the same discussion. He expressed the opinion that the United States "must cultivate a mental view toward world settlement after this war which will enable us to impose our own terms, amounting perhaps to a pax-Americana."[164] He went on to say that the nation must adopt a tough attitude toward its allies at the expected peace conference. Davis agreed with Strong, adding that the United States could "no longer be indifferent as to what happens in any part of the world."[165] Trouble must be nipped in the bud wherever it occurred.

The reason for this emphasis on global hegemony for the United States was the same one that the Council had stressed in 1940 and 1941: the economic life of American society as presently organized was very closely connected with the outside world. The economy of the nation, as it had been for some time, was geared to the need for large export markets, the loss of which—barring a transition to a form of socialism —would cause a lowering of the national income and greatly increased unemployment.[166] The haunting specter of depression and its political consequences made the planners pay careful attention to the relationship between international and domestic economic policies.[167]

Early in 1942 Leo Pasvolsky said that the close mutual "relation between international trade and investment on the one hand and the domestic recovery program of the United States on the other" was particularly important.[168] Herbert Feis, an active Council member and State Department economic adviser, expressed the problem in a similar way, saying that most countries lived in chronic fear of unemployment and so want foreign markets to avoid "drastic internal adjustments as a result of changes in external markets."[169] Two months later, Benjamin V. Cohen, a member of the Economic and Financial Group and a State Department postwar planner, asserted that the difficulty for the economy of the United States was "how to create purchasing power outside of our country which would be converted into domestic purchasing power through exportation. In practical terms, this matter comes down to the problem of devising appropriate institutions to perform after the war the function that Lend-Lease is now performing."[170] Pasvolsky also recognized this situation, saying in August 1942 that a solution had to be found to the existing condition in which some countries need more imports than they can pay for, while others can furnish exports without immediate payment.[171] This dual aspect, concern with foreign demand as well as internal needs, suggests that the Marshall Plan idea of overseas loans and gifts by the American government to stimulate United States exports had deep roots in the Lend-Lease experience.[172]

The first document produced by the economic subcommittee of the Advisory Committee on Postwar Foreign Policy stressed the danger of another world depression and the need to provide confidence in world economic stability.[173] This necessarily meant that American planners had to concern themselves with the politics and economies of other nations. At a minimum the United States had to be involved in the internal affairs of the key industrial and raw materials-producing countries. If one or a few of these nations did not cooperate in a new worldwide economic system, they might not develop rapidly enough to enlarge their purchases from the United States, thereby increasing the likelihood of a depression. The various countries' economies had also to be efficient; otherwise they could not pay for more imports. The political and security side was also connected with this basic economic dilemma. Davis's subcommittee laid great stress on "the impossibility of providing security to the world unless developments in other fields would be such as to provide a sound basis for international cooperation."[174]

The IMF and World Bank

Clarification of the objectives of American policy gave rise to ideas for specific methods of solving the concrete problems of American and world capitalism. Ideas for international economic institutions—the International Monetary Fund (IMF) and the International Bank for Reconstruction and Development (World Bank)—were worked out first.

The Council had proposed that economic means would play a key role in integrating the Grand Area.[175] In several recommendations during 1941, the CFR's War and Peace Studies groups proposed that international economic and financial institutions were needed to assure the proper functioning of the proposed world economy.[176] Recommendation P-B23 (July 1941) stated that worldwide financial institutions were necessary for the purpose of "stabilizing currencies and facilitating programs of capital investment for constructive undertakings in backward and underdeveloped regions."[177] During the last half of 1941 and in the first months of 1942, the Council developed this idea for the integration of the world.

In October 1941 Winfield W. Riefler of the Economic and Financial Group presented a design for an International Development Authority to stimulate private investment in underdeveloped areas. The Authority would be run by nine directors—three American, three British, and three representing international bodies. A new world judicial organization would settle disputes. The greater investment gained by international guarantees would develop resources and raise living standards in poorer regions and at the same time increase overseas purchasing power and, thus, the demand for United States exports.[178] Following Riefler's scheme was one which Alvin H. Hansen suggested on November 1, 1941: an international Reconstruction Finance Corporation should be jointly established by many governments during the war. This body would also promote investment, both in backward areas and in the more developed countries. The corporation would float bonds guaranteed by the government to tap private money now withheld from foreign investment because of the risk. To guide the investment, an international resources survey would be undertaken to discover where development might most usefully be initiated.[179]

The Council advanced these proposals by drafting a recommendation, dispatching it directly to President Roosevelt and the Department of State. This memorandum, dated November 28, 1941, was entitled "International Collaboration to Secure the Coordination of Stabilization Policies and to Stimulate Investment."[180] It stated that implementation of the economic goals of the Atlantic Charter depended on "effective anti-depression measures."[181] To prevent such economic downturns, a joint United States-United Kingdom board should be set up to advise on policy and devise plans for an "international investment agency which would stimulate world trade and prosperity by facilitating investment in developmental programs the world over."[182] Since depressions have political effects—the Council men argued that they had been one of the "chief factors" in Hitler's rise to power in Germany—all countries had a common interest in assuring economic stability and "reasonably continuous" full employment.[183]

Beginning in February 1942, the Economic and Financial Group became more specific and suggested what such an American-British board should recommend. Hansen and

Jacob Viner now recognized that separate institutions were needed for different functions. As Viner said early in February: "It might be wise to set up two financial institutions: one an international exchange stabilization board and one an international bank to handle short-term transactions not directly concerned with stabilization."[184] Here was the first specific mention of the need for both an International Monetary Fund and an International Bank for Reconstruction and Development. The Council followed this discussion with a memorandum, E-B49, to the department and the President. Dated April 1, 1942, it contained Hansen's statement on the necessity for an exchange stabilization fund to regulate international exchange rates, and Viner's ideas on promoting long-term world investment by establishing "multinational official agencies."[185] Thus the Council's planners first proposed multinational bodies to spur the worldwide development essential to sustain and increase American and British prosperity, as well as to integrate Germany and Japan into the expanded "Grand Area" which would result.

While it was the Council which initially proposed during 1941 and 1942 the idea of international economic institutions to integrate the new world order, it was Harry Dexter White of the Treasury Department who worked out the actual technical details which led to the International Monetary Fund and the World Bank. Although not a Council member, White probably had contact with its ideas, perhaps through Viner, who was a Treasury adviser, or through Hansen, who was active in many federal agencies. In any event, White produced a memorandum on the subject of both a monetary fund and bank by March 1942.[186] This was the plan which Secretary of the Treasury Morgenthau gave to Roosevelt in mid-May.[187] Following discussions with Secretary Hull, a special interdepartmental committee was established to refine the plan. This was the Cabinet Committee, which began meeting on May 25, 1942. The Cabinet Committee organized a group of experts, called the American Technical Committee, which did the actual planning work.[188] These two committees, largely responsible for the final form of the Monetary Fund and the World Bank, were centered in the Treasury Department and had only informal ties with the State Department's Advisory Committee on Postwar Foreign Policy. There was considerable overlapping of personnel, however, between the two groups. White served as the Treasury Department's man on the economic subcommittee of the Advisory Committee. Acheson, Berle, Feis, Pasvolsky of the State Department, and Cohen of the White House staff were on either the Cabinet Committee or the American Technical Committee, which White chaired. The Council was well represented on these latter two committees by the last three men and by Hansen, who attended many of the Technical Committee meetings.[189] A full-blown international conference to establish a monetary fund and world bank convened at Bretton Woods, New Hampshire, in 1944, creating institutions whose aim was integration of the expanded Grand Area to create one world economy dominated by the United States.

The Council and the Origins of the United Nations

Council leaders recognized that in an age of rising nationalism around the world, the United States had to avoid the onus of big-power imperialism in its implementation of the Grand Area and creation of one open-door world. Isaiah Bowman first suggested a way to solve the problem of maintaining effective control over weaker territories while avoiding overt imperial conquest. At a Council meeting in May 1942, he stated that the United States had to exercise the strength needed to assure "security," and at the same time "avoid conventional forms of imperialism."[190] The way to do this, he argued, was to make the exercise of that power international in character through a United Nations body.[191] As we shall see below, the Council planners had a central role in the creation of this United Nations organization.

The planning of the United Nations can be traced to the "secret steering committee" established by Secretary Hull in January 1943. This Informal Agenda Group, as it was later called, was composed of Hull, Davis, Taylor, Bowman, Pasvolsky, and, until he left the government in August 1943, Welles.[192] All of them, with the exception of Hull, were members of the Council on Foreign Relations. They saw Hull regularly to plan, select, and guide the labors of the department's Advisory Committee. It was, in effect, the coordinating agency for all the State Department postwar planning.[193]

The men of the Informal Agenda Group were most responsible for the final shape of the United Nations. Beginning in February 1943, members of the group met frequently with President Roosevelt, who called them "my postwar advisers."[194] They not only drew up policy recommendations, but also "served as advisers to the Secretary of State and the President on the final decisions."[195] In addition, they met frequently during 1943 for intensive work in connection with the Quebec and Moscow conferences, drafting the suggestions for the four-power agreement accepted by Britain and Russia.

By December 1943 the membership of the group included Hull, Davis, Bowman, Taylor, and Pasvolsky from the original six, as well as the new undersecretary of state, Edward R. Stettinius, Jr. Stettinius was a member of the Council on Foreign Relations, former top executive of United States Steel, and son of a partner in the J. P. Morgan Bank. Benjamin V. Cohen and Stanley K. Hornbeck, both with close ties to the Council, had also joined the Agenda Group along with James C. Dunn, Green H. Hackworth, and Notter from the staff of the department.[196] The Council's preeminence clearly remained. Seven of the eleven—Davis, Bowman, Taylor, Pasvolsky, Stettinius, Cohen, Hornbeck, and Dunn—were either present members of the Council or involved in the War and Peace Studies.[197] If others who were invited to join some of the meetings during this period are included, Council influence is even more striking. Joseph C. Green was added to the group in mid-March 1944. He was a Council member and regularly attended the gatherings of the Armaments Group.[198] Five military men were asked to conferences of the Agenda Group during March, April, and May 1944. One of these, Admiral Hepburn, was a Council member; two others, General Strong and Rear Adm. Roscoe E. Schuirmann of naval intelligence had been involved in the War and Peace Studies Project.[199]

Upon Hull's return from the Moscow conference in late 1943, the Agenda Group began to draft the American proposals for a United Nations organization to maintain international peace and security. The position eventually taken at the Dumbarton Oaks Conference was prepared during the seven-month period from December 1943 to July 1944. Once the group had produced a draft for the United Nations and Hull had approved it, the secretary requested three distinguished lawyers to rule on its constitutionality. Myron C. Taylor, now on the Council's board of directors, was Hull's intermediary to Charles Evan Hughes, retired chief justice of the Supreme Court, John W. Davis, Democratic presidential candidate in 1924, and Nathan L. Miller, former Republican governor of New York. Hughes and Davis were both Council members, and John W. Davis had served as president of the Council from 1921 to 1933 and as a director since 1921. The three approved the plan, and on June 15, 1944, Hull, Stettinius, Davis, Bowman, and Pasvolsky discussed the draft with President Roosevelt. The chief executive gave his consent and issued a statement to the American people that very afternoon.[200]

Although the Charter of the United Nations underwent

some modification in negotiations with other nations at the Dumbarton Oaks and San Francisco conferences during 1944 and 1945, one historian concluded that "the substance of the provisions finally written into the Charter in many cases reflected conclusions reached at much earlier stages by the United States Government."[201] The Department of State was clearly in charge of these propositions within the American government, and the role of the Council on Foreign Relations within the Department of State was, in turn, very great indeed.[202] The Council's power was unrivaled. It had more information, representation, and decision-making power on postwar questions than the Congress, any executive bureaucracy except the Department of State, or other private group.[203] It had a very large input into decisions on the International Monetary Fund, the World Bank, and the United Nations. The formulators of the Grand Area had indeed been able to gain positions of strength and put their plans for United States world hegemony into effect.

The CFR-Ruling Class Conception of the "National Interest"

Leaders of the United States have always declared that the foremost objective of their policies has been the promotion of the country's collective interest—the "national interest." As Secretary of State Charles Evans Hughes put it in the 1920s, "foreign policies are not built upon abstractions. They are the result of practical conceptions of national interest."[204] The national interest is rarely an objective fact, however, as is indicated by the truism that in every country it is always redefined after a revolution.

The very idea of "national" interest assumes that everyone's interests are identical, or nearly so, and this is far from true in a capitalist society. The working class and upper class have very different interests at home and abroad. The working class is most concerned with domestic society and change: redistribution of income and wealth, full employment, worker control of industry, and more egalitarianism generally. The capitalist class, on the other hand, has an interest in preventing basic changes in society, and a desire to maintain the socioeconomic system from which it greatly benefits. Since domestic problems can be solved through foreign expansion, without alteration of the existing domestic system from which the corporate upper class obtains its power and privilege, it has a much greater interest in foreign policy.

The concept of the national interest put forth by the Council on Foreign Relations laid the basis for American war aims in the Second World War. The nation's interest was first of all defined and discussed within an economic framework, focusing on the most basic facts and long-term trends: the type of economic structure existing in the United States, its requirements, and the regions of the world crucial to the satisfaction of these needs. It was therefore inherently a status quo formulation, aimed at preservation rather than change. If one accepts the set of assumptions, values, and goals implied in the Council's sketch of the national interest—a capitalist system with private ownership of the productive property of the society, resulting in inequality in the distribution of wealth and income and attendant class structure—the analysis cannot be refuted. The Council planners had identified the basic needs of such a system, and any discussion of the national interest necessarily had to address itself to these requirements. Since those in power define the national interest as the preservation of the existing set of economic, social, and political relationships and of their own rule, the national interest in a capitalist society is little more than the interest of its upper class. The Council, as a key organization of this class, was in the lead in defining its class interest. One has to transcend its values, assumptions, and goals in order to question its formulation of the national interest.

The American capitalist class, through the Council, had proposed to preserve and extend American capitalism by a policy of empire-building—overseas expansion of United States power. This necessarily meant conflict and possible war, since the ruling classes of certain other capitalist societies—Japan, for example—would not tolerate limitation by the United States. Given the serious potential consequences of the Council's analysis, it is appropriate to ask whether its definition of the national interest was the only one possible. It is clear that there was an alternative. The crux of the difficulty facing the American economy and society during 1940 and 1941—as the Council had pointed out—was that the economic isolation of the Western hemisphere would result in the loss of two-thirds of United States foreign trade. In essence, the Council argued that the way to resolve the problem was to assure unrestricted access to the raw materials and markets of Asia and the markets of Great Britain. Politically, this meant an alliance with the British Empire and war with Japan and Germany. The fact was, however, that the need for such export markets could be largely obviated by public ownership of the chief means of production, and democratic planning to assure all in the country both employment and adequate consumption.

The United States was the most self-sufficient nation in the world during the 1930s and 1940s. Council theorists recognized this fact during the depression. In 1937 Eugene Staley wrote a book called *Raw Materials in Peace and War* under the auspices of the Council-dominated American Coordinating Committee for International Studies. A study group under the supervision of James T. Shotwell, a founder of the Council, had been established to help Staley. This study group included Council leader Edwin F. Gay, as well as

Alvin H. Hansen, Jacob Viner, and other Council members. Staley concluded that in regard to raw materials the "United States is more nearly capable than any other great power (unless it be the Soviet Union) of meeting its normal demands from resources within its own boundaries."[205]

During the summer and fall of 1940, Council planners in the Economic and Financial Group recognized that Western hemisphere isolation was not impossible if the United States economy were adjusted to it. Studies were made on expansion of raw material production to replace sources outside the hemisphere. Expansion of Latin American tin, rubber, and manganese output could also provide a "substantial outlet" for United States surplus production of machinery, equipment, and vehicles, since such machines would be needed to increase production of these commodities.[206]

This possibility was never attempted, however, because it would have threatened the traditional capitalist form of American economic organization. Since the government would have been responsible for planning and coordination of the economy during peacetime, the power of the capitalist class to make decisions on economic development might have been limited. The alternative was to have a larger world area to work with, and the Council's Grand Area planning was based on this expansionistic assumption. As Riefler expressed it in mid-1941, the Council's task was to delineate "what 'elbow room' the American economy needed in order to survive without major readjustments."[207] Avoiding territorial restriction and the economic readjustment it would entail thus became a constant theme in the Council's planning and recommendations to the State Department and President Roosevelt during 1940 and 1941, as we have seen. By October 1940, for example, the Economic and Financial Group wrote a memorandum whose purpose was to show how the United States could "secure a larger area for economic and military collaboration, thus minimizing costs of *economic* readjustments that would be greater for a smaller area."[208] They added the observation that the alterations necessary in the American and other capitalist economies "obviously are reduced to a minimum if those economies can function in all the world outside of the German portion."[209]

The ruling class, through the Council, had successfully put forward a particular conception of the United States "national interest." This perspective did not in reality uphold the general interest of the people of the nation, but rather the special interests of a capitalist economic system controlled by and benefiting the upper class. Simply stated, the Council theoreticians argued that the United States needed living space to maintain the existing system without fundamental changes in the direction of socialism and planning. Council member Henry R. Luce put the issue more bluntly when he stated in his famous February 1941 *Life* article that "Tyrannies may require a large amount of living space. But Freedom requires and will require far greater living space than Tyranny."[210]

Suggested Readings

Although there is a voluminous body of literature on the Second World War, little exists on postwar planning or the actual long-range goals of the policymakers. Key primary sources include: CFR (1946b); Notter (1949); Hull (1948); and Israel (1966).

The best existing secondary sources are those by Kolko (1968); R. Gardner (1969); L. Gardner (1964 and 1970); and Divine (1967).

Useful specialized volumes exist on the following topics:

Postwar planning: Shoup (1974)
Formation of the United Nations: Russell (1958)
International Monetary Fund: Payer (1974)
World Bank: Hayter (1971)
United States entry into World War II: Russett (1972); Schroeder

(1958); Chadwin (1968); Offner (1971); and the Council-sponsored volumes by Langer and Gleason (1952, 1953). On the Marxist versus liberal debate over the question of whether the American economy as presently organized requires imperialism, see the exchange between Magdoff and Miller, Bennett, and Alapatt in Skolnick and Currie (1973).

Notes

1. John W. Davis and George O. May to Philip C. Jessup, June 22, 1941, Philip C. Jessup Papers, Box 114, MDLC.
2. William Diebold, Jr. interview, November 1, 1972; Isaiah Bowman to Lionel Curtis, November 2, 1939, Franklin D. Roosevelt Papers, President's Personal File 5575, FDRL.
3. George S. Messersmith, "Memorandum of Conversation, September 12, 1939," Decimal File 811.43 Council on Foreign Relations/220 Exhibit A, R.G. 59; Walter H. Mallory to Laurence H. Shoup, June 5, 1973.
4. Isaiah Bowman, Memorandum of Conversation with Walter Mallory, November 27, 1939, Isaiah Bowman Papers, Mallory File, JHUL.
5. Messersmith, "Memorandum of Conversation, September 12, 1939"; Notter, 1949:19; Hull, 1948 II:1625; Hamilton Fish Armstrong, "Memorandum for Under Secretary Stettinius from Mr. Armstrong," November 24, 1943, Decimal File 811.43 Council on Foreign Relations/220, R.G. 59.
6. Memorandum, "Council on Foreign Relations, Project for the Study of the Effects of the War on the United States and of the American Interest in the Peace Settlement," December, 1939, Stanley K. Hornbeck Papers, Box 133, HLWRP. A copy of the same memorandum may be found in Hanson Baldwin Papers, Box 115, YUL.
7. CFR, 1946(b):19-24.
8. Ibid.; the economist Arthur R. Upgren of the University of Minnesota and Council fellow William Diebold, Jr. were the research secretaries for the Economic and Financial Group during the 1940-1943 period. The political scientist Walter R. Sharp of the City College of New York served the Political Group in this role from 1941 on. Grayson Kirk, a Columbia University profes-

sor of international relations, did the same for the Armaments Group beginning in 1941, and the Cornell University historian Philip E. Mosely was the main research secretary for the Territorial Group. The Peace Aims Group, which concentrated on the goals of European nations, had several research secretaries.
9. Ibid., 4.
10. Ibid., 9-24.
11. Ibid.; Winant's name appears on the list of participants in the work of the Political Group during 1940.
12. Ibid., 12-13. The State, War, and Navy Departments were directly represented, Viner was a Treasury Department adviser during these years, Hansen headed postwar planning at the Federal Reserve Board, and Upgren joined the Commerce Department in 1941 to head postwar planning there.
13. Ibid., 10-11; Mallory to Shoup, June 5, 1973, and July 13, 1973; Mallory to Sumner Welles, December 4, 1940, Decimal File 811.43, Council on Foreign Relations/196, R.G.59.
14. Notter, 1949:56, footnote 24.
15. CFR, 1946(b):13.
16. Ibid., 15-16; memorandum T-B3, March 17, 1949, CFR, *War-Peace Studies*, NUL.
17. Roosevelt, 1972 XV-XVI:278-280; Link, 1963 II:485; Diebold interview, November 1, 1972.
18. Chadwin, 1968:32; Langer and Gleason, 1952:711. Warner joined the Council's board of directors in 1940, Riefler in 1945. Both were active in the War and Peace Studies as were Shepardson and Miller.
19. *St. Louis Post-Dispatch*, September 22, 1940:3C; Divine, 1965:90; Chadwin, 1968:74, 78, 86, and 94; Miller, 1971:95 and 102.
20. Divine, 1965:90; Chadwin, 1968:74, 78, 86, and 94; Miller, 1971:95, 98, and 102; Langer and Gleason, 1952:749-751.
21. Divine, 1965:90; see also Chadwin, 1968:74 and Fehrenbach, 1967:160.
22. Divine, 1965:91.
23. Heaton, 1952:237.
24. CFR, 1938; Francis P. Miller interview, October 18, 1972; Diebold interview, November 1, 1972.
25. "Progress Report of the Secretary, War and Peace Studies Project Council on Foreign Relations, December 15, 1939-July 1, 1940"

July 3, 1940, Hanson Baldwin Papers, Box 115, YUL; Mallory to Welles, December 4, 1940, Decimal File 811.43, Council on Foreign Relations/196, R.G.59.
26. "Report of the Secretary, War and Peace Studies Project, December 15, 1939 to September 1, 1940," Decimal File 811.43, Council on Foreign Relations/188, R.G.59; Memorandum E-A10, October 19, 1940, CFR, *War-Peace Studies,* Baldwin Papers, Box 117, YUL; "Memorandum of Discussions, First Plenary Session, Council on Foreign Relations, June 28, 1940," Baldwin Papers, Box 115, YUL.
27. "Progress Report of the Secretary, War and Peace Studies Project, Council on Foreign Relations, December 15, 1939-July 1, 1940," July 3, 1940, Baldwin Papers, Box 115, YUL.
28. "Memorandum of Discussions, First Plenary Session, Council on Foreign Relations, June 28, 1940," Baldwin Papers, Box 115, YUL.
29. Hull to Davis, November 12, 1940, Decimal file, 811.43, Council on Foreign Relations/191, R.G.59; Welles to Mallory, December 6, 1940, Decimal File 811.43, Council on Foreign Relations/196, R.G.59; CFR, 1937:53; Hull to Davis, October 1, 1941, Decimal File 811.43 Council on Foreign Relations/203B, R.G.59. For more details see Shoup, 1974:128, 189.
30. Memorandum E-B18, September 6, 1940, CFR, *War-Peace Studies,* NUL; memorandum E-B18, supplement I, September 6, 1940, CFR, *War-Peace Studies,* NUL. E-B18, supplement I is fifty pages long and illustrates well the very detailed work being done by the Group.
31. Ibid.
32. Memorandum E-B18, supplement I, September 6, 1940, CFR, *War-Peace Studies,* NUL.
33. Memorandum E-B18, supplement II, September 6, 1940, CFR, *War-Peace Studies,* NUL.
34. Ibid.
35. Ibid.
36. Memorandum E-B19, supplement I, October 9, 1940, CFR, *War-Peace Studies,* NUL.
37. Memorandum E-A10, October 19, 1940, CFR, *War-Peace Studies,* Baldwin Papers, Box 117, YUL.
38. Memorandum E-B19, October 19, 1940, CFR, *War-Peace Studies,* NUL.

39. Ibid.
40. Ibid.; Memorandum E-B19, supplement I, October 9, 1940, CFR, *War-Peace Studies*, NUL.
41. Memorandum E-B19, October 19, 1940, CFR, *War-Peace Studies*, NUL.
42. Ibid.
43. Ibid.
44. Ibid.
45. Ibid.
46. Ibid.
47. Memorandum E-A10, October 19, 1940, CFR, *War-Peace Studies*, Baldwin Papers, Box 117, YUL.
48. Memorandum E-A11, November 23, 1940, CFR, *War-Peace Studies*, HLWRP; a memorandum of the Territorial Group (T-B20, October 11, 1940) had previously raised this possibility, the aim being to stop Japanese expansion into the Western Pacific. It argued that such a move by Japan might cut off United States sources of raw materials in Southeast Asia.
49. Memorandum E-A11, November 23, 1940, CFR, *War-Peace Studies*, HLWRP; memorandum E-A12, December 14, 1940, CFR, *War-Peace Studies*, HLWRP.
50. Memorandum E-B24, November 23, 1940, CFR, *War-Peace Studies*, NUL.
51. Ibid.
52. Memorandum E-B24, supplement I, December 14, 1940, CFR, *War-Peace Studies*, NUL.
53. Memorandum E-A12, December 14, 1940, CFR, *War-Peace Studies*, HLWRP.
54. Ibid.
55. Ibid.
56. Ibid.
57. Memorandum E-B26, January 15, 1941, CFR, *War-Peace Studies*, NUL.
58. Ibid.
59. Ibid.
60. Ibid.
61. Ibid.
62. Ibid.
63. A copy of E-B26 with a note attached addressed to Secretary Hull

may be found in Hull Papers, Box 72, MDLC. The note, dated 1/28/41, states "This may interest you" and bears Pasvolsky's initials.
64. Langer and Gleason, 1953:490, fn. 62, 493. A total embargo on Japan was instituted by the United States, Britain, and the Netherlands in late July 1941.
65. Memorandum E-A17, June 14, 1941, CFR, *War-Peace Studies*, HLWRP.
66. Ibid.
67. Memorandum E-B34, July 24, 1941, CFR, *War-Peace Studies*, NUL.
68. Ibid.
69. Memorandum T-A14, June 17, 1941, CFR, *War-Peace Studies*, Baldwin Papers, YUL.
70. Memorandum E-B34, July 24, 1941, CFR, *War-Peace Studies*, NUL.
71. Ibid.
72. Ibid.
73. Memorandum T-A14, June 17, 1941, CFR, *War-Peace Studies*, Baldwin Papers, YUL.
74. Ibid.
75. Ibid.
76. Ibid.; memorandum E-B34, July 24, 1941, CFR, *War-Peace Studies*, NUL.
77. Memorandum E-B34, July 24, 1941, CFR, *War-Peace Studies*, NUL.
78. Memorandum E-A14, May 17, 1941, CFR, *War-Peace Studies*, HLWRP.
79. Memorandum E-A17, June 14, 1941, CFR, *War-Peace Studies*, Baldwin Papers, YUL.
80. Memorandum E-B31, March 7, 1941, CFR, *War-Peace Studies*, NUL.
81. Ibid. For evidence that the U.S. role in Vietnam during the 1950s and 1960s was based on such an analysis, see Chapter 6.
82. Ibid.
83. Memorandum E-B34, July 24, 1941, CFR, *War-Peace Studies*, NUL.
84. Ibid.; memorandum E-B28, March 17, 1941, CFR, *War-Peace Studies*, NUL; memorandum E-B28, supplement I, April 10, 1941, CFR, *War-Peace Studies*, NUL.

182 Imperial Brain Trust

85. Memorandum T-B8, May 20, 1940, CFR, *War-Peace Studies*, NUL.
86. Memorandum E-B27, February 15, 1941, CFR, *War-Peace Studies*, NUL.
87. Memorandum E-B31, March 7, 1941, CFR, *War-Peace Studies*, NUL.
88. Ibid.
89. Memorandum E-B26, January 15, 1941, CFR, *War-Peace Studies*, NUL.
90. Langer and Gleason, 1953:645.
91. Hull, 1948 II:1017.
92. Welles, 1951:89, 91.
93. Roosevelt, 1941:649-650.
94. Ibid.; Langer and Gleason, 1953:646; Jones, 1954:247; Grew, 1952 II:1259.
95. United States, Department of State, *Foreign Relations, 1941*, I:355-356.
96. Langer and Gleason, 1953:29, 52; Ike, 1967:78, 162.
97. Jones, 1954:224; Iriye, 1967:201, 207-209; Divine, 1969:115; Ike, 1967:XIX and 78-81.
98. Schroeder, 1958:52-53.
99. Ibid.; Welles, 1951:81; Roosevelt, 1941:650.
100. Langer and Gleason, 1953:862; Offner, 1971:149-153; Link, 1963, II:506-507; Schroeder, 1958:175-177.
101. Schroeder, 1958:177.
102. Memorandum E-B33, June 20, 1941, CFR, *War-Peace Studies*, NUL.
103. Leo Pasvolsky to Joseph W. Ballantine, November 12, 1941, Decimal File 711.94/2540-8/35, R.G.59.
104. Adolf A. Berle to Cordell Hull, December 15, 1941, Cordell Hull Papers, Box 49, MDLC.
105. Iriye, 1967:219; Hull, 1948 II:1083.
106. Langer and Gleason, 1953:915, 935; Sherwood, 1948:428.
107. Leopold, 1962:591.
108. Langer and Gleason, 1953:913, 932.
109. United States, Department of State, *Foreign Relations 1941*, IV:688.
110. Ibid., 689-694.
111. Ibid., 696.
112. Ibid., 677-680.
113. Langer and Gleason, 1953:860, 886-887; Leopold, 1962:592.

Shaping a New World Order 183

114. Esthus, 1971:217, 220.
115. Welles, 1951:182.
116. Memorandum, Pasvolsky to Hull, September 12, 1941, Harley A. Notter File, box 4, R.G.59.
117. Notter, 1949:466-467.
118. Ibid., 465.
119. Ibid., 467.
120. Armstrong to Bowman, December 12, 1941, Davis Papers, Box 2, MDLC.
121. Wilson, 1969:173.
122. Notter, 1949:64-65; CFR, 1946(b):19-23.
123. Notter, 1949:72-73.
124. Ibid., CFR, 1946(b):22.
125. Table compiled from Shoup, 1974:201-205.
126. Notter, 1949:172.
127. Ibid., 247.
128. Ibid., 73-77, 124.
129. CFR, 1946(b):20.
130. Armstrong to Davis, January 16, 1942, Davis Papers, Box 2, MDLC.
131. Ibid.
132. Notter, 1949:80.
133. Ibid., 151-152.
134. Minutes of the "Joint Organization Meeting of the Subcommittees on Political Problems, Territorial Problems, and Security Problems," February 21, 1942, Notter File, Box 77, R.G.59.
135. Ibid.
136. Ibid.
137. Ibid.
138. Ibid.
139. Ibid.; Notter, 1949:80.
140. Notter, 1949:80.
141. Ibid., 518-519, CFR, 1946(b):20-23; Decimal File 111.53/3a, 111.53/3b, 111.53/3c, 111.53/3d, R.G.59.
142. Notter, 1949:82, 518-519; CFR, 1946(b):23.
143. Minutes of the meeting of the "Advisory Committee on Postwar Foreign Policy," May 2, 1942, Hull Papers, Box 82, MDLC.
144. Notter, 1949:92; Divine, 1967:51.
145. "Staff Memorandum number 3," Division of Special Research, July 20, 1942, Notter File, Box 2, R.G.59.
146. Notter, 1949:117.

184 *Imperial Brain Trust*

147. Ibid.; CFR, 1946(b):23.
148. Memorandum, Notter to Pasvolsky, July 17, 1942, Notter File, Box 4, R.G.59.
149. Ibid.
150. Ibid.
151. Ibid.
152. Memorandum, Notter to Shaw, August 19, 1942, Notter File, Box 4, R.G.59.
153. Memorandum, Notter to Pasvolsky, September 14, 1942, Notter File, Box 4, R.G.59.
154. Ibid.
155. Ibid.
156. Ibid.
157. Ibid.
158. Memorandum E-A18, July 19, 1941, CFR, *War-Peace Studies*, Baldwin Papers, YUL.
159. Memorandum E-B32, April 17, 1941, CFR, *War-Peace Studies*, NUL.
160. Langer and Gleason, 1953:681; Wilson, 1969:173.
161. Bowman to Armstrong, December 15, 1941, Bowman Papers, Armstrong File, JHUL.
162. Memorandum T-A21, January 16, 1942, CFR, *War-Peace Studies*, Baldwin Papers, YUL.
163. Minutes S-3 of the Security Subcommittee, Advisory Committee on Postwar Foreign Policy, May 6, 1942, Notter File, Box 77, R.G.59. As early as October 1940, Davis had argued that the British Empire was collapsing and that the United States would be the "heirs of the Empire." See Hooker (ed.), 1956:333.
164. Minutes S-3 of the Security Subcommittee, Advisory Committee on Postwar Foreign Policy, May 6, 1942, Notter File, Box 77, R.G.59.
165. Ibid.
166. See Weinstein, 1968, for a detailed study of corporate upper class concern with this question during the early years of this century. See Williams, 1972, for the development of this dependency during the nineteenth and twentieth centuries.
167. This was true of top-level men like Cordell Hull, Sumner Welles, and Henry Morgenthau, Jr., as well as of the members of the State Department planning committees. Welles said, for instance, that economic barriers caused "the present world collapse." See

Shaping a New World Order 185

United States, Department of State, *Foreign Relations 1941,* I:353; for an example of Hull's view, see United States, Department of State, *Foreign Relations 1942,* I:201-202; Morgenthau stated in May 1942 that a lack of economic cooperation would cause another world war. United States, Department of State, *Foreign Relations 1942,* I:177.
168. Chronological Minutes E-1 of the Economic Subcommittee, Advisory Committee on Postwar Foreign Policy, February 20, 1942, Notter File, Box 91, R.G.59.
169. Feis, 1942:284.
170. Chronological Minutes E-3 of the Economic Subcommittee, Advisory Committee on Postwar Foreign Policy, March 6, 1942, Notter File, Box 91, R.G.59.
171. Memorandum, "Studies Necessary as a Basis for Economic Consultations under Article VII of the Lend-Lease Agreement," August 3, 1942, Leo Pasvolsky Office Files, Box 1, R.G.59.
172. See Eakins, 1969:143-169 for a careful tracing of the origins and basic ideas of the Marshall Plan to several upper-class planning bodies.
173. E-Document 1, "Postwar Economic Problems," February 19, 1942, Notter File, Box 88, R.G.59.
174. "S Minutes 16" of the Security Subcommittee, Advisory Committee on Postwar Foreign Policy, October 23, 1942, Notter File, Box 76, R.G.59.
175. Memorandum E-B34, July 24, 1941, CFR, *War-Peace Studies,* NUL.
176. Memorandum P-B23, July 10, 1941, CFR, *War-Peace Studies;* Memorandum E-B36, June 22, 1941, CFR, *War-Peace Studies,* NUL.
177. Memorandum P-B23, July 10, 1941, CFR, *War-Peace Studies,* NUL.
178. Memorandum E-A21, October 11, 1941, CFR, *War-Peace Studies,* Baldwin Papers, YUL.
179. Memorandum E-A22, November 1, 1941, CFR, *War-Peace Studies,* Baldwin Papers, YUL.
180. Memorandum E-B44, November 28, 1941, CFR, *War-Peace Studies,* NUL.
181. Ibid.
182. Ibid.
183. Ibid.

186 Imperial Brain Trust

184. Memorandum E-A26, February 7, 1942, CFR, *War-Peace Studies*, Baldwin Papers, YUL.
185. Memorandum E-B49, April 1, 1942, CFR, *War-Peace Studies*, NUL.
186. Young, 1950:779.
187. United States, Department of State, *Foreign Relations 1942*, I:174-177.
188. Notter, 1949:141-143; Young, 1950:779, 779, fn. 3.
189. Ibid.
190. Memorandum T-A25, May 20, 1942, CFR, *War-Peace Studies*, HLWRP.
191. Ibid.
192. Notter, 1949:169-170; entry for January 4, 1943 in Harley A. Notter, "Recollections: Notes January 1942-December 1943," Notter File, Box 1, R.G.59.
193. Notter, 1949:171.
194. Ibid., 107, 172; memorandum, Franklin D. Roosevelt to General Watson, February 20, 1943, Official File 4351 (January-March 1943), FDRL; memorandum, Sumner Welles to Roosevelt, March 18, 1943, President's Personal File 5575, FDRL.
195. Notter, 1949:226-227; Divine, 1967:136-137.
196. Notter, 1949:248.
197. CFR, 1937:46-53; CFR, 1940; CFR, 1946(b):19-24.
198. CFR, 1940. Green was present at all of the thirteen sessions of the Council's Armaments Group between November 29, 1943 and June 19, 1945. See memoranda A-A40 to A-A52, CFR, *War-Peace Studies*, HLWRP.
199. CFR, 1940; CFR, 1946(b):20.
200. Notter, 1949:247; Divine, 1967:192.
201. Russell, 1958:2.
202. Ibid., 21-22, 205.
203. The Council continued to have access to all top secret information during the 1942-1944 years, despite continued warnings by Pasvolsky to his staff about the need to maintain the "strictest confidence" about the postwar planning work of the department. Even the existence and organization of the committees, as well as their thinking, were "not under any circumstances to be the subjects of comment to anyone outside the members of the Division itself." Memorandum, Pasvolsky to staff members of the Division of Special Research, December 22, 1942, Notter File, Box 4, R.G.59.

204. Quoted in Beard, 1934a:1.
205. Staley, 1937:37.
206. Memorandum E-B12, June 7, 1940, CFR, *War-Peace Studies*, NUL.
207. Memorandum T-A14, June 17, 1941, CFR, *War-Peace Studies*, Baldwin Papers, YUL.
208. Memorandum E-B19, October 19, 1940, CFR, *War-Peace Studies*, NUL.
209. Ibid.
210. Luce, 1941:64. Luce's article is reprinted in Garraty and Divine, 1968:470-476.

5
Implementing the Council's World View: Case Studies in United States Foreign Policy

The War and Peace Studies Project marked the high point of the Council's intimacy and formal collaboration with the government in setting the pattern for United States foreign policy. The framework for foreign policy thus established was to remain virtually unchallenged for a quarter of a century. The expanded Grand Area became the "Free World" under United States leadership, and the guiding thread of American foreign policy was to defend this area against any incursion from forces which might disturb the established order. Such forces were quickly identified as subordinate to a Moscow-centered conspiracy, but actually they often were nationalist forces in the Third World. The Council on Foreign Relations continued its role of leadership, reinforcing, adapting, and implementing the foreign policy consensus it had molded. Its influence was felt through the presence of its members in key foreign policy posts. Its meetings and publications continued to guide foreign policy opinion and to keep it safely within the "reasonable" lines acceptable to the New York financial oligarchy.

To write the full story of Council influence during this

The Council's World View

quarter century of cold war is a task which must wait. For most of the period both Council and government archives are still closed. Moreover, Council influence was not concentrated in one project, as in the wartime War and Peace Studies Project, so that a study of Council influence is really a study of the whole range of United States foreign policy. There is enough information available, however, to give a preliminary picture of the extent and character of the Council role, through the examination of a number of case studies: Policy toward Germany, 1944-1946; United States intervention in Guatemala, 1954; the Cuban missile crisis, 1962; the shift in China policy, 1969-1972; and policy toward Southern Africa, 1961-1974. We have examined what had been written by others to try to identify the key issues and the key policymakers involved. We have then looked to see what information was available about Council studies related to these issues at the time and in years preceding the important decisions and tried to trace the role of these Council programs. To get at the informal influence of the Council community, we have also identified the Council members and leaders who were in key decision-making positions. The activities of other nongovernmental organizations which had something to do with the issues were also studied to determine the extent of their interlock with the Council.

Policy Toward Germany, 1944-1946

When the Grand Area concept was first formulated by Council planners during 1940-1941, German-controlled Europe was excluded. At a time of German strength the concept was limited by that reality, but once the victory of the Allies was in sight, the area included expanded accordingly. Among the most important areas to be included in the new world order was of course the territory of defeated Germany itself. The postwar treatment of Germany would be a test of the application of this new pattern.

The Council's concern with Germany had a long history. Its own formation was closely connected with discontent at the results of the Versailles Conference at the end of the First World War. Owen Young, a Council director, had been the guiding hand behind both the Dawes Plan and the Young Plan, both intended to deal with the problem of German reparations. A Council study group in the 1920s resulted in a book by James W. Angell on *Recovery of Germany*.[1] As the Second World War approached, Hamilton Fish Armstrong and Allen Dulles wrote, under Council auspices, on Hitler's Reich and on neutrality legislation. Leon Fraser, another Council director, served as the head of the Bank for International Settlements, which dealt with German reparations. For these men, the determination that the United States should not make the same mistakes again came from personal experience.

The framework set by the War and Peace Studies Project had clear implications for the treatment of Germany. Memorandum E-B63 of March 18, 1943, discussed the issue of reparations, and memorandum A-B124 of July 31, 1945, dealt with "The Postwar Treatment of Germany."[2] The stance which these documents took was in favor of a "moderate" peace: denazification, destruction of war potential, and some reparations to countries damaged by the war, but also the reintegration of Germany into the postwar European and world economies, and avoidance of any measures severe enough to exacerbate instability or cause unrest. The Soviet Union was interested in extensive reparations for war damages and in eliminating the possible resurgence of Nazism by attacking its primary base—German big business. While the Council envisaged denazification, this could not be permitted to interfere with the plans for a capitalist Germany integrated into the West. Nor could reparations measures be allowed to interfere with this overall perspective. The Council favored—as a priority over reparations from current production—exports from that production, so that imports from Western countries could be purchased. It insisted on the "first charge" principle, that exports should be available to pay for imports before reparations could be considered. In other words, of the claims on the German economy, those of American businessmen exporting to Germany should take priority over those of the Soviet Union, which was seeking to rebuild from the destruction of the war. The "moderates" also wished to minimize reparations which would remove capital equipment from Germany, on the grounds that this might weaken the German economy too much, causing unrest and delaying the time when Germany might again pay for imports from the West. In short, Germany should be reintegrated into the world capitalist economy, and any measures which promoted economic ties with the Soviet Union or encouraged a radical transformation of the German social order should be blocked.[3]

The "moderate" position gained acceptance in the early planning in the State and War Departments in 1943, although it had not yet received confirmation from the President, when Secretary of Treasury Henry Morgenthau, Jr. (not a Council member although his father had been) became involved with the subject in August 1944. Morgenthau still envisaged Germany as the principal potential threat to the United States, and advocated a harsh peace which would create a deindustrialized, agrarian Germany rendered incapable of conducting a war of aggression. Morgenthau's position agreed with the moderates in rejecting reparations to the Soviet Union from current production. However, the Morgenthau Plan's provisions for elimination of German heavy industry implied a much more favorable position toward another kind of reparations—the removal of capital equipment to the

Soviet Union. Moreover, his emphasis on Germany as the menace to world peace implied the importance of maintaining the wartime alliance with the Soviet Union. The moderates by no means shared this reluctance to antagonize the Soviet Union.

The high point of Morgenthau's influence came with the Quebec Conference in September 1944, when a Roosevelt-Churchill statement incorporated his point of view. Vigorous action by State and War, however, eventually resulted in a reversal of the President's decision, and in a compromise document (JCS 1067) which became the official directive for United States occupation authorities in Germany until July 1947. In the occupation itself, the implementation of policy by Gen. Lucius Clay, the deputy military governor, virtually eliminated any traces of the harsh line, even before Secretary Byrnes's speech of September 1946 made it clear that the harsh line did not apply.

Probably the most significant role of the Council in this issue was the early establishment, through the War and Peace Studies, of the conceptual basis for a moderate peace, implying the incorporation of Germany into a capitalist world order and resistance to the demands of the Soviet Union for reparations. But the Council and its members played more direct roles as well. Thus as early as 1943, the "relatively mild American position on German reparations, taken at the Moscow Foreign Ministers Conference in 1943, was blocked out on the basis of the Council's study of the problem."[4] Calvin Hoover, who had been involved in the Council's studies, served as chairman of the economic advisers to the Allied Control Commission in Germany, and was author of the controversial Hoover Report. This report suggested a level of industrial production for Germany which assumed very little dismantling of plants for reparations, and was accordingly attacked as too soft on Germany. Nevertheless, it was accepted as the basis of the official level-of-industry plan which oriented the occupation's economic programs.[5] Hoover joined the Council's War and Peace Studies Project in 1944, and later wrote that they were

> of immense psychological importance to me ... when by an unexpected turn of events I came to be responsible a year later for drawing up the details of the first reparations plan for Germany. The economists who worked on the Studies of American Interests in the War and Peace agreed that a Carthaginian peace settlement should not be imposed on Germany.... The memory of the conclusions of my associates in these studies sponsored by the Council on Foreign Relations was to strengthen greatly my confidence in the correctness of the economic terms of a reparations program which by contrast allowed some hope of a tolerable life to the German people.[6]

Council members were involved in policymaking on German issues at all levels. Of the thirty-nine policymakers identified as most involved from 1944 through 1946, one-third had been members of the Council and almost an additional one-third were shortly to join the Council.[7] In particular, four men influential in working against the Morgenthau Plan were Council members. Henry L. Stimson, the secretary of war, played a key role in persuading President Roosevelt to back off on his support of the plan, and was active in expressing his views to President Truman, who was ready to be convinced.[8] John J. McCloy, Stimson's right-hand man, was the key person in drafting the compromise memorandum, JCS 1067.[9] William L. Clayton, a Council member for over ten years and a friend of the Council's first president, John W. Davis, was one of the principal negotiators at Potsdam, chairman of the American group in the subcommittee on German economic problems. He was responsible for working out the compromise on reparations that resulted from the conference, and earlier had suggested that the "first charge" principle be adopted.[10] W. Averell Harriman, a longtime Council member, was ambassador to the Soviet Union, and pushed American resistance to the Soviet reparations claims. His influence during this period is generally regarded as quite significant.[11]

Other Council men involved in German affairs included Allen Dulles, Lewis W. Douglas, and James W. Angell. Dulles was the key OSS man dealing with German affairs from his post in Bern during the war, and his advice was bound to be crucial with respect to the occupation of defeated Germany.[12] Lewis Douglas, another Council director and brother-in-law of John J. McCloy, served for a short period of time as economic adviser to General Clay, and reported back on the necessity of building up Germany's economy. He was strongly opposed to any concessions to Morgenthau's ideas. Angell, who had written on Germany for the Council, negotiated the Paris agreement on reparations (which excluded the Soviet Union) in late 1945.

Following the initial period of occupation, during which the "hard peace" aspects of policy eroded away, the Council continued to concern itself with German matters. A study group was organized in late 1946 and early 1947 under the chairmanship of Allen Dulles. Its general focus was set out in an April 1947 article in *Foreign Affairs* by Allen Dulles: "Alternatives for Germany." The article emphasized the importance of integrating Germany into a European framework (i.e., a Western European framework), with such consequences, among others, as the restoration of the German economy along capitalist lines and strict limits on reparations. When John J. McCloy, who had been among the participants in the study group, went to Germany as American high commissioner in 1949, he took with him, according to Council member Joseph Kraft, "a staff composed almost exclusively of men who had interested themselves in German affairs at the Council."[13] It is hardly surprising that the policy followed was in congruence with that suggested by the study group. The ultimate result, since the

Soviet Union obviously could not accept that all of Germany follow this path, was a divided Germany, with the Federal Republic of Germany incorporated into the world capitalist economy and the smaller German Democratic Republic incorporated into the socialist camp.

United States Intervention in Guatemala, 1954

In June 1954 Col. Castillo Armas crossed the border into Guatemala from Honduras with his small army and in short order defeated the moderate nationalist regime of Jacobo Arbenz Guzman. The suspicions at the time that the coup was orchestrated by the United States Central Intelligence Agency have since been fully confirmed.[14] The reasons for the invasion were well described by Dwight D. Eisenhower, President at the time:

> In 1950 a military officer, Jacobo Arbenz Guzman, came to power and by his actions soon created the strong suspicion that he was merely a puppet manipulated by the Communists.... For example, on February 24, 1963, the Arbenz government announced its intention, under an agrarian reform law, to seize about 225,000 acres of unused United Fruit Company land.[15]

The conclusion that United States intervention was justified followed from the conception of United States interests that prevailed at the top of the administration. In the formation of this conception, or at least its perpetuation (for, after all, United States intervention in Latin America has a long history), the Council and its leaders were deeply involved. The early Council studies on Latin America had focused precisely on United States economic interests there.[16] In the War and Peace Studies Project, Latin America was from the start to be included in the Grand Area scheme of economic integration.

The Council apparently did not devote much formal study to Latin American issues in the years preceding the Guatemalan invasion. This may have been because there was already an implicit consensus on the character of United States interests and what should be done. In 1952 and 1953, Spruille Braden, former assistant secretary of state for inter-American affairs and a consultant for the United Fruit Company, led a Council study group on Political Unrest in Latin America. No books or articles appeared as a result of the group, and information on the discussions is accordingly limited, but it is known that the first meeting, in the fall of 1952, was devoted to Guatemala, with John McClintock of the United Fruit Company as the discussion leader. Adolf A. Berle recorded in his diary for October 17, 1952, with regard to overthrowing the Arbenz government, that the United States

> should welcome it, and if possible guide it into a reasonably sound channel. Certainly the Council on Foreign Relations the other night agreed generally that the Guatemalan government was Communist, and that it was merely carrying out the plan laid out for it by Oumansky ten years ago. I am arranging to see Nelson Rockefeller, who knows the situation and can work a little with General Eisenhower on it.[17]

Thus, even before the election of the new administration, the consensus for action was clear. The implementation was to be in the hands of men closely tied with the Council on Foreign Relations. Most important were President Eisenhower himself, the CIA head Allen Dulles, who continued on the Council's board of directors at the same time, and Frank Wisner, another Council member who was the CIA's deputy director for plans (the man in charge of clandestine operations). A shipment of arms from Czechoslovakia to Guatemala in May 1954 provided an excuse for invasion, but the plan was well under way long before then.[18]

Ambassador John E. Peurifoy had been sent to Guatemala

in November 1953 from his previous post in Greece, where he had had experience in counterinsurgency. Whiting Willauer, formerly with the Flying Tiger airlines in the Far East (which came under CIA control), became ambassador to Honduras. In testimony before the Senate Internal Security Subcommittee he testified that he was a member of a team working to overthrow the Arbenz government. He added that "of course, there were a number of CIA operatives in the picture."[19]

The public background was also being laid. Spruille Braden, leader of the CFR study group, in a speech on March 12, 1953, claimed that

> because Communism is so blatantly an international and not an internal affair, its suppression, even by force, in an American country, by one or more of the other republics, would not constitute an intervention in the internal affairs of the former.[20]

John Moors Cabot, assistant secretary of state for interAmerican affairs (and shortly to become a Council member), made the first official attack on Guatemala's regime on October 26, 1953, setting the stage for the Caracas Conference, where John Foster Dulles pushed through a resolution aimed particularly at Guatemala.

In December 1953 there appeared a public report by the National Planning Association on the Guatemala situation. The Association's Committee on International Policy was headed by Frank Altschul, secretary and vice-president of the Council. Of the twenty-two committee members signing the statement, fifteen were members of the Council. The statement concluded that "Communist infiltration in Guatemala constitutes a threat not only to the freedom of that country but to the security of all Western Hemisphere nations,"[21] and hinted that drastic action would probably be necessary to deal with the menace.

The number of people involved in the basic policy decisions on the Guatemalan intervention was by necessity quite small. Of the twelve people we identified as being involved at the top level, eight were Council members at the time or joined within the next few years. Besides the men already mentioned, these include Henry F. Holland, who succeeded John M. Cabot as assistant secretary of state in 1954, Walter Bedell Smith, a former director of the CIA serving as under secretary of state, and Henry Cabot Lodge, who as ambassador to the United Nations blocked the attempts of the Arbenz regime to bring the invasion to the attention of the world body.

The ties of the Council community to the intervention in Guatemala stand out as well in the triangular relationship of interlocks among the government officials involved, the Council, and the United Fruit Company. The government action and United Fruit were closely linked. Thus Miguel Ydigoras Fuentes, a future President of Guatemala, recorded that his cooperation in the coup was sought by Walter Turnbull, a former executive of United Fruit, who came accompanied by two CIA agents.[22] Of those openly involved, John Foster Dulles, while at Sullivan and Cromwell, had represented the United Fruit Company in negotiating a contract with Guatemala some years before. John M. Cabot's brother was a director and former president of the United Fruit Company. Spruille Braden served as a United Fruit Company consultant. Former CIA director Walter Bedell Smith, after leaving the government, became a director of United Fruit, as did Robert D. Hill, a participant in the operation as ambassador to Costa Rica.

The Council's links with United Fruit were also substantial. Whitney H. Shepardson, one of the Council's main leaders, was an officer of the International Railways of Central America, an affiliate of United Fruit Company. The Dulles brothers have already been mentioned. In 1953 the chairman of the board of United Fruit was T. Jefferson

The Council's World View 199

Coolidge, a relative of the first editor of *Foreign Affairs*. Also serving on the United Fruit board were three other Council members, including Robert Lehman. Lehman was related by marriage to Frank Altschul, the Council secretary who was also responsible for the National Planning Association report. The study group led by McClintock of United Fruit was thus only a small part of the network of relations linking the company and the Council.

It may well be that the Dulles brothers would have been just as eager to intervene if the company involved were one with which they had fewer close ties. Certainly such intervention fit well within the general view of United States interests promoted by the Council community. However, the network of relationships, direct or through the Council on Foreign Relations, linking them to the company involved in Guatemala, can hardly have failed to influence the balance of information they received, and the assumptions with which they interpreted and acted upon it. In the case of the Guatemalan intervention, personal and class interests, and the conception of the national interest formulated on behalf of the capitalist class, are all intertwined. Right in the center is the Council on Foreign Relations.

The Cuban Missile Crisis, 1962

Given the general framework of a postwar world order integrated into an economic system under United States leadership, it is logical that United States policy should enter into direct confrontation with the Soviet Union, as well as with left-oriented forces of all kinds throughout the world.[23] The United States failed to extend the Grand Area to Eastern Europe, and China had to be written off as "lost" after a few years, although the presence of the Taiwan regime on the

United Nations Security Council continued to symbolize the grandiose ambitions of the postwar planners. The containment policy, formulated in the famous "X" *Foreign Affairs* article, set the basic principles: establish the boundaries of the "free world" and permit no encroachment. The Council study on *Russia and America* in the mid-fifties summed up the assumption of the cold war: the Soviet Union was the omnipresent threat. Council Chairman John J. McCloy wrote in the foreword that the Soviet leadership "supports fanatically" the "long-range objective of world domination."[24]

The rapid development of the new nuclear technology meant, however, that continuous adjustments had to be made in the conception of how to deal with the Soviet "threat." One of the most influential attempts to define the new developments and the appropriate responses was a 1954-1956 Council study group on Nuclear Weapons and Foreign Policy. We have already mentioned the role of this study group in fostering the career of Henry A. Kissinger, but its importance also lies in its bringing together a set of assumptions about United States strategic policy which set the context for decisions in such crises as that of the missiles in Cuba in October 1962.

The book by Henry Kissinger on *Nuclear Weapons and Foreign Policy,* which emerged from the study group, is generally considered to be one of the most influential books published under the auspices of the Council. It received favorable reviews from all quarters and stayed on the bestseller list for fourteen weeks. Gordon Dean, chairman of the study group, writing in the foreword to the paperback edition, claimed that it had "an immediate and profound impact on American thinking about the political world in which we live with such terrible insecurity. Generals and statesmen studied it, Congressmen read it to their colleagues on Capitol Hill."[25] After making the necessary allowance for Dean's pride in the product of his study group, it is still clear that the book did have quite an impact.

Although Kissinger alone was the author and some of his more controversial conclusions (such as on the use of tactical nuclear weapons) may not have been shared by all those in the study group, the deliberations of the group were clearly the basis of the work. The study group had already been meeting for a year when Kissinger was appointed rapporteur. In the preface Kissinger noted that "their deliberations gave me a sense of the dimensions of the problem and of the considerations on which policy is based; this I could have acquired in no other way."[26]

Overall, the book was an attack on the massive retaliation doctrine, set forth by John Foster Dulles at a CFR meeting in January 1954, which left the United States vulnerable "to the preferred form of Soviet aggression: a strategy which seeks its objective by small increments of power, by avoiding 'all-out' provocations."[27] Dean's foreword notes that the book "was hopeful in showing a reasoned way between the alternatives of thermonuclear devastation and the prospect of being nibbled to death by the Russians."[28] Kissinger's solution called for "a military capacity which is truly graduated," and for leaving "no doubt about our readiness and our ability to face a final showdown."[29]

In the late fifties, the same point was hammered home in other contexts, each with close relations to the Council. Of particular importance were the voices of Gen. Maxwell D. Taylor, the report of the government-sponsored Gaither Committee, and the report of the Rockefeller Brothers Fund panel on *Prospect for America*. Taylor, upset with the policy of massive retaliation under the Eisenhower administration (among other points, such a policy downplayed the role of the army of which he was chief of staff), wrote articles after his retirement emphasizing the need for a flexible military capacity. The Gaither Committee report, leaked in November 1957, emphasized the danger of the increased vulnerability of the United States strategic force, and called for increased military spending to counter that danger, and to provide a capacity for limited warfare to counter "local aggression." The Rockefeller panel report called for a willingness and ability to resist aggression, and noted as one of the greatest threats "gradual Soviet infiltration and domination of vital areas through steps each of which is so small and seemingly so insignificant that it does not seem to justify overt intervention."[30]

Each of these voices was closely linked with the Council on Foreign Relations. Maxwell Taylor had been encouraged as early as 1956 to express his views in *Foreign Affairs* at the initiative of Hamilton Fish Armstrong, who, as Taylor stated, "was aware of the nature of my views from discussions in New York in the Council on Foreign Relations."[31] Although the administration did not allow him to publish his ideas while still in office, they became widely known in the foreign policy and political communities. The Gaither Committee (twenty-four men in all) included among its membership and advisers twelve members of the Council on Foreign Relations. These included John J. McCloy, then chairman of the board of the Council, as well as William C. Foster and James A. Perkins, who became Council directors in 1959 and 1963 respectively. Participants in both the Gaither Committee and the Council study group included James Perkins and Paul Nitze, later assistant secretary of defense and a decision-maker in the Cuban missile crisis.

The Rockefeller Brothers Fund panel was even more closely tied to the CFR. Of the general panel for the reports, twenty-one out of thirty-three were Council members. The chairman, Laurence Rockefeller, was not a Council member at the time, but his brother David was not only a Council vice-president, but also a member of the nuclear weapons study group. The panel on international security was composed of twenty men, ten of them Council members, and six of these ten participants in the Council's study group on nuclear weapons. They included the chairman of the group,

Gordon Dean, as well as Frank Altschul, another Council vice-president. The director of the Rockefeller project was Henry Kissinger, and it was he who wrote the report on international security for the panel.

With such "public" discussion of the issue building up, it is not surprising that an aspiring young politician should also make the issue his own. In a dramatic speech on August 14, 1958, John F. Kennedy outlined one of his major campaign themes, an attack on the inadequacies of Republican military policy. He painted a dire prospect of Western weakness and Soviet advance, echoing the themes of the Council study:

> Their missile power will be the shield from behind which they will slowly, but surely, advance—through Sputnik diplomacy, limited brushfire wars, indirect non-overt aggression, intimidation and subversion, internal revolution, increased prestige or influence, and the vicious blackmail of our allies. The periphery of the Free World will slowly be nibbled away. The balance of power will gradually shift against us. The key areas vital to our security will gradually undergo Soviet infiltration and domination. Each such Soviet move will weaken the West; but none will seem sufficiently significant by itself to justify our initiating a nuclear war which might destroy us.[32]

The solution, to put it briefly, was strength, firmness, and flexibility. Kennedy's speech quoted only two men by name: Kissinger and Gen. James Gavin, also a member of the Council study group.

The placement by the Soviet Union of missiles in Cuba in October 1962 was seen as just one such move by the Kennedy administration and the officials who gathered to make the crucial decisions in the National Security Council Executive Committee (EXCOMM).[33] Robert S. McNamara initially suggested that the additional missiles in Cuba no more changed the strategic balance than would a similar number within the borders of the Soviet Union. Ambassador to the United Nations Adlai E. Stevenson suggested that approaches be made to negotiate a withdrawal, perhaps in exchange for removing U.S. missiles in Turkey, which was already being envisaged. Such "soft" options did not fit the assumptions with which the policymakers saw strategic policy and were summarily rejected without consideration. The early consensus was that a firm stand must be taken: the Soviet Union must be forced to back down and remove the missiles. On the other hand, there was concern for a carefully graduated response, so that neither party would be forced to the ultimate decision of unacceptable defeat or all-out nuclear war. The major debate was whether to act at first by a direct air attack on the missiles, or by a blockade of Cuba, accompanied by a demand to the Soviet Union that those missiles already in Cuba be withdrawn. The decision was made for the blockade, in line with a strategy of graduated pressure. The Soviet ships did eventually turn back and an agreement was reached for the missiles to be withdrawn. The United States pledged not to invade Cuba, and it was also tacitly understood (but not as part of the public agreement) that the American missiles in Turkey would eventually also be removed. The basic point of the public conclusion was that the Soviet Union, faced with the United States ultimatum, backed down and withdrew the missiles. The Kennedy administration policymakers and their admirers have been congratulating themselves ever since.

The ties between the Council and the decisions in the Cuban missile crisis are not limited to the striking correspondence in assumptions. That correspondence, as is natural, is accompanied by a coincidence of personnel. Of the twenty-four men involved officially or unofficially in the EXCOMM meetings, eighteen were Council members at the time or shortly thereafter. Three of them, Paul Nitze, McGeorge Bundy, and Roswell Gilpatric, had been in the nuclear weapons study group. The Kennedy brothers themselves were apparently not Council members and Robert McNamara had not yet joined, but other key figures were Council men. One of the President's first moves, even before the initial meeting of the EXCOMM, was to contact John J. McCloy, the Council chairman. McCloy's position as chief of the "establishment" gave weight to his feeling that drastic action would have to be taken to get the missiles out of Cuba. A description of the decision-making process shows that Council members were involved on both sides of the debate between the "air-strike" and "blockade" options.[34] Among the most influential arguers for the blockade were McNamara and Robert Kennedy, neither of them Council members, but the turning point of the debate reportedly came when Douglas Dillon changed his mind, in turn persuading McGeorge Bundy and swinging the consensus in the direction of the blockade, which was presented to the President as the least dangerous first step.

Thus the Council's influence can be seen in the setting of a general climate of opinion, not only on the general aims of United States foreign policy ("containment"), but also on the type of stance necessary to react to challenges from the Soviet Union ("firmness" and "flexibility"). There is a close correspondence between the assumptions promoted by the Council and those which excluded any "soft" diplomatic option from serious consideration by EXCOMM. The overlap of personnel provides additional support for the role of the Council community in crystalizing and strengthening these assumptions.

From the three cases examined so far it is possible to derive a picture of the Council's success that would be misleading. In each case, reaching consensus within the Council met with no major obstacles. In each case, the Council's orientation rather quickly set the framework for the decisions within the government, and in each case, the foreign policy elite, in the Council and in the government, could point to success for their policy: the Federal Republic of Germany, a pillar of capitalist Western Europe; the elimination of the "communist" challenge in Guatemala; the Soviet Union backing down in public over the missiles. An activist, hard-line policy had the desired results: preservation of the expanded Grand Area, or, as it more commonly came to be called, the Free World.

This image of unanimity and success correctly reflects the general position of the Council in guiding the postwar hegemony of the United States, but it is not the whole picture. For, as Joyce and Gabriel Kolko have emphasized in their studies,[35] the world was not wholly malleable to American plans, even at the height of American power. The Free World under United States leadership suffered defeats, accelerating with the successful struggle of the liberation forces in Indochina. It was and is necessary for the rulers of imperialism to make some adjustment to the fact of setbacks and defeats. It is the Council's role in this process that has brought down upon it the fierce attacks from the extreme Right, which characterizes it as the nerve center of a "liberal" establishment with intentions of selling out the United States and the Free World to communism.[36]

For the Council, in addition to its commitment to the activist pursuit of a dominant world role for the United States, has had a certain commitment to realism, implying that the realities of the external world may necessitate adjustments in American policy. Thus, at the time when German power appeared invulnerable on the European continent, the Grand Area excluded that part of the world. In spite of postwar hopes for including much of Eastern Europe in the sphere of American influence, the orthodox policy backed by the Council did not countenance war with the Soviet Union to obtain this end. In the case of Cuba, in spite of the Bay of Pigs and the missile crisis, the United States government, with the general approval of the foreign policy establishment, stopped short of a full-scale invasion of the island to wipe out this "threat to the Free World."

This process of adjustment to adverse realities has not been easy. Admitting failure and reaching a consensus about new policies has been more difficult for the Council and the capitalist class. Right-wing recalcitrance has a strong base within the capitalist class itself, and not just among small businessmen, who are stereotyped as the supporters of the John Birch Society and related organizations.[37] The role of the Council in this process is illustrated in the remaining case studies: of Nixon's rapprochement with China, of the ambivalence of United States policy toward Southern Africa, and, in the next chapter, of United States involvement in Southeast Asia.

The Shift in China Policy, 1969-1972

The victory of the Chinese Revolution and the establishment of the People's Republic of China marked an end to China's role as the junior partner of the United States in Asia. When the United Nations was formed, the presence of China on the Security Council as one of five permanent members was conceded by the other powers, with the understanding that in practice this was just another vote for the United States. It did turn out that way, but the mockery of reality was even greater than anticipated as the Chiang Kai-shek regime, expelled from the mainland to the island bastion of Taiwan, retained China's United Nations seat. For twenty years, the United States government engaged in an attempt to deny the People's Republic of China any recognition on the world scene, to isolate and frustrate the Chinese Revolution. Republicans, including a young congressman named Richard

M. Nixon, castigated the Democrats for having "lost China." Not until this same Nixon became President was it to become thinkable in American politics to accept the existence of China and develop another set of relationships. The Council, through a series of studies on China, played a major role in this belated adjustment to world realities. The formation of a consensus took time, however, and was not seriously undertaken as a Council project until 1962, more than a decade after the initial "loss of China."

Council members were involved with China policy considerably before then. The three-man board appointed by Secretary of State and Council member Dean Acheson to recommend United States policy on China in 1949 were all active Council members: Raymond B. Fosdick, Philip C. Jessup (a Council director from 1934 to 1942), and Everett N. Case. While the initial view put forward by this group and adopted by the government was a policy of nonrecognition and isolation of the new regime in China, it was not intended to be a dogmatic unchangeable posture. The policy followed by the government, however, rapidly became caught up in attacks from the Right. The Korean war and the political activity of Senator Joseph R. McCarthy helped to close off options of flexibility. One of the primary targets of right-wing attacks was the Institute of Pacific Relations, with which Jessup and Case were closely associated. Partly as a result of the attacks, the Institute of Pacific Relations collapsed during the early 1950s, losing its funding from the Rockefeller Foundation (headed by Raymond Fosdick).

The Council community, the foreign-policy establishment, was thus under attack. And it is true that there was some openness in Council-related circles toward flexibility in China policy. In a 1950 poll taken by the Council of members of its affiliated committees on foreign relations, 64 percent of the respondents agreed that "American access to China, even on a limited basis, is so important to the American interest in

Asia as to warrant American initiative in seeking some degree of mutual toleration between the United States and the Chinese Communist regime."[38] Arthur H. Dean in 1954 and Eustace Seligman in 1958 came out for greater flexibility and adoption of a "two Chinas" policy. Dean, a Council director since 1955, chaired the Council's study group on Sino-Soviet relations. Seligman was also an active Council member. Both were law partners in the firm of Sullivan and Cromwell, the Dulles brothers' firm. In 1960 a Council book by Doak Barnett, stemming from a study group the previous year, took a similar qualified position in favor of a "two Chinas" policy, altering the basic posture of unqualified hostility to the Chinese regime.

But right-wing intransigence vis-à-vis China could not have obtained its public impact and reputation for effectiveness without a more basic factor at work. There were many within the foreign policy establishment who had their own reasons for a hard line and opposition to the relaxation of tensions which recognition of the Chinese government would imply.[39] In particular, at least two influential Council members did not agree with "flexibility." They were John Foster Dulles and Dean Rusk, who, between them, managed to fix China policy in an inflexible position during their long terms as secretaries of state. Although it is said by some that Foster Dulles was more flexible in private than he appeared to be in public, Doak Barnett and other Council members interviewed about the subject were skeptical. As for Rusk, at least one account of the origin of the Council's major China Study Project interprets it as a delaying move by Rusk, who, as an excuse for postponing consideration of new policy initiatives within the State Department itself, proposed "a series of studies of the China problem in all its ramifications, to be undertaken on the outside? By something solid like the Council on Foreign Relations?"[40]

The Council study on United States and China in World

Affairs was a turning point in the consideration of this issue. Two of the key people initiating the study were George S. Franklin, executive director of the Council, and Joseph Slater, a Council member who had just moved to the Ford Foundation from a position as deputy assistant secretary of state. The project, which ran from 1962 to 1966, was generously financed by the Ford Foundation, and was directed by a high-powered steering committee headed by Allen Dulles and other top Council leaders, together with China specialists Doak Barnett and Lucien Pye. The first director was Robert Blum, a former CIA official.

Although the position was maintained that the study committed the Council as a whole to no specific policy, the clear intent of the whole project was to open up new possibilities for relationships with China. In interviews Council members emphasized two kinds of influence which the study had. One was the impact of the public opinion survey, done as a part of the study, which showed an unexpected openness on the part of the public to new initiatives.[41] Secondly, the Council's consideration of the subject gave legitimacy to the possibilities of new options. The Council studies laid the basis for the change in policy, discussed in other, more public, forums in the following years and eventually implemented under the leadership of President Nixon and Council protégé Henry Kissinger.

It is surely no coincidence that, just as the Council studies were coming to an end, there emerged, also with Ford Foundation funding, the National Committee on U.S.-China Relations. The committee held its first national convocation in March 1969, bringing together more than 2,000 participants to listen to speakers on "The United States and China: The Next Decade." While diverse points of view were presented, the clear thrust of the event was toward increased openness to China.[42] The membership of this committee overlapped considerably with the Council. In 1970 the National Committee had twenty-seven members, twelve of them Council members, five of whom were participants in the Council's study groups on China. The next year, in spite of considerable turnover in committee membership, a similar pattern continued. If the leadership of the National Committee is considered, the close ties with the Council are even more apparent. The 1968-1969 chairman was Doak Barnett. Serving as vice-chairmen in 1970 were two directors of the Council, Lucien Pye and Robert Roosa (Pye directed the Council's China project after Blum's death). In 1971 Alexander Eckstein, a leader of the Council study, became chairman of the National Committee, and John Diebold, a Council member whose brother is a senior research fellow at the Council, became another vice-president of the National Committee. This committee was the leading group working publicly for new thinking on United States-China policy. As the *New York Times* commented, it had "quietly laid the groundwork and acceptance for a reexamination of China policy."[43]

Thus the climate for the change in policy was set. In February 1969 a Nixon memorandum instructed Kissinger to begin exploring all possibilities for reopening relationships with China.[44] By 1971 the public moves began, culminating in President Nixon's well-advertised trip to China in 1972. Within the administration itself, Council members, as expected, were prominent among the policymakers. Nixon himself, briefly a Council member during the mid-1960s, had written an article for *Foreign Affairs* in 1967, the year following the China Study Project. He noted that "taking the long view, we simply cannot afford to leave China forever outside the family of nations."[45] Kissinger's ties with the Council have been mentioned often enough to make repetition unnecessary; active in the Council's parallel Atlantic Study Project, he was not an active participant in the China studies. Of the lesser figures involved in making China policy, about one-third were Council members. One interesting case is that of Professor Richard H. Solomon, who joined Kissinger's staff, under a fellowship from the Council on Foreign Relations, to serve as a consultant in the planning of Nixon's visit to China.

This case of a shift in a long-established policy well illustrates the catalytic role the Council can have in changing a climate of opinion. With such artful preparation of the groundwork, the change seemed almost effortless. The feared right-wing reaction was reduced to a mere mutter, as the leaders of opinion were brought along with the new orientation. From a futile attempt to isolate the People's Republic of China, the policy shifted to Kissinger's complex balance of power schemes, in which China was to be one of the five players in a pentagonal power game.

Policy Toward Southern Africa

For the United states foreign policy elite the creation and the continued existence of the People's Republic of China represented an unwelcome reality to which some kind of adjustment eventually has to be made. Another unwelcome reality, as yet far from resolved, has been the potentially explosive situation in Southern Africa. There, the continued existence of racist and colonialist regimes has provoked the formation of national liberation movements, which enjoy the material support of the African and socialist countries, and the overwhelming moral support of the world community, as expressed in the United Nations.[46] Southern Africa forms part of the Western sphere of influence, with a strong traditional British interest, and substantial economic involvement from the rest of Western Europe and from the United States. The mineral wealth of the region is extraordinary, its gold alone serving as a primary base of the world's monetary system. South Africa's industrial economy is the most advanced in Africa. The extreme and obvious character of oppression in Southern Africa deprives it of all semblance of legitimacy and makes more likely the eventual emergence of revolutionary regimes with no enthusiasm at all for continuing to serve the interests of the Free World.

The adjustment to the revolution in China met with considerable delay. The adjustment to the far from complete revolution in Southern Africa is likely to be equally extended. There has been no such startling shift in United States policy in Southern Africa as in the case of China. Nor has the Council on Foreign Relations at any time dedicated itself to a major Southern Africa Study Project; however, the Council role has not been uninteresting, for all that. Council members, as usual, have played major parts in making policy toward that region, and Council studies have served to mark the outer limits of respectable debate about the issue.

Prior to 1961, the United States could hardly be said to have a policy on Southern Africa, or even on Africa as a whole. Considered a European responsibility, African affairs were subordinated to United States relationships with Western Europe. Not until 1958 did the State Department even have an assistant secretary of state for African affairs. Several Council groups during the 1950s served to acquaint some members with issues on the African continent, but attention to Southern Africa in particular was minimal. One of the leaders in at least one of the study groups was Wayne Fredericks of the Ford Foundation, who was later to play a leading role in the Africa Bureau under Kennedy and Johnson. Dean Rusk chaired a 1955 study group on the United States and the Issue of Colonialism, and Harold Hochschild chaired a group in 1958 and 1959 on Africa South of the Sahara. Hochschild was associated with American Metal Climax, which has major investments in the

Southern African region. Participating in this study group were several Council members who visited Africa, including David Rockefeller and four other Council directors.

Minutes or conclusions of these early discussion and study groups are not available, but there can be little doubt that there were at least two main themes. One was that it was necessary to pay some attention to Africa, and that the United States would eventually have to deal with independent African countries and not only with the European colonial powers. Among those involved in these discussions, Wayne Fredericks was well known for his energetic advocacy of this point during his later term of office. The second theme was an emphasis on economic interests in Africa. This is apparent from the composition of the study groups, which included many businessmen with African interests, and from the fact that the only book resulting from these studies was one by William Hance on *African Economic Development*.[47]

Similar currents of thought are reflected in the policy toward Southern Africa followed under Kennedy and Johnson. Broadly speaking, that course can be characterized as ritual opposition to colonialism and to racism, while refraining from any substantive actions which would cut off crucial economic and political ties with the key white regimes, South Africa and Portugal.[48] These policies were carried out by a set of officials who were, in large part, members of the Council. Of the twenty-eight officials most involved during the Kennedy and Johnson years, eighteen were members of the Council. Of those with particularly close ties to African strategy, Wayne Fredericks and W. Averell Harriman are especially noteworthy. Fredericks served as deputy assistant secretary of state for African affairs and was widely regarded as one of the most important men concerned with Africa policy (at least when he was not overruled by the more influential European interests in the State Department). Harriman held general responsibility for African affairs under

Johnson, among his other powers. During these years, especially under Kennedy, various public steps were taken against the white regimes—votes at the United Nations, supporting Great Britain on sanctions against the breakaway regime of Rhodesia, aid to Southern African refugees. At first the white regimes were annoyed, and African states and liberation movement leaders held hopes that United States influence might really be thrown against the continuation of the minority regimes, but disillusionment soon set in as symbolic steps failed to lead to practical actions. As the resolutions at the United Nations grew stronger, American abstentions and negative votes increased and "business as usual" economic policies led to an ever growing U.S. stake in Southern Africa. It is in this context that the Council for the first time focused specifically on Southern Africa in a 1964 discussion group.

The study was chaired by Waldemar A. Nielsen, president of the African-American Institute. Nielsen had worked for the Ford Foundation at the same time as Wayne Fredericks and drew on Fredericks and others who had participated in earlier study groups. Nielsen himself continued in the next few years to play a major role in the Council's programs dealing with Africa and authored two books for the Council on the subject.[49] The point of view expressed in Nielsen's books was mildly critical of the Kennedy-Johnson policies. He suggested a number of moves to weaken relationships with the white regimes and stressed the development of contacts with the nationalist movements, in particular increasing relief and educational assistance. (The African-American Institute served as one of the major channels for AID and CIA assistance along these lines to African nationalist movements.)

The rationale behind the Nielsen suggestions is indicated in his comment that the aid given under Kennedy and Johnson to the movements (scholarships, relief supplies) "has been insignificant in checking the drift of the nationalist movements into bitterness, extremism, and growing dependence on Communist support."[50] Thus, in the sixth meeting of the 1963-1964 study group, William Griffith, an MIT professor of political science, suggested that "the United States should consciously use scholarships to gain support among the African leadership and to divert students from Communist and guerrilla training."[51] Nielsen and other participants followed Griffith's remark with comments on the number of refugees and the kind of training that would be useful.

The Nielsen proposals formed a variant, but not a radical departure, from the established policy. The aim was to increase influence with nationalist groups, divert them from a revolutionary path, and maintain ties with the white regimes on a more low-key basis. The assumption was that the nationalist movements would eventually take over and that the United States should help mold the character of the transition.

The Nielsen books, it seems from subsequent events, had little influence in modifying policy, either under Johnson or subsequently. They served very well, however, to set the outer limits of "respectable" debate on the issue and to define the terms of the debate. The activities of the African-American Institute included not only its programs for African students, but others designed to inform and influence American opinion, through its magazine *Africa Report,* briefings for journalists, services for schools, conferences for congressmen with African leaders, meetings on the issue of investment in Southern Africa, and so on.[52] With an annual budget of over $6 million, it has undoubtedly been the best funded of United States groups dealing with Africa. Nielsen was its president from 1961 to 1970, and its board of trustees in 1971 included twelve CFR members among the total of thirty, as well as the wife of another CFR member. Six of the board members had been participants in one or more of the Council study groups on Africa. The influence of

The Council's World View   217

the Council studies can also be noted in a widely quoted 1971 report of the United Nations Association. The report largely followed the lines of Nielsen's books, while the panel of fourteen which had prepared the report included eight Council members, five of whom had participated in CFR groups dealing with Africa. Three, including Nielsen, were also on the board of the African-American Institute.

That the study groups served to delimit debate rather than to set policy should not be counted as a Council failure, for there is considerable evidence that, unlike the China Study Group or the War and Peace Studies Project, there was no Council consensus behind the Nielsen suggestions. The Ford Foundation and the Rockefeller Brothers Fund financed a book entitled *Southern Africa and the United States,* whose contributors (all participants in the Council study groups) were opposed to any disengagement of support for the white regimes.[53] The Nielsen study groups themselves had only minimal participation from top Council leadership. George F. Kennan, one of the editorial advisers for *Foreign Affairs,* spoke out in a January 1971 article for an American policy even more sympathetic to the white regimes.[54] David Rockefeller's Chase Manhattan Bank continued its heavy involvement in Southern Africa, and the combined economic investment of Council leaders in Southern Africa would be staggering if the full sum could be calculated.[55] Of the seven industrial corporations most closely tied to the Council, four (Mobil, IBM, ITT, and GE) are among the fifteen largest U.S. investors in Southern Africa; the other three are also involved, although to a lesser degree. In addition to loans made to South Africa by such banks as Chase and First National City, the Dillon investment firm was responsible for organizing the American-South African Investment Company, which has taken the lead in facilitating financial arrangements with South Africa.

A Council study in 1971-1972 is perhaps more indicative

of the general direction of Council thought. This project, by Donald F. McHenry, a State Department official, focused on United States business practices in South Africa, suggesting more "enlightened practices which would make more defensible the continued presence of American business in an essentially unjust political and social system and contribute substantially to improved economic, social, and, possibly, political conditions for non-whites."[56] Subsequent to this study, McHenry has been much in demand as an adviser to American corporations faced with growing criticism of their involvement in South Africa.

Thus it is not surprising that the change in Southern Africa policy which came with the Nixon administration took a different tack from that of the Nielsen books. Based on a Kissinger National Security Study Memorandum of 1969 (NSSM 39), a new policy of closer, but still low-key contacts with the white regimes was initiated.[57] The assumption was that the "whites are here to stay and the only way that constructive change can come about is through them." It was recognized, however, that the white regimes would have to be encouraged to undertake selected and gradual reforms to defuse world criticism and the revolutionary thrust of the liberation movements.

Although there is no poll to verify it, it seems plausible that the policies developed and implemented by Kissinger would meet with more approval among the Council's inner circle than the proposals based on adjustments to a future victory by African nationalist forces. The collapse of Portuguese colonialism in Africa does not yet seem to have shaken Kissinger's commitment to collaboration with the dominant white regime in South Africa. Africa-oriented policies on the Nielsen model continue to set the limits of debate among those with possible access to influence. Their adoption might be on the agenda of some future Democratic administration as the consequences of continued ties with the white regimes become more and more obvious. But, as was apparent in the case of China, adjustment to unpleasant realities is not easy for the foreign policy establishment. The Nielsen studies appear to have been little more than trial balloons, and as yet there is no news of more serious Council attention to Southern Africa. In spite of the liberation of Angola and Mozambique, there is no certainty about the timetable for the liberation of the rest of Southern Africa. It will be some time before the full history of United States response to revolution in Southern Africa has run its course.

Suggested Readings

For more detailed references on each of the case studies, see Minter (1973a). Among the more useful accounts of each case are:
Germany policy: Hammond (1963) and Kuklick (1972).
Guatemala: Barnet (1968) and NACLA (1974).
Missile crisis: Abel (1966) and Allison (1971).
China: Barnett (1971), Horowitz (1971), and Brandon (1973).
Southern Africa: Nielsen (1969), Minter (1973b), and *Southern Africa* magazine.

Notes

1. Angell, 1929.
2. Memorandum A-B124, July 31, 1945, CFR, *War-Peace Studies*, NUL; memorandum E-B63, March 18, 1943, CFR, *War-Peace Studies*, NUL. These documents, in spite of the late dates, were the fruit of earlier discussions in the Council's groups, and it should be remembered that digests of the discussions and drafts of memoranda were circulated to the State Department and President Roosevelt.
3. Among the most useful general sources on United States policy, see Kuklick (1972). Other references can be found in Minter (1973a: 242).

4. Kraft, 1958:67.
5. Ratchford and Ross, 1947.
6. Hoover, 1965:223.
7. The detailed lists of policymakers in this and the following case studies can be found in Minter, 1973a:246ff.
8. Stimson and Bundy, 1947:568-583.
9. Hammond, 1963:371-377.
10. United States, Department of State, *Foreign Relations, 1945*, III:453.
11. See especially Kuklick, 1972.
12. I. F. Stone, in *PM*, March 19, 1945:2.
13. Kraft, 1958:68.
14. The CIA involvement is discussed in Barnet, 1968, Tully, 1962, and Wise and Ross, 1964. Other sources on the intervention are noted in Minter, 1973a:243.
15. Eisenhower, 1963:421.
16. Bain and Reed, 1933; Feuerlein and Hannan, 1941; Burden, 1943.
17. Berle and Jacobs, 1973:611.
18. Tully, 1962:65.
19. United States, Senate Internal Security Subcommittee, 1961:865-866.
20. Braden, 1953.
21. Geiger, 1953:vi-vii.
22. Ydigoras Fuentes, 1963:49-50.
23. This thesis is systematically explicated in J. and G. Kolko, 1972.
24. Roberts, 1956:xi.
25. Kissinger, 1958:ix.
26. Kissinger, 1957:xiii.
27. Kissinger, 1958:23.
28. Ibid., x.
29. Ibid., 144.
30. Rockefeller Brothers Fund, 1961:113.
31. Taylor, 1972:43.
32. Kennedy, 1960:65.
33. The most detailed study of the missile crisis to date is Allison, 1971. Other important accounts are Abel, 1966, and Kennedy, 1968. Additional references can be found in Allison, 1971.
34. Abel, 1966:65.
35. Kolko, 1968; J. and G. Kolko, 1972.
36. Basic books in this tradition are Smoot, 1962, Courtney, 1968, and Allen, 1971. The contrast between the right-wing "conspiracy"

model and a model such as ours which sees the Council as one key organization of the United States capitalist class is helpfully discussed by Domhoff (1970). Our portrayal of the views of the Council also clearly shows the Council's commitment to the defense of United States capitalism.
37. See Hamilton, 1972:115 on the upper-middle-class support for Joseph McCarthy and in general on the social location of conservative views, particularly concentrated among upper-class white Protestants. Moreover, such avid supporters of right-wing causes as Howard Pew and H. L. Hunt can by no means be characterized as "small" businessmen.
38. Barber, 1950.
39. For more background on the forces at work on China policy at this time, see J. and G. Kolko, 1972, Thomas, 1974, and Koen, 1974.
40. Thomson, 1967:55.
41. Steele, 1966.
42. See the *New York Times*, March 20, 1969:24 and March 21, 1969:1 and 3.
43. The *New York Times*, May 2, 1971:8.
44. Brandon, 1973:183.
45. Nixon, 1967:121.
46. There is as yet no good overall account of the liberation struggles in Southern Africa, although Grundy (1973) contains much useful background material. There is much written on the separate countries involved: the ex-Portuguese colonies, Zimbabwe (Rhodesia), Namibia (South West Africa), and the Republic of South Africa. For current information the reader should follow *Southern Africa* magazine, published by the Southern Africa Committee in New York.
47. Hance, 1958.
48. On U.S. policy toward Southern Africa, Nielsen (1969) gives a convenient summary through the Johnson administration. Minter (1973b) deals with policy toward Portuguese colonialism.
49. Nielsen, 1965, 1969.
50. Nielsen, 1969:358.
51. From study group minutes provided to one of the authors.
52. On the activities of AAI, see Africa Research Group (1969, 1970) as well as the annual reports of AAI.
53. Hance, 1968.
54. Kennan, 1971.
55. On U.S. investments in Southern Africa, see National Council of Churches (1973) and sources cited there.

56. From McHenry's project proposal, a copy of which was made available to one of the authors.
57. Hultman and Kramer, 1975.

6
The Council and American Policy in Southeast Asia, 1940-1975

The full-scale intervention in the Vietnam war represents the most significant single event in United States foreign policy since the Second World War. The Council on Foreign Relations had a major part in defining the national interest of the United States in Southeast Asia. This chapter will explore the Council's role in the origins and development of American involvement and the reasons why the Council and American government felt that Southeast Asia, particularly Indochina, was important enough to commit United States power and prestige in this region of the world. What justified dispatching over 500,000 troops, sustaining over 56,000 deaths, 300,000 wounded, and spending almost $150 billion?

Much has been written about the United States intervention in Vietnam, exposing the deception practiced by policymakers, the step-by-step escalation of the war, and some of the debate within the government. It has been repeatedly noted that the basic assumptions of policy were rarely the subject of debate. How, then, was the American national interest in Southeast Asia defined? Why did ruling-class policymakers consider this region important? A focus on the activities of the Council makes it possible to answer this question and to discern the origins of American involvement from the early support for French colonialism to the full-scale war under Johnson and Nixon.

In sharp contrast to national policy in many other areas of the world, the American people as a whole had little interest in the fate of Southeast Asia prior to the mid-1960s. The Council and government therefore had a free hand in defining the national interest there as they wished. Three distinct periods stand out in the history of American involvement in Southeast Asia. During the 1940-1963 period, a consensus was developed which fixed the economic and strategic importance of Southeast Asia in the minds of national policymakers and opinion leaders. A second stage began in 1964 when the successes of Vietnamese revolutionaries made continued American dominance impossible without military intervention. Once the rulers of the United States were militarily committed to the war, it became a test of their will and prestige in Southeast Asia and the world. Finally, by 1968 the failure to win a military victory had provoked a crisis of confidence at home and abroad, and this failure was slowly and reluctantly accepted, resulting in a peace "settlement" in 1973, an agreement which proved to be only temporary.

The Council Forges a Consensus on the Importance of Southeast Asia, 1940-1963

As we have seen in Chapter 4, during 1940 and 1941 the Council's War and Peace Studies Project and the American government concluded that maintaining control of Southeast Asia was crucial enough to engage in war with Japan. The region's importance was seen in economic and strategic terms. One of the reasons why the Council considered the

Western hemisphere "inadequate" living space was that "it lacks important raw materials which we get from southeastern Asia."[1] The "strategic importance of converging sea and air routes" was also stressed by Council theorists.[2]

During the second half of 1943, as the end of the war approached, the Council's War and Peace Studies Project renewed its interest in Southeast Asia. In September 1943 a Council memorandum to President Roosevelt and the Department of State stressed again that the area constituted a "cheap source of vital raw materials" and that the American national interest demanded "placing political and economic control in hands likely to be friendly to the United States."[3] In this way "non-discriminatory trade policies and relationships" could be established "which will enable both the United States and other countries, in accord with the Atlantic Charter, to secure access to the trade and raw materials of the region, and to invest and do business in the area."[4] The Council also continued to emphasize the strategic importance of the Indochina area, asserting in a November 1943 memorandum that this region had served the Japanese "as a base of outstanding strategic and economic importance. The conquest of Malaya, Burma, and the Netherlands Indies was immeasurably eased by the ability to utilize Indo-China as a jumping-off point."[5] The perspective clearly stressed the strategic interdependence of the entire Southeast Asian area, and, as such, represented the beginnings of the "domino theory" linking the fate of Vietnam to Indochina and Southeast Asia as a whole.

During the late 1940s, the primary interest of the Council and the focus of American foreign policy was relations with the Soviet Union and Europe generally. The rest of the world was not neglected, however, and a CFR study group on Non-Self-Governing Territories was established in 1948, chaired by William L. Holland, a central figure in the Institute of Pacific Relations.[6] This group focused on Southeast

Asia in at least one of its meetings when Professor Rupert Emerson of Harvard led a discussion in February 1949 on United States interests and objectives in the area.[7] In March 1950, a few months after the victory of the Chinese Revolution, another study group, this one focusing exclusively on United States policy toward Southeast Asia, was formed, with Holland as chairman, "in response to the growing awareness of the importance of southeast Asia in world politics."[8] The conclusions of this group are unknown, since nothing was published and Council records after 1949 are presently closed to scholars, but it is clear that the Council was, by the 1949-1950 period, again taking a definite interest in Southeast Asia.

In 1951 the Council and Great Britain's Royal Institute for International Affairs—the Council's sister organization—formed a joint study group on Anglo-American relations, financed by a special grant from the Rockefeller Foundation. The Council half of the study group was chaired by the Council's president, Henry M. Wriston, and had as members three other Council officers as well as directors Hamilton Fish Armstrong, John W. Davis, Lewis W. Douglas, and Joseph E. Johnson.[9] The book produced by the joint study group in January 1953 defined the American national interest in Southeast Asia almost exactly as had the War and Peace Studies Project—in economic and strategic terms. The book argued that "Southeast Asia contributes some of the most critical raw materials needed by Western Europe and the United States. It also makes an essential contribution to the food supply of India."[10] Strategically, the "loss of any further portion" of the Far East in general "could well have decisive effects on the balance of world power in the years ahead."[11]

In October 1953 the Council organized a discussion group on political evolution in Southeast Asia which met during 1953 and 1954. It was chaired by Chester Bowles, former

American ambassador to India. A member of the Council staff, William Henderson, served as the research director. The group was made up of forty Council men—including several officers, directors, staff members, and the usual collection of corporate executives, foundation officials, lawyers, academics, and government officials.[12] The Council did not issue the official conclusions of this group, but its concerns are evident from a letter written by Council executive director George S. Franklin, and an article written by Henderson. In October 1953 Franklin wrote Columbia University professor Philip C. Jessup, a former Council director and State Department official, inviting him to participate in the discussion group's work, stating that "as you know, the strategic position and material resources of Southeast Asia have made it a factor of vital significance in world politics."[13] Franklin went on:

> The possibilities of Communist conquest or subversion are considerable. Since what happens in Southeast Asia has such significance for the United States, we believe it important for as many Americans as possible to increase their knowledge and understanding of this quarter of the globe, and to consider how we may help bring about a political evolution favorable to our national interest. It is the Council's hope that the group's discussions may contribute to these ends.[14]

The nature of the discussion group's conclusions about the United States national interest were clearly outlined in a March 1955 article which Henderson wrote for the Foreign Policy Association's Headline Series. The article stated at the outset that it was "based on a series of data papers which Mr. Henderson originally prepared for a discussion group on political evolution in Southeast Asia at the Council on Foreign Relations during 1953-54."[15] Henderson wrote that Southeast Asia was "vitally significant" to the United States as an "economic and strategic prize."[16]

As one of the earth's great storehouses of natural resources Southeast Asia is a prize worth fighting for. Five-sixths of the world's natural rubber and more than half of its tin are produced here. The region is also the main supplier of quinine and kapok and accounts for two-thirds of the world output of coconut products, one-third of the palm oil, and significant proportions of tungsten and chromium. It is a principal source of oil for the Far East, even though its oil production is less than 3 percent of the world total.

But proabably the most important export item is rice. Southeast Asia—particularly Burma, Thailand and (in normal times) Indochina—produces this vital staple in abundance. At present the region supplies fully 60 percent of all rice entering international trade. In a continent where rice is the principal item of the diet and where it has been chronically in short supply, the significance of Southeast Asia's rice supply need hardly be emphasized.

No less important than its natural wealth is Southeast Asia's key strategic position astride the main lines of communication between Europe and the Far East. If the Communists could gain control of this area they would literally cut the world in two.[17]

Many of the Council men involved in the 1953-1954 discussion group were invited to join a full-scale study group on "United States Policy and Southeast Asia," which met during 1954-1955. The chairman, Edwin F. Stanton, former American ambassador to Thailand, had been involved in the 1953-1954 meetings, as had seven of the twenty-five other participants.[18] In October 1954 Stanton wrote Philip C. Jessup inviting him to join the group, stating that "the emergence of Southeast Asia as an area of vital importance to the free world is one of the most significant developments of the postwar period ... because of the strategic position and rich material resources of this region, its future has become immensely important to all of us."[19] Stanton went on to ask what American objectives and policy should be. The purpose of the study group, he added, would be to answer such questions and "define the nature of the American interest in this area."[20]

Professor John Kerry King of the University of Virginia was awarded a Carnegie research fellowship to work as research secretary for the project. The Council itself never published a book as a result of this study group, but King did in 1956, with blessings from Stanton, the group's chairman, who wrote the foreword to the book. In the introduction King thanked Stanton and the Council on Foreign Relations for their help in the project. In his first chapter, entitled "The New Importance of American Interests in Southeast Asia," King argued that American interests in Southeast Asia have "become extremely significant, perhaps even decisive."[21] Why was Southeast Asia so important to the American national interest? King's answer was by now the traditional one—economic and strategic: "In geopolitical terms, Southeast Asia occupies a position of global strategic importance roughly comparable to Panama and Suez."[22] The strategic sea and air routes connecting the Pacific and Indian Oceans, King argued, must be kept from a hostile power. That the domino theory was perceived as a valid concept is evident from the fact that the entire Southeast Asian area was seen as "an interconnected strategic unit of far-reaching importance."[23] Economically, the American interest in Southeast Asia must

> be reckoned in strategic terms rather than in terms of volume or dollar value . . . in the case of two important strategic materials, tin and natural rubber, the United States depends wholly upon foreign imports for all its requirements. Of these materials, Southeast Asia supplies about 90 percent of the world's natural rubber, 55 percent of the world's tin.[24]

Other raw materials important to the American economy were produced in Southeast Asia, King pointed out, and despite the existence of synthetic rubber, "natural rubber also stands as a major strategic requirement."[25] King argued that the United States was a resource-deficient nation and was "heavily dependent on materials imported from abroad, especially from the so-called underdeveloped areas, to maintain an expanding and dynamic economy."[26] Since American needs would grow in the years to come, "an increase in the importance of Southeast Asia's raw material resources, as well as those of Latin America, Africa, and South Asia, certainly may be anticipated."[27]

Finally, King stressed the economic importance of Southeast Asia to the interdependent capitalist world as a whole:

> As long as Southeast Asia is important to the economic viability of western Europe and Japan, American interest in the area is compounded automatically. As keystones in its security and trade patterns, the United States has banked heavily on western Europe and Japan. In turn, dependence of these countries on trade with Southeast Asia enhances the American interest in Southeast Asian trade generally.[28]

In 1956 the Council established yet another Southeast Asian study group, this one on "United States Policy in Indo-China." Council Director Joseph E. Johnson was chairman and William Henderson again served as study director. The group planned to have Henderson write a book based on its work, but in January 1958 Henderson was appointed assistant executive director of the Council and his manuscript was never completed or published.[29]

It is clear that statements of key individuals associated with Council study groups on Southeast Asia derived in large part, if not entirely, from the currents of ideas and opinions circulating within the Council community. The Council on Foreign Relations as an organization, however, had not published anything on Vietnam, Indochina, or Southeast Asia by 1959. In that year the Council, "mindful of international events of grave significance," established yet another study group on United States policy in Southeast Asia, with the aim of publishing a book for dissemination beyond the Council community.[30] Syracuse University dean and former United Nations official Harlan Cleveland served as chairman of this group, and Professor Russell H. Fifield, on leave from the University of Michigan and a visiting fellow at the Council, was study director. Forty-three men were involved in the group's work during 1959 and 1960, including leaders of the Council and several who had been in previous study groups on Southeast Asia, such as William Henderson, John Kerry King, and John D. Rockefeller III.[31]

The Council published Fifield's book in 1963. Its purpose was "to set forth current conditions and problems and develop a rationale for American policy in Southeast Asia in the years ahead."[32] The book opens as follows: "Southeast Asia presents a challenge of major proportions to the United States—a challenge that poses diverse and complex questions affecting the future of the American people."[33] Why was this area so crucial? Fifield and the Council again stressed the strategic and economic importance of the region, arguing that it was "an area of great strategic, economic and demographic significance."[34] Strategically, its water passageways linking continents and worldwide trade, made Southeast Asia of "special significance in the world balance."[35] Economically, the "region has supplied the world with foodstuffs and raw materials, and among the exports rice, rubber, tin and petroleum may be singled out as having particular significance in international politics."[36] The other raw materials of the area should not be ignored either, argued Fifield, listing bauxite, tungsten, iron ore, and others in this category.[37] Despite the development of some synthetic products, "the basic significance of many items in the world economy will remain for the indefinite future."[38] In addition, the region's markets were "sure to grow in importance."[39] The problem in Southeast Asia, as Fifield and the Council perceived it, was that while "rich in resources and potentialities," it was weak in defense and therefore the Communist challenge to American interests "is acute and unrelenting."[40] China wanted to control the area for the same reasons the United States did—

China's growing industrialization "would be complemented by raw materials and markets of a dependent Southeast Asia."[41] The United States therefore had to be involved *militarily* in the region. As Fifield put it: "Military defense against direct and indirect aggression must be a fundamental U.S. objective in Southeast Asia, for without security all other goals collapse like a row of dominoes when the first is pushed over."[42]

It is clear from the evidence offered above that during the 1940-1963 period the Council on Foreign Relations paid an extraordinary amount of attention to the importance of Southeast Asia, with no less than five study and discussion groups focusing on the American policy in this region of the world during the 1950s alone. The consensus which quickly emerged and was repeatedly reinforced was that the area's economic and strategic value was crucially important to the United States and its allies. As we shall see below, this consensus was consistently reflected in government policy, to and including the full-scale intervention of the Johnson years.

The Council was also successful in promoting its view of the importance of Southeast Asia outside the Council membership. In late 1964, the Council conducted a survey of the opinions of the "community leaders" in thirty-three different cities, all connected with the CFR's committees on foreign relations.[43] Fully 80 percent of these nearly 600 leaders approved of the American objective of "assisting the South Vietnamese government to defend its independence and consolidate its authority over Viet-Nam south of the 17th Parallel."[44] But this was not all. The Council on Foreign Relations, through its members and leaders, was even more successful in forging a consensus on Vietnam and Southeast Asia among government policymakers during the 1950s and early 1960s.

The Identity of Government-Council Views on American National Interest in Southeast Asia, 1941-1963

Leaders and members of the Council on Foreign Relations were very active in governmental decision-making on Indochina and Southeast Asia and they inevitably dominate any listing of the major policymakers. Council member David Halberstam's "inside" story of American decision-making on the Indochina war, *The Best and the Brightest*, is one of the most widely acclaimed on the topic. The men referred to in its title are practically identical with the Council on Foreign Relations community; of those twenty-one men about whom Halberstam writes more than five consecutive pages, only a few politicians—Fulbright, Goldwater, Johnson, and Kennedy—were not Council members at some point in their careers. In this section the focus will be on the dominance of the Council men in decision-making and on the basis of government interest in Southeast Asia.

As we have seen in Chapter 4, key governmental policymakers, including not only Council members such as Henry L. Stimson, the secretary of war, and Sumner Welles, undersecretary of state, but also President Roosevelt and Secretary of State Cordell Hull, accepted during 1941 the Council's opinion on the importance of Southeast Asia and the need to prevent Japan's long-term domination of the area. The resulting policy led directly to United States entry into the Second World War.

After 1945 there was a relative lag in interest in Southeast Asia during the early years of the cold war. Following the 1949 "loss" of China, however, there was renewed concern. In January 1952 came the first full statement of American national interest in Southeast Asia by a top government official in a decade. It was by a member of the National Security Council, the government's highest-level foreign policymaking body. In a memorandum to President Truman, W. Averell Harriman, Truman's director of mutual security, defined American interests in a way identical to that of the Council itself. This was not surprising, since Harriman was a director of the Council on Foreign Relations at the time and a personal friend of many of the Council's study group members. Speaking of Southeast Asia, Harriman argued that in view of the strategic location of the area in relation to the

> Pacific lines of communication, its importance as a producer of rice, which is required as a basic food resource from India to Japan, its vast resources of tin, rubber, and numerous other strategic materials, and likewise, its manpower resources, the loss of this area to the free world would have the most serious consequences for the security of the United States.[45]

Harriman's memorandum was followed six months later by an official, presidentially approved "Statement of Policy" by the National Security Council (NSC). In 1952 the NSC was chaired by President Truman and included the secretaries of state and defense and the director of mutual security, and had as advisers the director of the Central Intelligence Agency and the chairman of the Joint Chiefs of Staff. Thus in the Truman administration the NSC included Council member Dean Acheson (secretary of state) and Council director Harriman (director of mutual security). National Security Council memorandum 124/1 (June 25, 1952) was entitled "United States Objectives and Courses of Action with Respect to Southeast Asia."[46] It stated that communist domination of the area, "would seriously endanger in the short term, and critically endanger in the longer term, United States security interests."[47] This was true for several reasons, the NSC argued. First, because of the strategic interdependence of the area, "the loss of any single country would probably lead to relatively swift submission to or an alignment with Communism by the remaining countries of this group," and "would in all probability" result in the loss

The Council and Southeast Asia   235

of the Middle East, thereby threatening Europe.[48] Second, the loss of Southeast Asia would make precarious the United States position in the Pacific offshore island chain and thereby threaten fundamental American security interests in the Far East.[49] Thirdly,

> Southeast Asia, especially Malaya and Indonesia, is the principal world source of natural rubber and tin, and a producer of petroleum and other strategically important commodities. The rice exports of Burma and Thailand are critically important to Malaya, Ceylon and Hong Kong and are of considerable significance to Japan and India, all important areas of free Asia.[50]

Finally, "the loss of Southeast Asia, especially of Malaya and Indonesia, could result in such economic and political pressures in Japan as to make it extremely difficult to prevent Japan's eventual accommodation to Communism."[51]

The implementation of these goals under Truman and during the first years of the Eisenhower administration involved backing French colonialism in Indochina. After 1950, the United States became the main prop of the French war to maintain control over the area, helping the French with billions of dollars in aid.

The Eisenhower administration, which entered office early in 1953, brought even more Council leaders and active members into top decision-making positions. The President himself had been an active Council member, chairing a study group and serving on the editorial advisory board of *Foreign Affairs*. The secretary of state, John Foster Dulles, was a long-time (since the 1920s) active member, and the director of the CIA, Allen W. Dulles, had been president of the Council and a director since 1927. All maintained their Council membership while in government service, and Allen Dulles continued to serve as a Council director.

It is hardly surprising, then, to find that the National Security Council, chaired by President Eisenhower and having as leading members or advisers the Dulles brothers, defined the United States national interest in Southeast Asia in a familiar way. A "Statement of Policy" on "United States Objectives and Courses of Action with Respect to Southeast Asia," NSC 5405, was approved by the President and issued on January 16, 1954.[52] Using the same analysis and similar language as NSC 124/1, NSC 5405 stated that the "loss" of Indochina and the impact of such a defeat on Southeast Asia would "have the most serious repercussions on U.S. and free world interests in Europe and elsewhere."[53] This statement of policy argued that the Southeast Asian nations were so interrelated that "effective counteraction would be immediately necessary to prevent the loss of any single country from leading to submission to or an alignment with communism by the remaining countries of Southeast Asia and Indonesia."[54] In NSC 5405, this "falling domino" principle was extended to India and most of the Middle East, and a realignment of these areas "would seriously endanger the stability and security of Europe."[55] Speaking of economics, NSC 5405 used language identical with that used in NSC 124/1:

> The loss of Southeast Asia would have serious economic consequences for many nations of the free world and conversely would add significant resources to the Soviet bloc. Southeast Asia, especially Malaya and Indonesia, is the principal world source of natural rubber and tin, and a producer of petroleum and other strategically important commodities. The rice exports of Burma, Indochina, and Thailand are critically important to Malaya, Ceylon and Hong Kong and are of considerable significance to Japan and India, all important areas of free Asia. Furthermore, this area has an important potential as a market for the industrialized countries of the free world.
>
> The loss of Southeast Asia, especially of Malaya and Indonesia, could result in such an economic and political pressure on Japan as to make it extremely difficult to prevent Japan's eventual accommodation to communism.[56]

National Security Council memorandum 5405 was the background for President Eisenhower's famous statement on

The Council and Southeast Asia   237

the economic and strategic importance of Indochina at a press conference in April 1954. Eisenhower said that the "possible consequences" of the "loss" of Indochina "are just incalculable to the free world," because of the "falling domino" principle and the importance of the raw materials, population, geographical position, and markets of the area.[57] The NSC statements of American policy on Southeast Asia during 1956, 1958, and 1960 were identical in content and stressed, as had NSC 5405, that the economic loss of access to raw materials and the geopolitical consequences of the "loss" of the area were serious.[58]

When the Kennedy administration took power in early 1961, a different group of Council members was brought into the government. Dean Rusk, a member active in Council programs during the late 1950s, became secretary of state; McGeorge Bundy, a Council member who had been a CFR employee during the late 1940s and involved in at least one Council study group during the late 1950s, became the President's national security adviser; and Council member John McCone took over from Allen Dulles at the CIA in the fall of 1961. These men fully accepted the twenty-year-old standing definition of the United States national interest in Southeast Asia. The Council-inspired consensus on the importance of the area was so well ingrained by 1961 that it did not have to be repeated. As one writer on Vietnam has said, "the Kennedy administration did not question (even privately) the *purposes* of the American involvement in Vietnam. Kennedy and his advisers went along with the inherited assumption that the perpetuation of a non-Communist regime in Saigon was vital to United States interests."[59] Arthur M. Schlesinger, Jr., the chronicler of the Kennedy administration, makes a similar point in *A Thousand Days,* stating that the correctness of the existing commitment to Diem and the Saigon government "had ceased by 1961 to be of interest to policymakers."[60] They agreed with the assumption of American vital interests in the area and concentrated on the means—economic, diplomatic, and especially military—to implement a long-established policy. It was under Kennedy that the early escalation of the war took place: large numbers of American "advisers" were sent to fight in the war, more sophisticated military technology was dispatched, and counterinsurgency techniques were applied on an increasing scale.

The Council's Attempt to Maintain a Consensus on the War, 1964-1968

Until 1964, with relatively limited involvement, the United States succeeded in keeping the South Vietnamese domino from falling. Preventing defeat, however, called for ever increasing military escalation from 1964 on. This escalation, with its high price in physical suffering not only for Vietnam but for the United States, eroded the domestic support needed to continue the war.

The Council on Foreign Relations had no study groups on Vietnam or Southeast Asia during the 1960-1968 period, because study groups during the 1950s had already definitely concluded that American interests were involved in Southeast Asia and that military efforts were therefore required to defend this interest. During the early 1960s, this consensus was virtually unchallenged. As the war was escalated in 1964-1965, however, students throughout the United States began to voice doubts through teach-ins and demonstrations. At the same time, an active Council member, Undersecretary of State George W. Ball, defected from the existing consensus regarding United States policy. President Lyndon B. Johnson then called in a group of "establishment advisers" from outside the government to discuss Ball's dissent. Dominated by Council leaders and members, they overruled Ball and

The Council and Southeast Asia 239

supported the decision to escalate the war.[61] As one writer later put it: "The President had called in what amounted to a steering committee of its [the establishment's] elder statesmen to pass on his policies, and in effect to deal with a rebellion on the part of Ball."[62]

Council leaders were evidently concerned over both the domestic unrest and Ball's dissent, however, for they had a continuous parade of government leaders—mainly Council members—come to Council headquarters to discuss Vietnam policy. John J. McCloy, Council chairman during those years, expressed the question of the Council's Vietnam role during the mid-1960s as follows: "Certainly we had all the Bunkers and Lodges and the generals up explaining it."[63] During 1964-1965, for example, Henry Cabot Lodge, former United States ambassador to Saigon, General Maxwell Taylor, at that time current ambassador to south Vietnam, and McGeorge Bundy, the President's special assistant for national security affairs, all spoke before Council meetings on the subject of Vietnam.[64] During 1965-1966, the secretary of state, Dean Rusk, the chiefs of staff of the army and air force, Henry A. Kissinger, W. Averell Harriman, and Walt W. Rostow, special adviser to President Johnson on national security, addressed the Council on Vietnam and related topics.[65] In addition, William P. Bundy became a Council director in 1964, the same year he was appointed assistant secretary of state for Far Eastern affairs, remaining in that key position throughout the Johnson administration and continuing as Council director into the 1970s. With William Bundy as a director, the Council had yet another direct link with Vietnam policymaking. As David Halberstam has written:

> The job of Assistant Secretary of State for Far Eastern Affairs is a crucial one, perhaps on the subject of Vietnam the most crucial one. If there were doubts on Vietnam, they should have been voiced first of all by State. And in the case of Vietnam the position of the Assistant Secretary of FE was particularly vital.[66]

In September 1965, Council leaders also took the lead in organizing a national committee to support the government's Vietnam policies. Headed by Council director Arthur H. Dean, it was called the Committee for an Effective and Durable Peace in Asia. Six other leading members were CFR directors, including chairman McCloy, vice-president David Rockefeller, and treasurer Gabriel Hauge. Almost one-half of the total committee membership were Council members. The committee stated that its aims were to support President Johnson "in combatting Communism in Southeast Asia," adding that Johnson "acted rightly and in the national interest" in committing American forces in Vietnam.[67]

Thus the hard-line consensus on Vietnam was maintained during the 1965-1967 period. Some dissent within the government continued during those years, however, as did the resistance of the Vietnamese people and the deepening opposition of students and other Americans at home.

The crucial period of change took place between November 1967 and March 1968. The group of establishment advisers mentioned above and now called the Senior Advisory Group on Vietnam, met with President Johnson in November 1967 and again supported existing policy.[68] On a deeper level, however, there was evidently an unease and an increase in concern within ruling-class circles over the stalemate in Vietnam and the domestic conflicts it was engendering. The Council's annual report for 1967-1968 stated that Vietnam was "part of many conversations at the Council" during the year.[69] Henry Cabot Lodge, Herman Kahn, Robert G. K. Thompson, Graham A. Martin, Wesley R. Fishel, Maj. Gen. William G. DuPuy, Chester L. Cooper, Senator Thruston B. Morton, George W. Ball, William P. Bundy, and others all addressed the Council on Vietnam during 1967-1968.[70] The highlight was the equivalent of a debate before the Council between Ball and William Bundy on the Vietnam question. Ball, who had resigned as undersecretary of state but had not

The Council and Southeast Asia 241

spoken publicly against the war, spoke privately to the Council on December 6, 1967, on "Viet-Nam from the Perspective of U.S. Global Responsibilities," downplaying Vietnam's overall importance.[71] Bundy, whose title was now assistant secretary of state for East Asian and Pacific affairs, spoke on December 8, 1967, on "United States Objectives in Vietnam: A Progress Report," stressing the general picture of "progress" and successes of American policy.[72]

During 1967-1968, the Council also carried on two separate study groups reassessing American foreign policy as a whole. Vietnam policy critic Hans J. Morgenthau of the University of Chicago, a visiting senior fellow at the Council, together with Council director Joseph E. Johnson, conducted a study group on "A Re-examination of American Foreign Policy."[73] At the same time, Ball led a discussion group on American Foreign Policy which was "composed largely of members who have in the past been actively engaged in the conduct of American policy. A general reappraisal of American foreign policy was undertaken."[74] Although a list of participants in these two groups has not yet been revealed by the Council, both, and particularly Ball's, undoubtedly discussed Vietnam and had important individuals as participants.

Then, in February 1968, came the successful Tet offensive by the National Liberation Front and the North Vietnamese. This offensive set in motion a series of events leading to one of the most remarkable turnarounds in the history of American foreign policy. These events, which took place during March 1968, began with the simultaneous swearing in of Clark Clifford as the new secretary of defense, and the request by American military leaders for 206,000 troops for assignment to Vietnam, in addition to the over 500,000 already there.

President Johnson asked the new defense secretary to be chairman of an ad hoc government task force to decide the troop-level question.[75] Clifford broadened the issue to include the overall course the United States was following in Vietnam. His thirteen-man task force, seven of whom were CFR members, met during early March, but soon hit a "discordant note" and could not come to a consensus.[76] Council members stood on both sides of the stalemate.

In mid-March came Eugene J. McCarthy's strong showing in the New Hampshire primary and Robert F. Kennedy's declaration of his presidential candidacy. President Johnson responded to these events forcefully, taking a hard line on the war. On March 18, the President made a tough speech, ridiculing critics who would "tuck our tails and violate our commitments" in Vietnam.[77] Yet, the doubts of Clifford, Arthur J. Goldberg, United States ambassador to the United Nations, and others within the government had to be resolved before decisions on future policy could be made. Johnson summoned the Senior Advisory Group on Vietnam, the secret body of "elder statesmen," sometimes called the "wise men," who had advised Johnson on the war at least once a year since 1965, and who had, as we have seen, approved renewed escalation of the war as recently as November 1967.[78] As could be expected, twelve of the fourteen were members or leaders of the Council on Foreign Relations. John J. McCloy, the chairman of the Council's board, was present, as were Council directors Douglas Dillon, Cyrus R. Vance, and Arthur H. Dean. Dean Acheson, George Ball, and McGeorge Bundy, key figures in the "wise men's" deliberations, were long-standing Council men, and Bundy and Ball were very active ones.[79] The only two non-Council members were Abe Fortas, LBJ's alter ego, and Gen. Omar Bradley.

The members of the Senior Advisory Group met at the State Department and White House on March 25 and 26. During these two days, they heard briefings from State Department, CIA, and military experts, and had dinner with the principal cabinet officers and presidential advisers, questioning them at length. They then discussed and debated the issues late into the evening.[80] During the deliberations, these men felt "a pervasive awareness that the enterprise in Vietnam stood at a historical turning point."[81] When the time came to meet with the President, only a few stood for existing policy, none of them leaders of the CFR.[82] Council directors Dillon and Vance and members Acheson, Bundy, and Ball were strong for dramatic change. The reasons for the change in the position of these leading "wise men" are important to note. First, they realized that the previous policy was failing due to the resistance of the Vietnamese. A military solution involving escalation was obviously no longer feasible.[83] Second, domestic unrest and disaffection within the United States threatened long-term ruling-class control over the nation. Third, the economic implications—domestic and international—of continued escalation were serious. Finally, American relations with other countries were being adversely affected by the war. As Cyrus Vance put it:

> We were weighing not only what was happening in Vietnam, but the social and political effects in the United States, the impact on the U.S. economy, the attitude of other nations. The divisiveness in the country was growing with such acuteness that it was threatening to tear the United States apart.[84]

The American antiwar movement had thus played a decisive role in forcing ruling-class leaders to alter their views on American policy.

The "wise men's" meeting with the President, at which Johnson queried each man as to his personal view, left Johnson "deeply shaken."[85] He was "visibly shocked by the magnitude of the defection."[86] There was no doubt that a large majority felt that a significant change in American policy was necessary. The President was particularly impressed that Acheson, McGeorge Bundy, Dillon, and Vance had become "doves" on the Vietnam question.[87] That such ruling-class leaders had shifted positions carried significantly "more weight than something like the New Hampshire primary," one "close observer" later pointed out.[88] The result was that on March 31, only five days after the President's meeting with the Senior Advisory Group on Vietnam, Johnson, heretofore an unreconstructed hawk, announced a de-escalation of the war and his own retirement from public life. Johnson's announcement that he would not seek reelection, wrote the *New York Times,* was a "stunning surprise even to close associates."[89] There is no question that his decisions were heavily influenced by the views of the Senior Advisory Group on Vietnam, a body almost entirely composed of leaders and members of the Council on Foreign Relations.

Construction of a New Consensus, 1968-1973

Leaders and key members of the Council on Foreign Relations, through the Senior Advisory Group on Vietnam, had rejected continued escalation aimed at a military solution to the Vietnam conflict. They were unclear, however, as to the nature of a political settlement short of victory. To work out the details of such an agreement to end the war, the Council organized, in the spring of 1968, a study group on "Viet Nam Settlement." Headed by Council director and former undersecretary of the treasury Robert V. Roosa, its purpose was to "explore possible paths toward a settlement."[90] The group had as members by early 1969 Senior Adviser and Council director Cyrus Vance, who had been deputy negotiator at the Paris peace talks during the Johnson administration, Council director and MIT professor Lucian Pye, two Council staff members, and several other academics and former government officials.[91] The Council group developed a proposal endorsed by the majority of participants which "envisioned a standstill ceasefire and a division of power based on a recognition of territory controlled by the Saigon government and the Vietcong—a formula the framers conceded was 'rigged' to favor the Government."[92] In May 1969 the group met at the Cosmos Club in Washington with Undersecretary of State Elliot Richardson and Henry A. Kissinger, special assistant to President Nixon for national security affairs, to give them their conclusions. The Council's proposal, said one official, "was received with all the pomp and circumstance accorded a communication from a foreign government."[93] The same official added that the proposal was "then filed and largely forgotten."[94] If it was forgotten, it was only for a short time. When President Nixon announced his own five-point peace plan in October 1970, it included many aspects of the Council group's plan, including the two key sections—a standstill cease fire and a political settlement based on "the existing relationship of political forces in South Vietnam."[95] Vance later said in regard to the Council's Vietnam study group, "I think we had some influence."[96] The government's negotiating position had conformed to the recommendations of the Council, and the peace treaty eventually worked out by Council member Henry A. Kissinger and signed in January 1973 was identical with the two key aspects of the Council plan—standstill ceasefire and division of South Vietnam based on the existing spheres of control. The Council had indeed achieved its goal of devising "a formula that might break the deadlock in Paris."[97]

Conclusion

The Council's impact on American policy in Southeast Asia during the 1940-1973 period was clearly very great. If we focus on the twenty-five central figures in government

Table 6-1
Key Government Decision-Makers on American Policy in Southeast Asia, 1940-1973[98]

Name	Primary occupation(s)	Primary government position	CFR member?
Acheson, Dean	Corporate lawyer	Sec. of state	Yes
Ball, George W.	Corporate lawyer, investment banker	Undersecretary of state	Yes, active
Bundy, McGeorge	Academic, foundation official	Special Asst. to president for national security	Yes, active
Bundy, William P.	Government official, editor	Asst. sec. of state	Yes, active
Clifford, Clark	Corporate lawyer	Sec. of defense	No
Dillon, Douglas	Investment banker	Sec. of treasury	Yes, active
Dulles, Allen W.	Corporate lawyer	CIA director	Yes, active
Dulles, John Foster	Corporate lawyer	Sec. of state	Yes, active
Eisenhower, Dwight D.	Career military	President	Yes, active
Harriman, W. Averell	Investment banker	Director of mutual security	Yes, active
Hull, Cordell	Politician	Sec. of state	No

Name	Occupation	Government position	CFR member
Johnson, Lyndon B.	Politician	President	No
Kennedy, John F.	Politician	President	No
Kissinger, Henry A.	Academic	Special asst. to president for national security	Yes, active
Knox, Frank	Newspaper owner and publisher	Sec. of navy	No
McCloy, John J.	Corporate lawyer, banker	Presidential adviser	Yes, active
McNamara, Robert S.	Corporation executive	Sec. of defense	Yes
Nixon, Richard M.	Politician, corporate lawyer	President	Yes
Roosevelt, Franklin D.	Politician	President	No
Rostow, Walt W.	Academic	Special asst. to president for national security	Yes
Rusk, Dean	Academic, foundation official	Sec. of state	Yes, active
Stimson, Henry L.	Corporate lawyer	Sec. of war	Yes, active
Truman, Harry S.	Politician	President	No
Vance, Cyrus	Corporate lawyer	Deputy sec. of defense	Yes, active
Welles, Sumner	Government official	Undersecretary of state	Yes

decision-making on United States policy in Southeast Asia during those years, we find that the Council, and the class it represents, were definitely in control. Table 6-1 lists these decision-makers, including all the presidents, the long-term secretaries of state (Hull, Acheson, Dulles, Rusk), presidential advisers, and others known to have played an important part. Eighteen of the twenty-five (72 percent) were members of the CFR at some point in their career, and most of these were active participants in the Council's work. In terms of class position, these men were overwhelmingly members of the corporate upper class, as measured by occupation and wealth level (relationship to the means of production), listing in the *Social Register,* membership in elite clubs, and attendance at elite schools (part of a social set of interacting and intermarrying "high society" families). At minimum, twenty-one of the twenty-five (84 percent) were clearly part of this capitalist class, a socioeconomic group which makes up only 1 or 2 percent of the American population. The remaining four represent no possible alternative to the control of this class, and at least two of them were closely linked to it. These two were Rusk and Kissinger, who, while apparently having neither the wealth nor the social position to be considered directly, originally, or independently upper class, both worked for the Rockefeller family—Rusk as president of the Rockefeller Foundation during the 1950s and Kissinger as Nelson Rockefeller's foreign policy adviser during the 1960s.

It has been amply illustrated here that contrary to both public discussion of American war aims at the time and conventional explanations since, which variously stress irrational anticommunism, liberal idealism, and vague security interests as the basis for policy, the real concerns of both Council and government decision-makers were economic and geopolitical. The substantive private discussion at the CFR and within the government focused on the desire to maintain control over an area perceived as an economic and strategic "prize" because of its raw materials, food production, population, markets, and importance as an air and sea communication route. The loss of the area, its withdrawal from the American empire, was thus seen as having serious consequences: decreasing the economic living space and power of the United States vis-à-vis potential enemies. The domino theory postulated that additional losses might follow, possibly extending to Japan, the Middle East, and even Europe. Such a development would in turn limit the economic living space of the American capitalist system to the Western hemisphere and perhaps necessitate a transformation of that system.

Suggested Readings

A basic primary source on United States policy in Southeast Asia is the Pentagon Papers. There are several versions, the most complete of which are the twelve-volume House Committee on Armed Services edition, *United States-Vietnam Relations 1945-1967* (1971), and the five-volume Senator Gravel edition, *The Pentagon Papers* (1971-1972).

Among the secondary works written on this major episode in American foreign policy, of particular note are Halberstam (1972), Schurmann (1974), Cooper (1972), Hoopes (1969), Ellsberg (1972), Chomsky (1973), and Fitzgerald (1972).

Notes

1. Memorandum E-B34, July 24, 1941, CFR, *War-Peace Studies*, NUL.
2. Memorandum T-B8, May 20, 1940, CFR, War-Peace Studies, NUL.
3. Memorandum T-B67, September 14, 1943, CFR, *War-Peace Studies*, SUL.

4. Ibid.
5. Memorandum T-B69, November 16, 1943, CFR, *War-Peace Studies*, SUL.
6. CFR, 1950:18. Three departments of government were regularly represented in the meetings of this group, along with academics, lawyers, businessmen, and other Council members with "diversified interests." A list of the study group's members during 1948-1949 may be found in the Philip C. Jessup Papers, Box 114, MDLC.
7. George S. Franklin to Philip C. Jessup, January 27, 1949, Jessup Papers, Box 114, MDLC.
8. CFR, 1950:18-19.
9. Roberts and Wilson, 1953:vi-vii.
10. Ibid., 120.
11. Ibid., 122.
12. CFR, 1954:20-22; CFR memorandum, "Discussion Group on Political Evolution in Southeast Asia," November 30, 1953, Jessup Papers, Box 115, MDLC.
13. Franklin to Jessup, October 1, 1953, Jessup Papers, Box 115, MDLC.
14. Ibid.
15. Henderson, 1955:2.
16. Ibid., 3-4.
17. Ibid., 4-6.
18. CFR, "Study Group on United States Policy and Southeast Asia," third meeting, January 18, 1955, Jessup Papers, Special Correspondence, Box 7, MDLC.
19. Edwin F. Stanton to Jessup, October 26, 1954, Jessup Papers, Special Correspondence, Box 7, MDLC.
20. Ibid.; See also CFR, 1955:15.
21. King, 1956:3.
22. Ibid., 7.
23. Ibid.
24. Ibid., 9.
25. Ibid.
26. Ibid.
27. Ibid.
28. Ibid., 9-10.
29. CFR, 1958:18.
30. Fifield, 1963:viii.
31. Ibid., viii-ix.
32. Ibid., viii.

33. Ibid., 3.
34. Ibid., 4.
35. Ibid.
36. Ibid., 5.
37. Ibid.
38. Ibid.
39. Ibid.
40. Ibid., 6.
41. Ibid., 9.
42. Ibid., 407. William Henderson, in a book he edited in 1963, put the issue in even stronger terms, saying the "loss" of Southeast Asia "would be an irreparable blow." See Henderson, 1963:253. In the same book (pp. 134-136), Frank N. Trager, another participant in several of the Council's study groups on Southeast Asia, relates in detail what a valuable economic and strategic "prize" the area represented.
43. Bushner, 1965:1.
44. Ibid.
45. Memorandum, W. Averell Harriman to Harry S. Truman, January 5, 1952, Harry S. Truman Papers, Official File 355 B, HSTL. Reprinted in Gardner, 1974:282.
46. NSC 124/1, June 25, 1952, *United States-Vietnam Relations 1945-1967* (12 volumes, study prepared by Department of Defense, Committee Print, House Committee on Armed Services, 92nd Congress, 1st Session, Washington, D.C., 1971), VIII, 522. This is the official version of the Pentagon Papers. Southeast Asia was defined in NSC 124/1 as Burma, Thailand, Indochina, Malaya, and Indonesia.
47. Ibid.
48. Ibid.
49. Ibid., 523.
50. Ibid.
51. Ibid.
52. NSC 5405, January 16, 1954, *United States-Vietnam Relations 1945-1967*, IX, 220. Southeast Asia was defined as Burma, Thailand, Indochina, and Malaya.
53. Ibid.
54. Ibid., 221.
55. Ibid.
56. Ibid., 221-222.
57. Eisenhower's statement is reprinted in Gardner, 1974:215-216.

58. See NSC 5612/1, September 5, 1956, *United States-Vietnam Relations 1945-1967*, X, 1083; NSC 5809, April 2, 1958, *United States-Vietnam Relations 1945-1967*, X, 1115; NSC 6012, July 25, 1960, *United States-Vietnam Relations 1945-1967*, X, 1281.
59. Donovan, 1974:196.
60. Schlesinger, 1965:537.
61. Hodgson, 1973:21.
62. Ibid.
63. Lukas, 1971:126.
64. CFR, 1965:14-15.
65. CFR, 1966:14-15, 44.
66. Halberstam, 1972:461.
67. *New York Times*, September 9, 1965:30.
68. Hoopes, 1969:207.
69. CFR, 1968:40.
70. Ibid., 40, 47, 48, 64.
71. Ibid., 48.
72. Ibid.; William P. Bundy to Laurence H. Shoup, September 17, 1975.
73. CFR, 1968:27.
74. Ibid., 26.
75. Clifford, 1969:609; Donovan, 1974:246; Gardner, 1974:20.
76. Donovan, 1974:246-247; Gardner, 1974:23.
77. Gardner, 1974:27.
78. Hoopes, 1969:207; Donovan, 1974:248; Hodgson, 1973:22.
79. The list of "wise men" was taken from Hoopes, 1969:215-215, and Gardner, 1974:29-30. The list of Council members and leaders was taken from CFR, 1967:72-84 and CFR, 1973:94.
80. Hoopes, 1969:215.
81. Ibid.
82. Ibid.
83. Donovan, 1974:249, 251; Hoopes, 1969:216-217.
84. Hoopes, 1969:215-216.
85. Ibid., 217; Gardner, 1974:30; *New York Times,* July 4, 1971: section I, 17.
86. Hoopes, 1969:217.
87. Ibid., 217, 224; Gardner, 1974:30.
88. Quoted in Gardner, 1974:30.
89. *New York Times*, April 1, 1968:1.
90. CFR, 1968:28.
91. For a full listing see Lukas, 1971:34.

92. Ibid.
93. Ibid.
94. Ibid.
95. Ibid.
96. Ibid.
97. Ibid.
98. Compiled from *The Social Register Locator* for various years, biographical sources such as *Who's Who* and *Current Biography*, as well as membership lists of clubs and the *Annual Reports* of the Council on Foreign Relations.

7
Toward the 1980s: The Council's Plans for a New World Order

We have shown in the previous case studies that the Council on Foreign Relations planned the post-World War II global order and tried to preserve it against challenges from the Third World and the Left. What of the future? The Council's 1974 Annual Report began with a description of a new CFR program which for the next several years "will be by far the largest operation at the Council and, because of its range and complexity, many other Council activities will be geared into it."[1] The 1980's Project has as its aim nothing less than the creation of a new global political and economic system to replace the existing one. The present, American-dominated, international capitalist system has been slowly disintegrating since the late 1960s under the impact of competition within the advanced capitalist world, the war in Vietnam, poverty and revolution in the Third World, inflation, monetary problems, the success of the oil cartels, and global power shifts. The timeliness of such a project is thus evident to Council leaders. As the Council's president, Bayless Manning, expressed it:

The last systematic, overall examinations of the international system—its structure, key relationships, rules, processes and institutions—took place during the Second World War and in the early years of the cold war. Since then there have been some adjustments, but no thoroughgoing attempts to re-examine the pattern as a whole. Much has happened since the late 1940's and early 1950's, and many new demands have been put on the international system: scientific and economic developments have eroded the traditional insulators of time and space and given rise to new interdependencies, population has soared, power has shifted, new states have proliferated, and the number and importance of non-state actors in international affairs have increased. The institutional components of the post-World War II era, such as GATT, the IMF, and NATO, increasingly seem out of gear with changed conditions. The time is ripe for an attempt to analyze the characteristics of the kind of international system that would be suited to deal with the conditions and problems of the upcoming decade. Systematic intellectual effort is required to identify the changes in policies, institutions, and attitudes that such an international system would imply and to suggest ways to bring about those changes. The Council's 1980's Project will undertake that effort.[2]

The 1980's Project is thus an attempt to duplicate the success the Council had during World War II when its War and Peace Studies Project played a key part in constructing a new world order. The comparison of the two programs is conscious on the part of the Council. President Manning stated that there is a "similarity in conception between the 1980's Project and the War and Peace Studies undertaken by the Council during the Second World War."[3] In the world of the 1970s, the capitalist system faces, as it did in the 1940s, a serious crisis and the Council, true to form, is responding to this situation. As a "systematic endeavor to develop guidelines for orienting and managing change in the international system during the course of the next decade" the 1980's Project is "concerned with positing goals and objectives for a changing international system and charting the behavior for attaining those goals."[4] The project plans to "deal with the major issues likely to characterize international relations ten to fifteen years from now."[5]

A March 1975 Council memorandum visualizes three stages in the life of the 1980's Project. First, looking at the totality of the global system, it will outline "the characteristics of a desirable international environment."[6] The idea is to ask "where would we like to be a decade from now?"[7] Secondly, the constraints preventing the achievement of these desired conditions will be analyzed.[8] The relationship between a desirable and a feasible global order will be dealt with in this stage. Thirdly, strategies will be developed and implemented to achieve Council goals. This final stage will involve achieving consensus about the new world order on a global scale. A Council memorandum stated that the 1980's Project must

> come to grips with strategies for *modifying the behavior of all the relevant actors in the international community* — individuals, governments, agencies within governments, elite groups, industrial firms, interest groups, mass societies, and other groups and organizations at the subnational and transnational levels.[9] (emphasis added)

Thus the ultimate goal of the Council is wide-ranging influence over the thought and action of people on a world scale. This extravagant ambition, along with the other goals of the 1980's Project, makes it the most important project which the Council has undertaken since the War and Peace Studies Project.

For the 1980's Project the Council has organized an operating structure having four main elements: a full-time staff, a core Coordinating Group, twelve working groups, and numerous domestic and foreign advisers, experts, and small ad hoc bodies.[10] The first two will be "the main intellectual driving force of the Project."[11] The real locus of power will be in the Coordinating Group, fourteen men who will meet frequently to guide the entire 1980's Project. They will

Toward the 1980s 257

approve policy targets and give advice on the feasibility of policy choices and methods of implementation. The Coordinating Group will also provide "the central integrating functions of the Project—resolving conflicts engendered when choices regarding goals in one area of behavior clash with goals and requisite behavior in other areas."[12] The group is composed of persons from a limited number of prestigious backgrounds—academic, business, government. They were chosen "for their capacities as policy 'conceptualizers' but also for their sense of the politics and processes of policymaking and their ability to think about the wide range of problems to be explored by the Project."[13] Almost all of them have earned Ph.D. degrees from Harvard, Princeton, or Columbia.

Three of the fourteen group members are corporate leaders—Council director W. Michael Blumenthal, chairman of Bendix Corporation, Stephen Stamas, vice-president of Exxon, and Council director Edwin K. Hamilton, president of Griffenhagen-Kroeger Inc. One member is from government, Bruce K. MacLaury, president of the Federal Reserve Bank, Minneapolis. Ten are university professors—Council director Marshall D. Shulman, former director of Columbia University's Russian Institute; economists Richard N. Cooper and Carlos Diaz-Alejandro of Yale; Harvard government professors Stanley H. Hoffman, Joseph S. Nye, and Samuel P. Huntington; international lawyer Richard A. Falk (Princeton); environmental studies professor Gordon J. MacDonald (Dartmouth); and Ali Mazrui and Alan S. Whiting, professors of political science at the University of Michigan.[14]

These fourteen men interlock with an impressive array of other organizations with an interest in foreign policy. Two—MacDonald and Whiting—are consultants to the Department of State, and MacDonald is a member of the Defense Department's defense science board. Nye is the chairman of the Committee for Economic Development's Research Advisory

Board and Cooper is a member of that body. Huntington is an editor of *Foreign Policy* magazine and Falk, Cooper, Nye, and Hoffman are on the editorial board of that magazine. Falk is the director of the North American section of the World Order Models Project, a group of scholars from around the world who have been studying world organization since 1967. Falk appears to be the sole representative of an approach to world order not beholden to the interests of the multinational corporations. A prominent critic of the United States government's war crimes in Vietnam, Falk favors what he calls "global populism," defined in terms of peace, economic equity, social and political dignity, and ecological balance.[15] He argues that such a world order cannot be brought into being by multinational corporations.[16]

Under the supervision of the staff and Coordinating Group, the twelve working groups, each having about twenty members, will focus on an equal number of broad policy issues. Economic questions dominate the list of issues to be studied, with security and international-organizational questions next in importance respectively. Six of the twelve working groups focus on aspects of the international economy and three of these appear to be particularly important:

North-south relations. This group is concerned with the economic aspects of relations between the developed, industrial states and developing nations, including the desire of raw material buyers for an assured, predictable supply and the demands on the part of the Third World for a larger share of global wealth and power.[17]

Macroeconomic policy and international monetary relations. This group focuses on relationships among the advanced industrial capitalist societies—North America, Western Europe, and Japan particularly. A crucial issue here is the choice between "retaining a high degree of national autonomy in economic decision-making and new forms of international policy coordination and integration."[18]

Industrial policy. This term is used in a broad sense, covering all kinds of economic activity, especially bringing together issues of trade policy and investment policy. This working group will also concern itself with both broad allocation of economic activities in the world and the interplay of national measures that respond to local needs but affect other countries. Thus the group will go

> to the heart of questions of the international order, including autonomy and interdependence. In another dimension, it provides a framework within which one can take account of a number of kinds of activities that are of major importance to the international division of labor and the shaping of the world economy but which might otherwise escape attention.[19]

The working group on institutional issues also appears to be central. Reform of international institutions is a recognized need and will be systematically examined, especially in the later stages of the project.[20]

The other three economic working groups will focus on principles of international trading arrangements, multinational enterprise and investment, and the global commons (airspace, oceans, outer space, Antarctica, and the North Polar icecap). The three security-oriented working groups are concerned with nuclear and other weapons of mass destruction, armed conflict, and transnational terrorism and subversion. The remaining two groups are on organization of United States foreign policymaking for the issues of the late 1980s and on human rights.[21]

In addition, the staff and outside experts will research topics which will, at least at first, be tied to no working groups. The topics in this category include the shape of the international system as a whole and the nature and configuration of power in that system. Another focus will be "collective identity," the trends, strengths, and direction of the loyalties that people have, particularly in the Third World. Food, raw materials, East-West trade, services in the international economy, environmental issues, developments in science and technology, and population growth round out the list of topics to be studied.[22]

The work of the 1980's Project will cost more than $1.33 million for three years. The Ford Foundation, Lilly Endowment, Mellon Foundation, and the Rockefeller Foundation had by the summer of 1975 already contributed over $1 million, the bulk of the resources needed to finance the project.[23]

While the most important, the Council's 1980's Project is not the only ruling-class attempt to do long-range planning to deal with the present capitalist world crisis. As previously mentioned, a separate body, called the Trilateral Commission, was established in 1973 on the initiative of Council chairman David Rockefeller. Rockefeller proposed setting up such a body in the spring of 1972 and provided the initial financial support until foundation funding could be obtained.[24] Initial meetings of Trilateral leaders, in July 1972 and March 1973, were held at Rockefeller's New York estate, Pocantico.[25] The commission brings together 180 leaders from the three main industrial capitalist regions: North America, Western Europe, and Japan. There are close ties between the Council and the commission. The majority of U.S. commissioners are CFR members and no less than eleven Council directors sit on the commission. Council director Zbigniew Brzezinski is the director of the commission; Council member Gerard C. Smith is North American chairman of the commission; and Council director George S. Franklin is North American secretary of the commission.[26] David Rockefeller continues to play a central role, serving on the executive committee and on a small, informal steering group which advises the officers of the commission.[27]

There are also numerous interlocks of personnel between the Trilateral Commission and the 1980's Project. The fourteen-man coordinating group for the 1980's Project has two Trilateral commissioners—Yale economist Richard N. Cooper and banker Bruce K. MacLaury. Another member of the Coordinating Group—Samuel P. Huntington of Harvard—helped write a book for the Trilateral Commission.[28] Several Trilateral commissioners sit on the Council's Committee on Studies, which was a prime mover in establishing the 1980's Project. These include Cooper, Brzezinski, and banker Robert V. Roosa, the chairman of the Committee on Studies.[29]

While a full-scale study of the power structures of Western Europe and Japan is not possible here, the Japanese and European members of the Trilateral Commission represent in their respective countries a sector of society identical with that which the Council represents in the United States. The case of Japan's Trilateral commissioners is the most obvious. Japan has long had the reputation for government by financial interest groups, the famous "Zaibatsu." The main such financial-industrial combines in contemporary Japan seem to be the Mitsubishi Group, the Sumitomo Group, the Mitsui Group, and the Fuyo Group, organized around the Fuji Bank. These Zaibatsu, in cooperation with several business federations like "Keidanren" (Federation of Economic Organizations), are said to rule Japan. This supposition fits very well with the Japanese personnel on the Trilateral Commission. Commission members include Toshio Doko, the president of Keidanren; Kogoro Uemura, honorary president of Keidanren; Toshio Nakamura, president of Mitsubishi Bank; Chujiro Fujino, chairman of Mitsubishi Corporation (who also sits on Chase Manhattan Bank's International Advisory Commission); Fumihiko Kono, counselor, Mitsubishi Heavy Industries; Shoyo Hotta, chairman of Sumitomo Bank; Norishige Hasegawa, president of Sumitomo Chemical Company; Kunihiko Sasaki, chairman of Fuji Bank (Fuyo group); and the president of SONY, the chairman of Nissan Motor, the chairman of Nippon Steel, the chairman of the Bank of Tokyo, and the president of Toyota Motor Company.

European commissioners include Giovanni Agnelli, president of FIAT (who also sits on Chase's International Advisory Commission); Alwin Münchmeyer, president of the German Banking Federation; John Loudon, chairman of Royal Dutch Shell Petroleum Company (also on Chase's International Advisory Commission); Edmond de Rothschild, president of the Compagnie Financière Holding; Hans-Gunther Sohl, president of the Federal Union of German Industry and president of the board of directors of August Thyssen Hütte A. G.; and A. F. Tuke, chairman of Barclays Bank International.[30] Thus Rockefeller's statement about wanting to bring the "best brains in the world" together to plan for a new world order is, to put it mildly, inaccurate.[31] Rather, these are mainly the most *affluent* brains from North America, Western Europe, and Japan, although there are some good academic minds on the commission, as well as some parliamentary and labor leaders. The commission represents an attempt by the leading sectors of the ruling classes of these three areas to reconcile their differences and create the conditions for a stable world capitalist economy.

What Kind of World Order?

As this is written in July 1976, the 1980's Project has been under way only three years and the Trilateral Commission only four. Their work is still developing. Despite the newness and ongoing nature of both efforts, enough material has been published or made available to discern the main trends and directions of the Council's planning efforts and thus gain an insight into what kind of future international system the Council wants.

For the past several years there has been, within the Council and among ruling-class leaders, a "great debate" over

Toward the 1980s 263

the future of American foreign policy. Two main conceptions have emerged. The first, the "power-realist" or balance-of-power approach, stresses national sovereignty and the traditional concerns of international relations—the balance of power and maintenance of stability and military strength. Secretary of State Kissinger and conservative nationalists generally have been leading exponents of this perspective. Kissinger's policy, central in his term of office, of manipulating the balance of power—especially the United States–Soviet–Chinese triangle—is a classic example of this approach. It attempts to combine the flexibility of a Bismarck within a Metternichian alliance framework, to have the best of both worlds.

The second perspective, liberal internationalism or "transnationalism," is now emerging as dominant within the CFR. It sees the era of the nation-state drawing to a close and transnational forces joining various regions of the world together in political and economic federation.[32] Arguing that the world is becoming increasingly economically and environmentally interdependent, it places primary emphasis on cooperative relations with Western Europe and Japan, as well as certain compromises with the Third World. Trilateral commissioners Zbigniew Brzezinski, George W. Ball, Edwin O. Reischauer, and, on a practical level, David Rockefeller are a few of the leading exponents of this perspective.

Brzezinski, Ball, and Reischauer have all criticized Kissinger's balance of power approach in recent articles or books.[33] Council director Brzezinski is representative of the approach of the Trilateral Commission, which he directs. Writing in *Foreign Policy* magazine, Brzezinski argues that Kissinger has neglected both the Third World and traditional allies in his efforts to achieve détente with the Soviets and Chinese and in relations with the Middle Eastern nations. Summarizing present world trends, Brzezinski states that a "profound transformation" of the present global order is now taking place and nation-states are losing their centrality, although for the present time their role remains crucial.[34] There is a basic crisis in the present international system because of the challenge of a stronger Western Europe and Japan, and because of an upheaval in economic relations between the rich advanced capitalist nations of the North and the poor Third World nations of the South. Because of these trends, Brzezinski concludes, the old political and economic system created by the United States during and after the Second World War is now "severely shaken."[35] The power realist approach is inadequate in a rapidly changing world; restructuring and rebuilding is now needed, including new institutions, which require "architecture" to shape the future, not the short-term tactical "acrobatics" which Kissinger is so good at.[36] This dispute over goals and tactics does not mean that the Brzezinski-Ball-Reischauer-Rockefeller view is not presently being heard by the government. On the contrary, Ball and Rockefeller are part of a foreign policy advisory group which has been meeting "occasionally" with Kissinger since September 1973 to advise him on such key questions as solving the Mideast stalemate.[37] It does mean that there is at present some divergence between this group and Kissinger over long-range issues.

The emerging Council perspective is thus one of transnationalism. This has been made even more evident in the first publication of the 1980's Project, *The Management of Interdependence; A Preliminary View,* by Miriam Camps. Camps, a senior research fellow at the Council, wrote the book after heading a CFR study group on the subject, which met for almost two years in 1971-1973. Many of the personnel of this study group are playing key roles in the 1980's Project: Camps and William Diebold, Jr. are project staff members, and Richard N. Cooper, Joseph S. Nye, and Stanley Hoffmann are members of the project's Coordinating Group.[38] The director of the 1980's Project, Professor

Richard H. Ullman of Princeton, wrote in the preface to Camps's book that the work "is the first in a series of Council publications addressed to the basic problems of the next decade," an "important first publishing step in, and a catalyst for, what promises to be a long and searching enquiry into the prospective international environment of the 1980's and the policy choices that will face the United States and other societies."[39]

Central to Camps's book is a vision of a world political economy where power to manage or "steer" the global order is shared by the United States, Western Europe, and Japan. In her conclusion, called "Collective Management," Camps argues that the international system requires leadership, steering, planning, "a capacity for anticipating problems, sounding early warnings, seeing interconnections between issue-areas, deciding which of a half-dozen possible agencies should act, pushing for needed new codes and other institutional reforms—in short, seeing to it that the system works."[40] Camps argues that no nation today can play the determining role that the United States has played in the past and that therefore collective management on the part of the advanced industrial capitalist powers is required. The "United States, Western Europe, and Japan will in effect share leadership."[41] These three regions, the "Trilateral World," make up the core of the highly industrialized, rich capitalist nations.

Camps outlines two different ways of providing the necessary international management of the world economy. Both are based on the assumption that the objective is a global system. The first she obviously considers the ideal one, with the second a more realistic fall-back position. The favored conception assumes that

> the rules, goals, and procedures that the advanced countries adopt to govern economic relationships with one another should be the norms of the global system. In other words, the arrangements among the advanced countries would be the central core of the

wider system; other countries would be expected in time to join the central core.[42]

The "advanced countries" are defined as the Trilateral World plus a few other industrialized capitalist nations.[43] The Soviet Union, Eastern Europe, and Third World countries would, in this perspective, eventually integrate with the Trilateral World to make up one world economy. Such a world order would be designed by and for the Trilateral World, although Camps adds that "the needs of other groups would not be ignored."[44] The obvious drawback to this pattern would be Third World resentment of "arrangements so plainly dominated by the advanced countries."[45]

This and other considerations suggest to Camps a second possibility:

> That the advanced countries, because of their high degree of economic interdependence and interaction, will want and will need to go further than other countries in coordinating policies and in adopting codes of conduct which apply within the group. But there would be no presumption that these codes and procedures would, over time, be the rules of the wider system, although they might in fact become so.[46]

Whichever option is eventually adopted, a global system is the goal, with far-reaching coordination of domestic and foreign policy among the advanced capitalist nations—collective management—and the "steering" of the structure by the Trilateral World—the United States, Western Europe, and Japan.[47] A free-trade perspective is also evident. This, Camps argues, would be "desirable on many grounds."[48]

The project's working group on macroeconomic policy and international monetary relations is also pointing to similar conclusions. The group stated in the summer of 1975 that existing trends are toward more and more economic integration among the Trilateral World and that this "severely impinges upon the effectiveness of national policies."[49] Domes-

Toward the 1980s 267

tic policies are now international in scope and this implies that the Trilateral World's governments *"ought* to coordinate their policies on an exclusive basis."[50] The working group plans to examine alternative new institutions and institutional rules "for coordinating policies among the advanced industrialized societies and for creating desirable ... centralized supranational institutional mechanisms."[51] If achieved, CFR planners hope that the economic unification of the advanced capitalist world would have the practical effect of creating a unit so large that it would exert a strong gravitational pull economically on the rest of the world, resulting in one world economy with the Trilateral World at the center.

The Trilateral Commission's analysis of the problem and proposed solutions are virtually identical to those put forth by the Council and the 1980's Project. The commission also recognizes that the existing global order is in crisis. Its executive committee adopted a resolution in December 1974 which stated: "The international system is undergoing a drastic transformation through a number of crises."[52] The commission also believes that fundamental to any solution is "collective management" of the world capitalist system by the United States, Western Europe, and Japan, with an assist from Canada. As the commission's second publication stated:

> The international system, which depended heavily upon U.S. leadership and sustenance, now requires a truly common management to which North America, the European Community and Japan must—in view of their large economic power—make a special contribution. For the United States, this means a sense of loss of power because decisions have to be shared more than in the past; for the European Community and Japan it means a sense of burden, because new responsibilities have to be assumed and, in some cases, paid for.[53]

Thus a "shift from a leadership system to one of genuine collective management" is required.[54] The consequences of a failure to act are seen as disastrous. A commission publication expressed it thus:

> The energy crisis has propelled the industrial nations into a situation to which other factors were also bringing them though more slowly: a situation in which they have to set the lines of basic policy together or succumb to chaotic national competition and a destruction of the fundamentals of a rational world order.[55]

A basic purpose of the work of the Trilateral Commission is thus also revealed—it is not only a policy planning body, but also an operating organization to bring about the practical policy unification of the Trilateral World. In a 1973 memorandum, Brzezinski states that the underlying purpose of the commission and its policy program is to

> cultivate among concerned Americans, Japanese, and Europeans the habit of *working together on a trilateral basis* in the formulation of joint policies on matters of common concern, to promote a *shared understanding* of the central issues involved in their relations among themselves and in their relations with other countries, to arrive at agreed and workable *trilateral policies* designed not only to enhance closer trilateral cooperation but also to progress *towards a more just global* community, and to inform the publics and governments concerned about pertinent conclusions and recommendations (sic).[56]

The overall goal of the commission is thus to minimize the friction and competition within the Trilateral World, unifying it as much as possible.

Leaders of the commission clearly want to subordinate territorial politics to their transnational economic goals, and many fear that governments have become "too democratic" and beholden to domestic constituencies whose interests conflict with the multinational corporate ideology which they most represent.[57] The commission published a study, *The Crisis of Democracy,* in October 1975, which concluded that authority has been delegitimized too much and that democratic demands on government are now too great, undermining the capacity of governments to deal with problems. In the words of the study, "the balance has tilted too far against governments in Western Europe and the United States."[58] These two regions must "restore a more equitable relationship between government authority and popular control, and Japan will probably face this necessity in the not-too-distant future."[59] There was some dissent within the commission concerning this authoritarian trend in the commission's thinking, and at least one commissioner argued that excess on the part of the governors might be a more appropriate focus than a presumed excess on the part of the governed.[60] Other Trilateral commissioners have, in the past, however, spoken out against egalitarianism generally. Harold Brown, president of California Institute of Technology, said in a June 1974 meeting of the commission that "unfortunately, in my view, there is an increasing tendency toward egalitarianism" in the United States.[61]

The 1980's Project is also concerned with the problem of "governability." It too desires to limit democracy and equality. The project wants to "depoliticize" key issues, take them out of the area of democratic political control. One of the project's working groups thus plans to concern itself with "various methods of defusing or depoliticizing issues such as inflation or unemployment, and also of depoliticizing intergovernmental relationships."[62]

Another of the central focuses of the Council-Trilateral Commission's planning for the future concerns the role of the Third World in the new international economy. Active Council member C. Fred Bergsten, a former National Security Council staff member under Kissinger and presently a senior fellow at the Brookings Institution, has taken the lead in defining the importance of and the "threat" from the Third World. Bergsten chaired a discussion group at the Council during 1972 and 1973 on "American Interests in the Third World," and continued as the discussion leader of a similar

Council group during 1974-1975.[63] Bergsten published his views in the summer of 1973, criticizing the Nixon administration's neglect of the Third World and its treatment of this region of the globe "solely as pawns on the chessboard of global power politics."[64] Bergsten argued that the Third World is currently very important to the United States, Europe, and Japan. The United States "is rapidly joining the rest of the industrialized countries in depending on the Third World for a critical share of its energy supplies and other natural resources."[65] Oil, copper, natural rubber, bauxite, timber, and other Third World raw materials were mentioned as vitally important to the Trilateral World. American investments in the Third World are of "strategic importance" for the United States balance of payments and important for corporate profit levels.[66] The real market value of American investments in the Third World is "at least" $46 billion.[67] The United States, Bergsten concluded, faces a serious threat from the Third World. Supplies could be withheld or the Trilateral World could be forced to compete for scarce resources, dividing the Trilateral World and driving up prices. The Third World, therefore, should be higher on the list of American foreign policy priorities.[68] Trilateral Commission director Brzezinski also said at the commission's spring 1975 meeting in Japan: "The main axis of conflict at most international conferences today is not between the Western world and the Communist world but between the advanced countries and the developing countries."[69] The Third World wants an equal distribution of gains from a world economic system, and its general strategy is to use its control over many raw materials to break the traditional patterns of world trade and thus create a new international economic order.[70]

Due to pressure from the Third World, magnified by the success of the Organization of Petroleum Exporting Nations (OPEC), the Council's world planners of the 1980's Project and Trilateral Commission are evidently now willing—for a price—to offer some minor concessions to the Third World. Thus Camps talks of the desirability of "some shift of real resources from the rich countries to the poor countries."[71] The way to do this, she adds, is to give trade advantages to the developing world and to accept some shifts in production from the Trilateral World to the Third World.[72]

The Trilateral Commission has a similar thrust, making the point that "an international economic system cannot successfully endure unless both rich and poor countries feel they have a stake in it."[73] The commission goes on to argue that both sides need each other:

> The developing countries need the aid, technology, know-how and markets of the Trilateral World. The Trilateral countries increasingly need the developing countries as sources of raw materials, as export markets, and ... as constructive partners in the creation of a workable world order.[74]

The United States, while the least dependent of the Trilateral World on its foreign economic relations, still finds itself relying on those relations in key ways. As commission leaders put it:

> All its [U.S.] major corporations are deeply committed to foreign investment and markets, its balance of payments heavily depends on their income, its people expect freedom to consume foreign goods, its industry needs foreign fuels and raw materials, and their relative cost and weight in the economy is bound to grow. The whole dynamic of business activity is moving toward greater, not less, international involvements.[75]

These facts give the Third World great potential power. As Brzezinski pointed out in spring 1975, the Third World has negative power, the ability to deny cooperation in maintaining world order, thereby encouraging violence and chaos.[76] Camps similarly fears any division between rich and poor nations "that would breed long-term trouble."[77] Further polarizations of rich-poor relationships are thus to be avoided.

272 Imperial Brain Trust

This threat from the Third World has led the Council and Trilateral Commission to stress heavily the themes of interdependence, mutuality of interests, and cooperation between the rich northern part of the world and the poorer southern section. Thus, the Commission's Executive Committee, in a statement on December 2, 1975, argued that "the reshaping of the world economy requires new forms of international cooperation for managing the world's resources for benefit of both the developed and developing countries."[78] Terms like "social contract," "world order bargain," "collective responsibilities," and "new accommodation," are now used with increasing regularity in the literature. For example, as part of a "world order bargain" the Trilateral Commission demands rules on access to raw material supplies. The Commission's third publication states:

> New rules and arrangements governing access to supplies should be part of a new system of relations between developed and developing countries ... developing countries as a group are as dependent on developed countries for supplies of food and manufactured goods as developed countries are dependent on them for supplies of energy and raw materials. The logic of interdependence suggests the need for agreed limits on the ability of producers to cut off the essential supplies of others for political or economic reasons.[79]

Thus the "world order bargain" would involve trading access to supplies for access to markets, technology, and capital.[80] Council planners favor a one-world economy, based on free trade, with all nations interdependent, including the Soviet Union and China as well as the Third World. Camps, for example, recognizes that the Third World nations have, "not, in fact, been full members of the global economic system that we have had, in theory, since 1945. And a central task of the next couple decades is to bring them into the global system and to make them fully functioning parts of the world economy."[81]

All of this makes evident that the Council's present plans for the Third World involve no real changes in the global distribution of wealth and power. The most that can possibly be expected by the Third World from Council blueprints is more access to the markets of the advanced countries, some shift in older industrial technology from the Trilateral World to the Third World, higher raw material prices, a somewhat greater voice in the management of some world economic institutions, and little else. Developing nations are still viewed primarily as sources of raw materials and export markets for the Trilateral World. An international division of labor would be maintained which would give the Third World little chance to develop the manufacturing which produces wealth. The overall aim of Council planning efforts for a new world economy is, thus, to preserve, as much as possible, the existing structure of Western power and predominance. Council plans include, as a prime goal, increasing integration of the world capitalist system, a structure which perpetuates underdevelopment in the Third World and, because of its individualistic and private profit orientation, cannot provide the ideological or organizational basis for mass development projects.[82]

There is a large body of evidence, conveniently ignored by Council theorists, that the actual result of multinational corporate capitalism in the Third World is poverty and repressive governments. That poverty is the main product of multinational corporate power has been convincingly argued by numerous scholars, including Richard Barnet and Ronald Müller, Andre Gunder Frank, Paul Baran, and Pierre Jalée.[83] Evidence of multinational corporations requiring and scheming, directly and indirectly, to achieve repressive, reactionary governments is also substantial. The influence of Anaconda, Kennecott, and International Telephone and Telegraph in Chile in 1970-1973, and of the United Fruit Company in Central America are but two examples. Instances of bribery and corruption of government officials are numerous. The actions of the CIA in various parts of the world have frequently directly served the interests of multinational corporations.[84] The success of China, formerly a very poor nation, in eliminating social evils and the extremes of wealth and poverty is instructive when compared to the present plight and suffering of most Third World peoples. The real problem, which Council leaders in general cannot recognize because of their class interests, is that it is capitalism itself and capitalist institutions like the IMF which perpetuate poverty and underdevelopment.[85]

Security concerns make up a final element in the Council's plans for a new world order. In her book, Camps sees the search for security in a new stage. Five major power blocs now exist: the United States, the Soviet Union, China, Western Europe, and Japan. Avoidance of a major war depends "on a combination of countervailing power and self-restraint."[86] The first of these, power itself, will be supplied by a commanding military posture on the part of the United States, joined with a strengthening of ties within the Trilateral World. The latter involves, in addition to the economic measures mentioned above, maintaining the major American alliances with Western Europe and Japan.[87]

"Self-restraint" involves convincing all five major power centers that "certain areas of the world should be, quite deliberately, removed from the area of major power competition."[88] Such a "spheres of restraint" policy would, in Camps's view, take Latin America, Black Africa, and Southeast Asia out of the area of big-power competition. The advantages of such an agreement among the major powers would be economic as well as political. The escalation of small wars could be prevented and multilateral economic relations encouraged instead of spheres of influence.[89] In this scheme détente is to be extended and Soviet and Chinese backing of liberation movements undermined.

Initial Success

Despite the newness of the Council-Trilateral Commission plans for a new world order, there is already evidence that its overall perspective is being implemented by government action. Press reports have described the commission as "highly influential."[90] Several Trilateral commissioners—William T. Coleman, Elliot L. Richardson, and William W. Scranton—have been chosen for high posts in the Ford administration. Representative commissioners, led by David Rockefeller, met in late 1974 with President Ford, Secretary Kissinger, and Interior Secretary Rogers Morton about energy policy, and in 1975 with the French prime minister and with the Japanese prime minister and foreign minister.[91] This supports Brzezinski's statement in early 1974 that he and his fellow commissioners were "confident that we have direct access to the governments of our countries ... we think we will have an audience."[92]

Council leaders and Trilateral commissioners have also been active during the 1976 election year. As this is written in July 1976, the presidential contest continues. But it can already be said that the biggest surprise of the year has been the emergence of James E. Carter, Jr., former governor of Georgia, as the Democratic nominee for President. Carter's rise was no surprise to the Trilateral Commission, however, since he has been a member since David Rockefeller and Zbigniew Brzezinski first chose the commissioners nearly four years ago. Senator Walter F. Mondale, Carter's choice for vice-president, is both a commission and a Council member. Carter's foreign policy advisers include Brzezinski, Cyrus R. Vance, and Paul C. Warnke, all Trilateral commissioners and directors of the Council; George W. Ball and Richard N. Gardner, both active in the commission and the Council; and CFR members Paul Nitze, Charles Yost, and Dean Rusk.[93] These advisers, especially the first five, are likely to fill key roles in a Carter administration.

Carter's ties with the Council and commission help explain his extensive support, good media coverage, and extraordinary success.[94] Several of his campaign speeches and statements indicate that he has been influenced by the emerging CFR perspective. In his primary campaign, for example, Carter argued that balance-of-power politics must give way to "world-order politics." He also stressed the need to "recement strained relationships with our allies."[95] Regardless of who wins the 1976 presidential election, however, those installed in key advisory positions in the new administration are likely to be associated with the CFR. The reader can compare top officials of the next administration with the Trilateral commissioners, Council leaders, and members listed in the appendixes at the end of the book to see the degree of overlap and thus the likelihood of their plans for a new world order being implemented in the next administration.

Further evidence of current Council-Trilateral Commission influence can be seen in regard to various policies now evolving. In June 1974 for example, the commission published "Energy: The Imperative for a Trilateral Approach." This pamphlet recommended "a master strategy" to "set broad lines of policy for the Trilateral countries on the energy problem. An energy agency, logically one associated with the O.E.C.D., is required for consultation and coordination of policies."[96] In November 1974 an International Energy Agency, associated with the OECD, was established by seventeen Trilateral nations meeting in Paris.[97] The commission's pressure was also instrumental in altering Secretary of State Kissinger's "hard line" against the oil-producing nations in late 1974, and in bringing the policies of France and the United States into accord at the summit meeting between President Ford and French President Giscard d'Estaing at Martinique in December 1974.[98] A Trilateral Commission publication later stated:

> A persistent theme in ... trilateral discussions was the essentially complementary—and not conflicting—character of the French and

American positions ... Commissioners had the opportunity to present these views in a meeting with President Ford and a dinner hosted by Secretary of State Kissinger, and we have reason to believe that our emphasis had some bearing on the outcome of the Ford-Giscard meeting in Martinique later that week.[99]

Another decision in which the influence of the commission is evident is the World Bank's decision in July 1975 to proceed with the new "Third Window" lending facility. This was recommended in a commission resolution in December 1974 and in a commission publication in early 1975.[100] The commission, in its magazine, *Trialogue,* claimed credit for initiating the idea.[101] In the area of international monetary reform, Trilateral commissioner and 1980's Project leader Richard N. Cooper stated that much progress has been made, "generally along the lines recommended in our report," since the commission's 1973 report on the subject.[102]

The Commission's *Crisis of Democracy* report has also had an impact. One of its authors, Samuel P. Huntington, also a member of the 1980's Project's Coordinating Group, recently argued that the report has been important, "particularly in lowering public expectations of what governments can achieve."[103] Huntington cites as examples the administrations of governors Brown of California and Dukakis of Massachusetts and Carter's success on the national level.[104]

Finally, and in more general terms, the November 1975 summit meeting held at Rambouillet, France, brought together the leaders of six top Trilateral nations—the United States, West Germany, Japan, France, Great Britain, and Italy—to discuss economic cooperation. The Trilateral Commission saw this as "an official endorsement of the trilateral approach."[105] The commission welcomed the progress made at the meeting "toward closer coordination of domestic economic policies among the trilateral governments, and in particular the pledge by them to refrain from restrictive actions affecting international trade."[106] The commission's hope for future meetings has been fulfilled by the seven-nation

(Canada has been added) economic summit held, appropriately enough, at a Rockefeller resort in Puerto Rico in the summer of 1976.

In terms of future policies, it is clear that Council theorists intend to maintain economic and, insofar as possible, political control over as much of the world as possible. Apparent "concessions," such as adopting a "spheres of restraint" policy in areas like Southeast Asia, where American imperial control is waning, or economic measures, such as agreeing to already inevitable raw materials price rises, are both more to maintain the old system of Western power than to create a new system based on justice. Assuming that consensus on Council goals can be developed within the Trilateral World, the real question then becomes: Can the Council's plans for a new world order be successfully reconciled with the Third World's real needs and conception of a just world order?

Concluding Reflections

This study has revealed the roots of United States imperialism in the economic, political, and strategic needs of the dominant sector of the American ruling class, led by the Council on Foreign Relations. Their will to power, a drive for world hegemony, has made the United States the largest imperial power in human history, deploying forces on every continent and controlling the economics and politics of much of the world. The basic reason for these policies has been, as we have shown in our case studies, the need of American capitalism for a world order open and receptive to its expansion. In contrast to the die-hard ultra-right perspective of laissez-faire and nationalistic competition, there is a measure of realism on the part of the Council in accepting irreversible changes, rejecting the extreme anti-communist "roll-back" position, and showing a willingness for détente. But there is an equally firm determination to maintain a world in which United States capitalism will feel at home. War in Indochina, the fantastic waste of vast military spending, the encouragement of assassinations of foreign leaders, support of reactionary regimes the world over, bribes and corruption, as well as the domestic repression necessary to maintain imperialism abroad—political trials of dissenters, FBI-CIA harassment of radicals, and wiretaps—are all the result of and testimony to the destructive nature of imperialism.

We have shown that the Council is a central link binding American foreign policy formulation to the corporate upper class and, in particular, to the leading sector of that class located in the New York financial community. The Council on Foreign Relations community has consistently provided a substantial proportion of the policymakers who have made, and continue to make, United States foreign policy. The organization itself has also taken a leading role in formulating general directions and foreign policy options. The Council, through its membership and on occasion through more formal ties, is also pivotally connected to organizations involved in molding American public opinion on foreign policy issues. Thus what emerges from our study is a model of a ruling capitalist class, dominating, through direct and indirect means, foreign policy formation.

In the Council on Foreign Relations the leading sector of the upper class has a very useful instrument. There it can get together, and bring in others of its choice recruited from academia and government service, to discuss just what sort of foreign policy it judges to be reasonable. There corporate leaders can set the agenda of issues to be discussed and the terms of debate. Through their media connections and in other ruling class-sponsored organizations they can widen the debate. When Council leaders take up government office, they have the opportunity to implement the ideas of the capitalist class, while keeping in touch with their peers currently not in government office. If it does happen that a policy alternative emerges from some other source that deviates too radically from their assumptions, the weight of ruling-class opinion can be brought to bear to label it foolish and unrealistic, unworthy of serious consideration. It is these men who deem themselves competent to judge what is the "national interest" in foreign relations. If, as invariably happens, their idea of the national interest corresponds with what serves their own interests as a class, then to such men this state of affairs is only natural, and the way things should be.

The Council's War and Peace Studies Project established the framework for a stable capitalist world under United States leadership following World War II. This framework lasted almost a quarter of a century, although the world's self-appointed policeman was unable to enforce complete stability on a troubled world. By the 1970s the postwar system was obviously inadequate, and the opinion leaders of the United States ruling class are, with the 1980's Project and the Trilateral Commission, planning a new global structure, engineering a new consensus which might ensure another quarter century of relative stability, enhancing cooperation among the advanced capitalist powers, and attempting to hold off revolutionary change for yet another generation.

Suggested Readings

To follow the development of the Council's present planning and consensus-building efforts, one should see the publications of the Trilateral Commission and the Council and follow the debates in *Foreign Affairs* and *Foreign Policy* magazines. Among recent books of special significance for revealing the perspectives developing are Camps (1974), Brown (1974), Chace (1973), Reischauer (1973), Diebold (1972), Cooper (1973), and Crozier, Huntington and Watanuki (1975).

For a good example of writing with a different perspective, linking the interests of the United States working class with the working class of other countries, see the pamphlet by Zimmerman (1972). Discussion of how a socialist foreign policy for a developed country would work can be found in Mandel (1968):605ff., and in Barratt-Brown (1972): 79ff. Lerner (1973) makes the general case for socialism in the United States in clear terms. But the continuing debate on strategy and tactics can only be followed in the various periodical and pamphlet publications of a widely fragmented Left.

Notes

1. CFR, 1974:4.
2. Ibid., 1-2.
3. Ibid., 2.
4. CFR, 1975a:1.
5. CFR, 1975c:37.
6. Ibid., 2.
7. CFR, 1974:3.
8. CFR, 1975a:2.
9. Ibid., 3.
10. Ibid., 6-8; CFR, 1974:3.
11. CFR, 1974:3.
12. CFR, 1975a:7.
13. Ibid.
14. CFR, 1975c:38.
15. Falk, 1975:1017.
16. Ibid., 1004-1008.
17. CFR, 1975b:3b, 15.
18. Ibid., 20.
19. Ibid., 26-27.
20. Ibid., 32.
21. Ibid., 2.
22. Ibid., 34-39.
23. Ibid., 43; CFR, 1975a:10.
24. Trilateral Commission, 1973a:Annex 2:1.
25. Ibid.
26. Trilateral Commission, 1974a:43. There also are numerous inter-

282 *Imperial Brain Trust*

   locks of personnel between the Bilderberg group and the Trilateral commissioners.
27. Trilateral Commission, 1973a:7. The other U.S. members of the steering group are Brzezinski, Smith, and Professor Edwin O. Reischauer of Harvard.
28. Crozier, Huntington, and Watanuki, 1975.
29. CFR, 1974:1, 95; Trilateral Commission, 1974a:43-44.
30. List of Trilateral Commission members taken from Trilateral Commission, 1974a:45-48.
31. Trilateral Commision, 1973d:2.
32. Chace, 1973:24-26. Chace is managing editor of *Foreign Affairs*.
33. Brzezinski, 1974; Reischauer, 1973; Ball, 1976. Reischauer is on the executive committee of the Trilateral Commission.
34. Brzezinski, 1974:53.
35. Ibid., 54.
36. Ibid., 54-55.
37. *New York Times*, April 2, 1975:3.
38. Camps, 1974:104; CFR, 1974:4; CFR, 1975c:38.
39. Camps, 1974:3.
40. Ibid., 97.
41. Ibid.
42. Ibid., 45.
43. Ibid., 43, footnote 3.
44. Ibid., 45-46.
45. Ibid., 46.
46. Ibid.,45
47. Ibid., 54.
48. Ibid., 48.
49. CFR, 1975d:4.
50. Ibid.
51. Ibid., 9.
52. Trilateral Commission, 1974d:3.
53. Trilateral Commission, 1973b:14.
54. Ibid.
55. Trilateral Commission, 1974b:30.
56. Trilateral Commission, 1973c:1.
57. Falk, 1975:1004-1006.
58. Crozier, Huntington, and Watanuki, 1975:173.
59. Ibid., 174.
60. Trilateral Commission, 1975a:10.
61. Trilateral Commission, 1974e:17.

62. CFR 1975d:12.
63. CFR, 1974:52; CFR, 1975c:49.
64. Bergsten, 1973:104-105.
65. Ibid., 107.
66. Ibid., 112.
67. Ibid.
68. Ibid., 108-109, 124.
69. *Newsweek*, June 16, 1975:37. See also Trilateral Commission, 1975a:12.
70. *New York Times*, February 5, 1975:8.
71. Camps, 1974:52.
72. Ibid., 53.
73. Trilateral Commission, 1974c:11.
74. Ibid.
75. Trilateral Commission, 1973b:14.
76. *Newsweek*, June 16, 1975:37; Trilateral Commission, 1975a:12.
77. Camps, 1974:58.
78. Trilateral Commission, 1975d:3.
79. Trilateral Commission, 1974c:22.
80. Ibid., 23.
81. Camps, 1974:77.
82. See Jalée, 1968.
83. See Barnet and Müller, 1974; Baran, 1957; Frank, 1967; and Jalée, 1968.
84. See Agee, 1975; Wise and Ross, 1964; Marchetti and Marks, 1974.
85. See Payer, 1974.
86. Camps, 1974:21.
87. Ibid., 21-22.
88. Ibid., 32.
89. Ibid., 33.
90. *New York Times*, January 5, 1975, section 3:63.
91. The Trilateral Commission, 1974d.1, 10, the Trilateral Commission, 1975a:1; *New York Times*, December 12, 1974:82.
92. Darby, 1974:79.
93. *Newsweek*, May 10, 1976:38; *Time*, March 8, 1976:19; *New Republic*, April 12, 1975:19.
94. At least two sources of support for Carter's candidacy appear to be linked with this membership in the commission. *Time* magazine has given Carter very favorable coverage and *Time*'s editor-in-chief is Hedley Donovan, a director of the CFR and member of the commission. The United Auto Workers gave Carter support at key points in the primary campaign, especially in Iowa, Florida,

and Michigan. UAW President Leonard Woodcock, a Carter supporter, is a member of both the Council and commission.
95. Taken from Carter campaign literature and *Newsweek*, March 29, 1976:17.
96. Trilateral Commission, 1974b:8. The OCED is the Organization for Economic Cooperation and Development, based in Paris.
97. *New York Times*, February 6, 1975:5.
98. Barraclough, 1975:26-27.
99. Trilateral Commission, 1974d:10.
100. Trilateral Commission, 1975b:6; Trilateral Commission, 1975c; *New York Times*, December 27, 1974:3.
101. Trilateral Commission, 1975b:6.
102. Trilateral Commission, 1976a:2.
103. Ibid., 10.
104. Ibid., 10-11.
105. Ibid., 1.
106. Trilateral Commission, 1975d:3.

Postscript

This book, based on extensive research in the National Archives, Library of Congress, private papers in university and other manuscript collections, published articles, books, and interviews, was completed early in December 1975. Shortly before completion of the manuscript, we learned that the Council's own archives, heretofore entirely closed to those outside the organization, would be opened up to a limited degree. Accordingly, one of the authors traveled to New York in January 1976 to review the newly available resource material for possible inclusion in this book. The results were disappointing. All records less than twenty-five years old were entirely closed. What the Council defines as "substantive" records were open if they were more than twenty-five years old. "Substantive" records included only three categories: records of groups, records of meetings, and records of conferences. All records of the meetings of the board of directors, the meetings of all Council committees (Executive, Studies, Membership, Finance and Budget, etc.), the records of the editor of *Foreign Affairs,* are entirely closed.

In addition, a release had to be signed, agreeing not to "directly or indirectly attribute to any living person any assertion of fact or opinion" based on the Council's records without first obtaining written permission from that person. Due to these restrictions, we have not made reference to records held by the Council and only available there. Our prior research enabled us to construct independently a picture of the organization and its activities which is only confirmed by additional details from the records newly made available by the Council.

July 1976

Appendices

Appendix 1
Key Leaders of the Council, 1921-1973

	Council office	Dates director	Occupation	New York Social Register	Century Assoc.	Wealth level
Frank Altschul	Secretary-Vice-president	1934-1972	Banker	Yes	Yes	Contributed $200,000 to CFR
Hamilton Fish Armstrong	Editor—*Foreign Affairs*	1928-1972	Editor	Yes	Yes	$300,000 at death
Elliot V. Bell	Treasurer	1953-1966	Editor, corp. director	No	Yes	Unknown
Isaiah Bowman	Vice-president	1921-1950	College pres.	No	Yes	Over $50,000 at death
Archibald Cary Coolidge	Editor-*Foreign Affairs*	1921-1928	College prof.	No	Yes	Unknown
Paul D. Cravath	Vice-president	1921-1940	Wall St. lawyer	Yes	Yes	Over $125,000 in tax in 1925
John W. Davis	President	1921-1955	Wall St. lawyer	Yes	Yes	Over $1.8 million at death
Norman H. Davis	President	1921-1944	Banker, speculator	Yes	Yes	Over $650,000 at death
Arthur H. Dean	Committee chairman	1955-1972	Wall St. lawyer	Yes	Yes	Unknown
Hedley Donovan	Committee chairman	1969-	Editor	No	Yes	Unknown
Allen W. Dulles	President	1927-1969	Wall St. lawyer	Yes	Yes	Over $350,000 at death
George S. Franklin, Jr.	Executive director	1972-	Executive dir.	Yes	Yes	Unknown
Edwin F. Gay	Vice-president	1921-1945	Scholar-educator	No	Yes	Had $12,000 at death
Gabriel Hauge	Treasurer	1964-	Banker	No	Yes	Unknown
Clarence E. Hunter	Treasurer	1942-1953	Banker	No	No	Unknown
Devereux C. Josephs	Vice-president	1951-1958	Corporate exec., banker	Yes	Yes	Unknown

Grayson L. Kirk	Vice-chairman of board	1950–1973	College pres.	Yes	Unknown
Russell C. Leffingwell	Chairman of the board	1927–1960	Banker	Yes	Over $6 million at death
Walter H. Mallory	Executive director	1945–1968	Executive dir.	Yes	Unknown
Bayless Manning	President	1971–	Scholar-educator	No	Unknown
George O. May	Committee chairman	1927–1953	Corporate dir.	Yes	Unknown
John J. McCloy	Chairman of the board	1953–1972	Lawyer, banker	Yes	Unknown
Alfred C. Neal	Committee chairman	1967–	Economist, banker	No	Unknown
Frank L. Polk	Vice-president	1921–1943	Wall St. lawyer	Yes	Over $140,000 at death
David Rockefeller	Chairman of the board	1949–	Banker	Yes	Est. at $100–200 million
Elihu Root	Honorary president		Wall St. lawyer	Yes	Unknown
Whitney H. Shepardson	Treasurer	1921–1966	Lawyer, corp. executive	Yes	Over $225,000 at death
George W. Wickersham	President	1921–1936	Wall St. lawyer	Yes	Unknown
Carroll L. Wilson	Committee chairman	1964–	Engineering exec.	No	Unknown
Henry M. Wriston	President	1943–1967	College pres.	No	Son worth over $2 million

*This table has been compiled from the following sources: Shoup, 1974:25-37; Social Register Association, 1939:197; Social Register Association, 1940:23, 177, 198, 235, 466, 530, 624, 711; Social Register Association, 1974:19, 282, 391, 593, 619, 694, 959; Court records located at Alexandria, Virginia; Baltimore, Maryland; Washington, D.C.; Mineola, New York; New York, New York; and Los Angeles, California; CFR, 1975c; and *Who's Who in America*

Appendix 2

Trilateral Commission Membership
(as of August 15, 1975)

Gerard C. Smith, North American chairman
Max Kohnstamm, European chairman
Takeshi Watanabe, Japanese chairman
François Duchêne, European deputy chairman
Zbigniew Brzezinski, Director
George S. Franklin, North American secretary
Christopher J. Makins, Deputy director
Tadashi Yamamoto, Japanese secretary

North American Members

*I. W. Abel, *President, United Steelworkers of America*
David M. Abshire, *Chairman, Georgetown University Center for Strategic and International Studies*
Graham Allison, *Professor of Politics, Harvard University*
Doris Anderson, *Editor,* Chatelaine *Magazine*
John B. Anderson, *House of Representatives*
Ernest C. Arbuckle, *Chairman, Wells Fargo Bank*
J. Paul Austin, *Chairman, The Coca-Cola Company*
George W. Ball, *Senior Partner, Lehman Brothers*
Russell Bell, *Research Director, Canadian Labour Congress*
Lucy Wilson Benson, *Former President, League of Women Voters of the United States*
W. Michael Blumenthal, *Chairman, Bendix Corporation*
*Robert W. Bonner, Q.C., *Bonner and Foulks, Vancouver*
Robert R. Bowie, *Clarence Dillon Professor of International Affairs, Harvard University*
John Brademas, *House of Representatives*
*Harold Brown, *President, California Institute of Technology*
James E. Carter, Jr., *Former Governor of Georgia*

* Executive Committee
† Currently in Government Service

Appendix 2

Lawton Chiles, *United States Senate*
Warren Christopher, *Partner, O'Melveny and Myers*
†William T. Coleman, Jr., *Secretary, Department of Transportation*
Barber B. Conable, Jr., *House of Representatives*
Richard N. Cooper, *Frank Altschul Professor of International Economics, Yale University*
John C. Culver, *United States Senate*
Gerald L. Curtis, *Director, East Asian Institute, Columbia University*
Lloyd N. Cutler, *Partner, Wilmer, Cutler and Pickering*
Archibald K. Davis, *Chairman, Wachovia Bank and Trust Company*
Emmett Dedmon, *Vice-President and Editorial Director, Field Enterprises, Inc.*
Louis A. Desrochers, *Partner, McCuaig and Desrochers*
Peter Dobell, *Director, Parliamentary Center for Foreign Affairs and Foreign Trade*
Hedley Donovan, *Editor-in-Chief, Time, Inc.*
Daniel J. Evans, *Governor of Washington*
Gordon Fairweather, *Member of Parliament*
Donald M. Fraser, *House of Representatives*
Richard N. Gardner, *Henry L. Moses Professor of Law and International Organization, Columbia University*
*Patrick E. Haggerty, *Chairman, Texas Instruments*
William A. Hewitt, *Chairman, Deere and Company*
Alan Hockin, *Executive Vice-President, Toronto-Dominion Bank*
Richard Holbrooke, *Managing Editor,* Foreign Policy
Thomas L. Hughes, *President, Carnegie Endowment for International Peace*
J. K. Jamieson, *Chairman, Exxon Corporation*
Lane Kirkland, *Secretary-Treasurer, AFL-CIO*
Sol M. Linowitz, *Senior Partner, Coudert Brothers*
Bruce K. MacLaury, *President, Federal Reserve Bank of Minneapolis*
Claude Masson, *Professor of Economics, Laval University*

Paul W. McCracken, *Edmund Ezra Day Professor of Business Administration, University of Michigan*
Walter F. Mondale, *United States Senate*
Lee L. Morgan, *President, Caterpillar Tractor Company*
Kenneth D. Naden, *President, National Council of Farmer Cooperatives*
Henry D. Owen, *Director, Foreign Policy Studies Program, The Brookings Institution*
David Packard, *Chairman, Hewlett-Packard Company*
*Jean-Luc Pepin, P.C., *President, Interimco, Ltd.*
John H. Perkins, *President, Continental Illinois National Bank and Trust Company*
Peter G. Peterson, *Chairman, Lehman Brothers*
*Edwin O. Reischauer, *University Professor, Harvard University; former U.S. Ambassador to Japan*
†Elliot L. Richardson, *United States Ambassador to the United Kingdom*
*David Rockefeller, *Chairman, Chase Manhattan Bank*
Robert V. Roosa, *Partner, Brown Brothers Harriman and Company*
*William M. Roth, *Roth Properties*
William V. Roth, Jr., *United States Senate*
Carl T. Rowan, *Columnist*
*William W. Scranton, *Former Governor of Pennsylvania*
*Gerard C. Smith, *Counsel, Wilmer, Cutler and Pickering*
Anthony Solomon, *Consultant*
Robert Taft, Jr., *United States Senate*
Arthur R. Taylor, *President, Columbia Broadcasting System, Inc.*
Cyrus R. Vance, *Partner, Simpson, Thacher and Bartlett*
*Paul C. Warnke, *Partner, Clifford, Warnke, Glass, McIlwain and Finney*
Marina von N. Whitman, *Distinguished Public Service Professor of Economics, University of Pittsburgh*
Carroll L. Wilson, *Professor of Management, Alfred P. Sloan School of Management, MIT*
Arthur M. Wood, *Chairman, Sears, Roebuck and Company*
Leonard Woodcock, *President, United Automobile Workers*

Appendix 2

European Members

*Giovanni Agnelli, *President, FIAT, Ltd.*
Raymond Barre, *Former Vice-President of the Commission of the European Community*
Piero Bassetti, *President of the Regional Government of Lombardy*
*Georges Berthoin, *Former Chief Representative of the Commission of the European Community to the U.K.*
*Kurt Birrenbach, *Member of the Bundestag; President, Thyssen Vermögensverwaltung*
Franco Bobba, *Company Director, Turin*
Frederick Boland, *Chancellor, Dublin University; former President of the United Nations General Assembly*
René Bonety, *Représentant de la CFDT*
Jean-Claude Casanova, *Director of Studies, Fondation Nationale des Sciences Politiques, Paris*
Umberto Colombo, *Director of the Committee for Scientific Policy, OECD*
Guido Colonna di Paliano, *President, La Rinascente; former member of the Commission of the European Community*
*Francesco Compagna, *Undersecretary of State, Ministry of the Mezzogiorno*
The Earl of Cromer, *Former British Ambassador to the United States; Partner, Baring Brothers and Company, Ltd.*
Michel Debatisse, *Président de la F.N.S.E.A.*
*Paul Delouvrier, *Chairman, French Electricity Board*
Barry Desmond, *Member of the Lower House of the Irish Republic*
Fritz Dietz, *President, German Association for Wholesale and Foreign Trade*
Werner Dollinger, *Member of the Bundestag*
*Herbert Ehrenberg, *Member of the Bundestag*
Pierre Esteva, *Directeur Général de l'U.A.P.*
*Marc Eyskens, *Commisary General of the Catholic University of Louvain*
M. H. Fisher, *Editor,* Financial Times

Appendix 2   295

Francesco Forte, *Professor of Financial Sciences, University of Turin*
Jacques de Fouchier, *Président, Banque de Paris et des Pays-Bas*
Michel Gaudet, *Président de la Fédération Francaise des Assurances*
Sir Reay Geddes, *Chairman, Dunlop Holdings, Ltd.*
Giuseppe Glisenti, *Director of General Affairs, La Rinascente*
Lord Harlech, *Former British Ambassador to the United States; Chairman, Harlech Television*
Karl Hauenschild, *President, German Chemical-Paper-Ceramics Workers' Union*
Jozef P. Houthuys, *President, Belgian Confederation of Christian Trade Unions*
Daniel E. Janssen, *Deputy Director General, Belgian Chemical Union, Ltd.*
Pierre Jouven, *Président de Pechiney Ugine Kuhlmann*
Karl Kaiser, *Director of the Research Institute of the German Society for Foreign Policy*
Michael Killeen, *Managing Director, Industrial Development Authority, Irish Republic*
André Kloos, *Chairman of the Socialist radio and television network "V.A.R.A."; former chairman of the Dutch Trade Union Federation*
*Max Kohnstamm, *President, European Community Institute for University Studies*
Baron Léon Lambert, *President, Banque Lambert, Brussels*
Count Otto Lambsdorff, *Member of the Bundestag*
Arrigo Levi, *Director, La Stampa, Turin*
Eugen Loderer, *President, German Metal Workers' Union*
†John Loudon, *Chairman, Royal Dutch Petroleum Company*
Evan Luard, *Member of Parliament, U.K.*
Robert Marjolin, *Former Vice-President of the Commission of the European Community*
Roger Martin, *Président de la Cie Saint-Gobain-Pont-à-Mousson*
Reginald Maudling, *Member of Parliament; former Cabinet Minister, U.K.*

F. S. McFadzean, *Managing Director, Royal Dutch Shell Group*
Cesare Merlini, *Director, Italian Institute for International Affairs*
Alwin Münchmeyer, *President, German Banking Federation*
†Ivar Norgaard, *Minister of Foreign Economic Affairs and Nordic Affairs, Denmark*
Michael O'Kennedy, *Shadow Minister of Foreign Affairs, Irish Republic; former Cabinet Minister*
Bernard Pagezy, *Président Directeur Général de la Paternelle-Vie*
Pierre Pescatore, *Luxembourg; Member of the European Court of Justice*
Sir John Pilcher, *Former British Ambassador to Japan*
Jean Rey, *Former President of the Commission of the European Community*
Julian Ridsdale, *Member of Parliament, U.K.; Chairman of the Anglo-Japanese Parliament Group*
Sir Frank K. Roberts, *Advisory Director of Unilever, Ltd.; Adviser on International Affairs to Lloyds of London*
*Mary T. W. Robinson, *Member of the Senate of the Irish Republic*
Sir Eric Roll, *Executive Director, S. G. Warburg and Company*
Edmond de Rothschild, *Président de la Compagnie Financière Holding*
John Christian Sannes, *Director, Norwegian Institute of International Affairs*
Gerhard Schröder, *Member of the Bundestag; former Foreign Minister of the Federal Republic of Germany*
Roger Seydoux, *Ambassador of France*
Andrew Shonfield, *Director, The Royal Institute of International Affairs*
Hans-Günther Sohl, *President, Federal Union of German Industry; President of the Board of Directors of August Thyssen Hütte A.G.*
Theo Sommer, *Editor-in-Chief,* Die Zeit

Appendix 2   297

Myles Staunton, *Member of the Lower House of the Irish Republic*
Thorvald Stoltenberg, *International Affairs Secretary, Norwegian Trade Union Council*
G. R. Storry, *St. Antony's College, Oxford (Far East Centre)*
J. A. Swire, *Chairman, John Swire and Sons, Ltd.*
*Otto Grieg Tidemand, *Shipowner; former Norwegian Minister of Defense and Minister of Economic Affairs*
A. F. Tuke, *Chairman, Barclays Bank International*
Heinz-Oskar Vetter, *Chairman, German Federation of Trade Unions*
Luc Wauters, *President, Kredietbank, Brussels*
Otto Wolff von Amerongen, *President, Otto Wolff A.G.; President, German Chamber of Commerce*
*Sir Kenneth Younger, *Former Director of the Royal Institute of International Affairs; former Minister of State for Foreign Affairs, U.K.*
*Sir Philip de Zulueta, *Chief Executive, Antony Gibbs Holdings, Ltd.; former Chief Assistant to the British Prime Minister*

Japanese Members

Isao Amagi, *Director, Japan Scholarship Foundation; former Vice-Minister of Education*
Yoshiya Ariyoshi, *Chairman, Nippon Yusen Kaisha*
Yoshishige Ashihara, *Chairman, Kansai Electric Power Company, Inc.*
Toshio Doko, *President, Japan Federation of Economic Organizations (Keidanren)*
Jun Eto, *Professor, Tokyo Institute of Technology*
Shinkichi Eto, *Professor of International Relations, Tokyo University*
*Chujiro Fujino, *Chairman, Mitsubishi Corporation*
Shintaro Fukushima, *President, Kyodo News Service*

Noboru Gotoh, *President, TOKYU Corporation*
Toru Hagiwara, *Advisor to the Minister of Foreign Affairs; former Ambassador to France*
Sumio Hara, *Chairman, Bank of Tokyo, Ltd.*
*Yukitaka Haraguchi, *Chairman, All Japan Federation of Metal and Mining Industries Labor Unions*
Norishige Hasegawa, *President, Sumitomo Chemical Company, Ltd.*
*Yoshio Hayashi, *Member of the Diet*
Teru Hidaka, *Chairman, Yamaichi Securities Company, Ltd.*
*Kazushige Hirasawa, *Radio-TV news commentator, Japan Broadcasting Inc.*
Hideo Hori, *President, Employment Promotion Project Corporation*
Shozo Hotta, *Chairman, Sumitomo Bank, Ltd.*
Shinichi Ichimura, *Professor of Economics, Kyoto University*
Hiroki Imazato, *President, Nippon Seiko K.K.*
Yoshihiro Inayama, *Chairman, Nippon Steel Corporation*
Kaoru Inoue, *Chairman, Dai-Ichi Kangyo Bank, Ltd.*
Rokuro Ishikawa, *Executive Vice-President, Kajima Corporation*
Tadao Ishikawa, *Professor, Department of Political Science, Keio University*
Yoshizane Iwasa, *Chairman of the Advisory Committee, Fuji Bank, Ltd.*
Motoo Kaji, *Professor of Economics, Tokyo University*
Fuji Kamiya, *Professor, Keio University*
*Yusuke Kashiwagi, *Deputy President, Bank of Tokyo, Ltd.; former Special Advisor to the Minister of Finance*
Ryoichi Kawai, *President, Komatsu Seisakusho, Ltd.*
Katsuji Kawamata, *Chairman, Nissan Motor Company, Ltd.*
Kazutaka Kikawada, *Chairman, Tokyo Electric Power Company, Inc.*
Kiichiro Kitaura, *President, Nomura Securities Company, Ltd.*
Koji Kobayashi, *President, Nippon Electric Company, Ltd.*
Kenichiro Komai, *Chairman, Hitachi, Ltd.*

Fumihiko Kono, *Counselor, Mitsubishi Heavy Industries, Ltd.*
Masataka Kosaka, *Professor, Faculty of Law, Kyoto University*
Fumihiko Maki, *Principal Partner, Maki and Associates, Design, Planning and Development*
Shigeharu Matsumoto, *Chairman, International House of Japan, Inc.*
Masaharu Matsushita, *President, Matsushita Electric Company, Ltd.*
†Kiichi Miyazawa, *Minister of Foreign Affairs*
Akio Morita, *President, SONY Corporation*
Takashi Mukaibo, *Professor, Faculty of Engineering, Tokyo University*
*Kinhide Mushakoji, *Director, Institute of International Relations, Sophia University*
Yonosuke Nagai, *Professor of Political Science, Tokyo Institute of Technology*
Shigeo Nagano, *President, Japan Chamber of Commerce and Industry*
Eiichi Nagasue, *Member of the Diet*
Toshio Nakamura, *President, Mitsubishi Bank, Ltd.*
Ichiro Nakayama, *President Janpa Institute of Labor*
Sohei Nakayama, *President, Overseas Technical Cooperation Agency*
Yoshihisa Ohjimi, *Adviser, Arabian Oil Company, Ltd.; former Administrative Vice Minister of International Trade and Industry*
*Saburo Okita, *President, Overseas Economic Cooperation Fund*
Kiichi Saeki, *Director, Nomura Research Institute of Technology and Economics*
Kunihiko Sasaki, *Chairman, Fuji Bank, Ltd.*
*Ryuji Takeuchi, *Advisor to the Ministry of Foreign Affairs; former Ambassador to the United States*
Eiji Toyoda, *President, Toyota Motor Company, Ltd.*
Seiji Tsutsumi, *President, Seibu Department Store, Inc.*

Kogoro Uemura, *Honorary President, Japan Federation of Economic Organizations (Keidanren)*
Tadao Umezao, *Professor of Ethnology, Kyoto University*
*Nobuhiko Ushiba; *Former Ambassador of Japan to the United States*
Jiro Ushio, *President, Ushio Electric Inc.*
Shogo Watanabe, *President, Nikko Securities Company, Ltd.*
*Takeshi Watanabe, *Chairman, Trident International Finance, Ltd., Hong Kong; former President, the Asian Development Bank*
Kizo Yasui, *Chairman, Toray Industries, Inc.*

Appendix 3
Council Directors, 1921-1975

Isaiah Bowman	1921-1950	Charles P. Howland	1929-1931
Archibald Carey Coolidge	1921-1928	Walter Lippmann	1932-1937
Paul D. Cravath	1921-1940	Clarence M. Woolley	1932-1935
John W. Davis	1921-1955	Frank Altschul*	1934-1972
Norman H. Davis	1921-1944	Philip C. Jessup	1934-1942
Stephen P. Duggan	1921-1950	Harold W. Dobbs	1935-1943
John H. Finley	1921-1929	Leon Fraser	1936-1945
Edwin F. Gay	1921-1945	John H. Williams*	1937-1964
David F. Houston	1921-1927	Lewis W. Douglas	1940-1964
Otto H. Kahn	1921-1934	Edward Warner	1940-1949
Frank L. Polk	1921-1943	Clarence H. Hunter	1942-1953
Whitney H. Shepardson	1921-1966	Myron C. Taylor	1943-1959
William R. Shepherd	1921-1927	Henry M. Wriston*	1943-1967
Paul M. Warburg	1921-1932	Thomas K. Finletter*	1944-1967
George M. Wickersham	1921-1936	William A. M. Burden*	1945-1974
Allen W. Dulles	1927-1969	Walter H. Mallory*	1945-1968
R. C. Leffingwell	1927-1960	Philip D. Reed*	1945-1969
George O. May	1927-1953	Winfield W. Riefler	1945-1950
Wesley C. Mitchell	1927-1934	David Rockefeller	1949-
Owen D. Young	1927-1940	W. Averell Harriman	1950-1955
Hamilton Fish Armstrong	1928-1972	Joseph E. Johnson*	1950-1974

301

Appendix 3

Grayson Kirk*	1950–1973	Zbigniew Brzezinski	1972
Devereux C. Josephs	1951–1958	Elizabeth Drew	1972
Elliott V. Bell*	1953–1966	George S. Franklin	1972
John J. McCloy*	1953–1972	Marshall D. Shulman	1972
Arthur H. Dean*	1955–1972	Martha R. Wallace	1972
Charles M. Spofford*	1955–1972	Paul C. Warnke	1972
Adlai E. Stevenson	1958–1962	Peter G. Peterson	1973
William C. Foster*	1959–1972	Robert O. Anderson	1974
Caryl P. Haskins*	1961–1975	Edward K. Hamilton	1974
James A. Perkins	1963	Harry C. McPherson, Jr.	1974
William P. Bundy	1964–1974	Elliot L. Richardson	1974–1975
Gabriel Hauge	1964	Franklin Hall Williams	1974
Carroll L. Wilson	1964	Nicholas deB. Katzenbach	1975
Douglas Dillon	1965	Paul A. Volcker	1975
Henry R. Labouisse*	1965–1974		
Robert V. Roosa	1966		
Lucian W. Pye	1966		
Alfred C. Neal	1967		
Bill D. Moyers	1967–1974		
Cyrus R. Vance	1968		
Hedley Donovan	1969		
Najeeb E. Halaby	1970–1972		
Bayless Manning	1971		
W. Michael Blumenthal	1972	* Directors Emeriti	

Bibliography

Abbreviations

FDRL — Franklin D. Roosevelt Library, Hyde Park, New York
HLWRP — Hoover Library on War, Revolution and Peace, Stanford, California
HSTL — Harry S. Truman Library, Independence, Missouri
JHUL — Johns Hopkins University Library, Baltimore, Maryland
MDLC — Manuscript Division, Library of Congress, Washington, D.C.
NUL — Northwestern University Library, Evanston, Illinois
PUL — Princeton University Library, Princeton, New Jersey
RG59 — Record Group 59, Records of the Department of State, National Archives, Washington, D.C.
SUL — Stanford University Library, Stanford, California
YUL — Yale University Library, New Haven, Connecticut

I. Personal Papers

Baldwin, Hanson W., Papers. Sterling Library, Yale University, New Haven, Connecticut.
Bowman, Isaiah, Papers. Johns Hopkins University Library, Baltimore, Maryland.

Davis, Norman H., Papers. Manuscript Division, Library of Congress, Washington, D.C.
Green, Joseph C., Papers. Princeton University Library, Princeton, New Jersey.
Hornbeck, Stanley K., Papers. Hoover Institution on War, Revolution and Peace, Stanford University, Stanford, California.
Hull, Cordell, Papers. Manuscript Division, Library of Congress, Washington, D.C.
Jessup, Philip C., Papers. Manuscript Division, Library of Congress, Washington, D.C.
Roosevelt, Franklin D., Papers. Franklin D. Roosevelt Library, Hyde Park, New York.
Sweetser, Arthur, Papers. Manuscript Division, Library of Congress, Washington, D.C.
Truman, Harry S., Papers. Harry S. Truman Library, Independence, Missouri.

II. Unpublished United States Government Records

Department of State, Decimal File, Record Group 59, National Archives, Washington, D.C.
Department of State, Harley A. Notter File, Record Group 59, National Archives, Washington, D.C.
Department of State, Leo Pasvolsky Office File, Record Group 59, National Archives, Washington, D.C.

III. Unpublished Court Records

Estate Records of the Corporation Court, Alexandria, Virginia. 1945.
Estate Records of the Orphans Court, Baltimore, Maryland. 1950.
Estate Records of the Probate Court of the United States District Court, District of Columbia. 1953, 1969.
Estate Records of the Superior Court, County of Los Angeles, California. 1947.

Bibliography 305

Estate Records of the Surrogate's Court, County of Nassau, New York. 1960, 1964.

Estate Records of the Surrogate's Court, County of New York, New York. 1943, 1966.

IV. United States Government Publications

United States. *Statutes at Large.* LIV 1939-1941. Part 1.

———. Department of State. *Foreign Relations of the United States 1941* (7 volumes). Washington, D.C., 1956-1963.

———. Department of State. *Foreign Relations of the United States 1942* (7 volumes). Washington, D.C., 1960-1963.

———. Department of State. *Foreign Relations of the United States 1945* (9 volumes). Washington, D.C., 1967-1969.

———. House of Representatives, Committee on Armed Services. *United States-Vietnam Relations 1945-1967.* 92nd Congress, 1971.

———. House of Representatives, Committee on Banking and Currency. *Commercial Banks and Their Trust Activities: Emerging Influence on the American Economy.* Staff Report for the Subcommittee on Domestic Finance. 90th Congress, 2nd Sess., 1968.

———. Senate, Committee on Government Operations. *Disclosure of Corporate Ownership.* 93rd Congress, 2nd Session, 1974.

———. Senate, Committee on the Judiciary, Internal Security Subcommittee. *Hearing,* Part 13. 87th Congress, 1st Sess. (July 27), 1961.

V. Council on Foreign Relations Publications

Documents

Council on Foreign Relations. *Studies of American Interests in the War and the Peace.* 1939-1945. (The War-Peace Studies) Northwestern University Library, Evanston, Illinois; Hoover Institution on War, Revolution and Peace, Stanford, California; Stanford University Library, Stanford, California.

306   Bibliography

1975a "The 1980's Project," March 7, 1975. Draft memorandum.
1975b "The 1980's Project: An Interim Report," June 1975. Draft memorandum.
1975d "Working Group on Macro-Economic Policy and International Monetary Relations." Working Paper, June 12, 1975.

Publications

Council on Foreign Relations
   1919 *Handbook.* New York.
   1922 *By-Laws with List of Officers and Members.* New York.
   1924 *By-Laws with List of Officers and Members.* New York.
   1937 *The Council on Foreign Relations: A Record of Fifteen Years.* New York.
   1938 *By-Laws with List of Officers and Members.* New York.
   1940 *Annual Report of the Executive Director.* New York.
   1943 *Annual Report of the Executive Director.* New York.
   1946a *Annual Report of the Executive Director.* New York.
   1946b *The War and Peace Studies of the Council on Foreign Relations, 1939-1945.* New York.
   1947a *Annual Report.* New York.
   1947b *The Council on Foreign Relations: A Record of Twenty-five Years 1921-1946.* New York.
   1948-1974 *Annual Reports.* New York.
   1975c *Annual Report.*

VI. Council Members and Leaders Interviewed

John Bennett	Council member	Sept. 23, 1972
David MacEachron	Deputy executive director	Sept. 26, 1972
A. William Loos	Council member	Sept. 28, 1972
William Diebold, Jr.	Senior research fellow	Sept. 29, 1972 Nov. 1, 1972
George S. Franklin, Jr.	Former executive director	Oct. 2, 1972 Nov. 17, 1972

Francis P. Miller	Former organizational director	Oct. 18, 1972
Richard J. Barnet	Council member	Nov. 13, 1972
Richard A. Falk	Council member	Nov. 14, 1972
Louis G. Cowan	Council member	Nov. 18, 1972
Henry M. Wriston	Honorary president	Mar. 28, 1973
Frank Altschul	Secretary	Mar. 29, 1973
Bayless Manning	President	Mar. 29, 1973
A. Doak Barnett	Council member	Apr. 2, 1973

VII. Letters to Authors

Bundy, William P. Editor, *Foreign Affairs*. September 17, 1975.
Mallory, Walter H. Former executive director of the Council on Foreign Relations. June 5, 1973; July 13, 1973.

VIII. Books and Articles

Abel, Elie
    1966 *The Missile Crisis*. New York.
Acheson, Dean
    1969 *Present at the Creation*. New York.
Africa Research Group
    1969 *The Extended Family*. Cambridge Mass.
    1970 *Africa Retort* (rev. edition of *The Extended Family*). Cambridge, Mass.
Agee, Philip
    1975 *Inside the Company: CIA Diary*. Harmondsworth, England.
Allen, Gary
    1971. *None Dare Call It Conspiracy*. Rossmoor, California.
Allen, Michael Patrick
    1974 "The Structure of Interorganizational Elite Cooptation: Interlocking Corporate Directorates," *American Sociological Review* 39 (June):393-406.

Allison, Graham T.
  1971 *Essence of Decision.* Boston.
Alperovitz, Gar
  1967 *Atomic Diplomacy: Hiroshima and Potsdam.* New York.
Angell, James W.
  1929 *The Recovery of Germany.* New Haven, Connecticut.
Armstrong, Hamilton Fish
  1971 *Peace and Counterpeace.* New York.
Armstrong, Hamilton Fish (ed.)
  1947 *The Foreign Affairs Reader.* New York.
Bain, H. Foster
  1927 *Ores and Industry in the Far East.* New York.
Bain, H. Foster and T. T. Read
  1933 *Ores and Industry in South America.* New York.
Baker, Newton D.
  1936 *Why We Went to War.* New York.
Ball, George W.
  1976 *Diplomacy for a Crowded World.* Boston.
Baltzell, E. Digby
  1958 *Philadelphia Gentlemen.* Glencoe, New York.
  1964 *The Protestant Establishment.* New York.
Barber, Joseph (ed.)
  1950 *American Policy Toward China.* New York.
Baran, Paul
  1957 *The Political Economy of Growth.* New York.
Barnet, Richard J.
  1968 *Intervention and Revolution.* New York.
  1972 *Roots of War.* New York.
Barnet, Richard and Ronald E. Müller
  1974 *Global Reach: The Power of the Multinational Corporation.* New York.
Barnett, A. Doak
  1971 *A New U.S. Policy Toward China.* Washington.
Barraclough, Geoffrey
  1975 "Wealth and Power: The Politics of Food and Oil," *The New York Review of Books* (August 7, 1975):23-30.
Barratt-Brown, Michael
  1972 *Essays on Imperialism.* Nottingham, England.
Beard, Charles A.
  1934a *The Idea of National Interest.* New York.
  1934b *The Open Door at Home: A Trial Philosophy of National Interest.* New York.

Bell, Daniel
1973 *The Coming of Post-Industrial Society.* New York.
Bergsten, C. Fred
1973 "The Threat from the Third World," *Foreign Policy* 11 (Summer):102-124.
Berle, A. A. and Gardiner C. Means
1932 *The Modern Corporation and Private Property.* New York.
Berle, Beatrice B. and Travis B. Jacobs (eds.)
1973 *Navigating the Rapids 1918-1971, From the Papers of Adolf A. Berle.* New York.
Birmingham, Stephen
1967 *Our Crowd.* New York.
Bottomore, T. B.
1966 *Classes in Modern Society.* New York.
Bowman, Isaiah
1922 *The New World: Problems in Political Geography.* New York.
1928 *The New World: Problems in Political Geography* (4th edition). New York.
Braden, Spruille
1953 "The Communist Threat in the Americas," *Vital Speeches of the Day* 19 (May 1):432-437.
Brandon, Henry
1973 *The Retreat of American Power.* Garden City, New York.
Braverman, Harry
1974 *Labor and Monopoly Capital.* New York.
Brown, Seyom
1974 *New Forces in World Politics.* Washington, D.C.
Brzezinski, Zbigniew
1974 "The Deceptive Structure of Peace," *Foreign Policy* 14 (Spring):39-55.
Bukharin, Nikolai I.
1925 *Historical Materialism: A System of Sociology.* New York.
Burden, William A. M.
1943 *The Struggle for Airways in Latin America.* New York.
Bushner, Rolland H.
1965 *American Dilemma in Viet-Nam: A Report on the Views of Leading Citizens in Thirty-Three Cities.* New York.
Byrnes, James F.
1947 *Speaking Frankly.* New York.
Campbell, John C.
1947 *The United States in World Affairs.* New York.

1948 *The United States in World Affairs.* New York.
Campbell, John Franklin
    1971 "The Death Rattle of the Eastern Establishment," *New York* (September 20):47ff.
Camps, Miriam
    1974 *The Management of Interdependence: A Preliminary View.* New York.
Canfield, Cass
    1971 *Up and Down and Around: A Publisher Recollects the Time of His Life.* New York.
Century Association
    1937 *Elihu Root.* New York.
Chace, James
    1973 *A World Elsewhere: The New American Foreign Policy.* New York.
Chadwin, Mark L.
    1968 *The Hawks of World War II.* Chapel Hill, North Carolina.
Chomsky, Noam
    1973 *For Reasons of State.* New York.
Clay, Lucius D.
    1950 *Decision in Germany.* Garden City, New York.
Clifford, Clark M.
    1969 "A Viet-Nam Reappraisal," *Foreign Affairs* 47 (July): 601-622.
Cohen, Bernard C.
    1963 *The Press and Foreign Policy.* Princeton, N.J.
    1973 *The Public's Impact on Foreign Policy.* Boston.
Cohen, Saul B.
    1963 *Geography and Politics in a World Divided.* New York.
Coolidge, Archibald Cary
    1908 *The United States as a World Power.* New York.
Cooper, Chester L.
    1972 *The Lost Crusade.* New York.
Cooper, Richard N.
    1973 *A Reordered World.* Washington, D.C.
Courtney, Phoebe
    1968 *America's Unelected Rulers: The CFR.* New Orleans.
    1971 *Nixon and the CFR.* New Orleans.
Crozier, Michel J., Samuel P. Huntington, and Joji Watanuki
    1975 *The Crisis of Democracy: Report on the Governability of Democracies to the Trilateral Commission.* New York.

Dahrendorf, Ralf
   1959 *Class and Class Conflict in Industrial Society.* Stanford, California.
Darby, Edwin
   1974 "A New Brain Trust to Tackle the Future," *Chicago Sun-Times* (February 24):79.
Dickson, Paul
   1971 *Think Tanks.* New York.
Diebold, William, Jr.
   1972 *The United States and the Industrial World: American Economic Policy in the 1970's.* New York.
Divine, Robert A.
   1965 *Reluctant Belligerent: American Entry into World War II.* New York.
   1967 *Second Chance: The Triumph of Internationalism in America.* New York.
Divine, Robert A. (ed.)
   1969 *Causes and Consequences of World War II.* Chicago.
Domhoff, G. William
   1967 *Who Rules America?* Englewood Cliffs, N.J.
   1970 *The Higher Circles.* New York.
   1972 *Fat Cats and Democrats.* Englewood Cliffs, N.J.
   1974 *The Bohemian Grove and Other Retreats.* New York.
   1975 "Social Clubs, Policy-Planning Groups, and Corporations: a Network Study of Ruling-Class Cohesiveness," *The Insurgent Sociologist* 5 (Spring special issue):173-184.
Domhoff, G. William and Hoyt B. Ballard (eds.)
   1968 *C. Wright Mills and the Power Elite.* Boston.
Donovan, John C.
   1974 *The Cold Warriors: A Policy-Making Elite.* Lexington, Mass.
Dooley, Peter C.
   1969 "The Interlocking Directorate," *American Economic Review* 59 (June):314-323.
Dulles, Allen W. and H. F. Armstrong
   1936 *Can We Be Neutral?* New York.
DuPont
   1974 *Annual Report.* New York.
Dye, Thomas R., Eugene R. DeClerq, and John W. Pickering
   1973 "Concentration, Specialization, and Interlocking Among Institutional Elites," *Social Science Quarterly* 54 (June): 8-28.

Dye, Thomas R. and L. Harmon Zeigler
 1970 *The Irony of Democracy: An Introduction to American Politics.* Belmont, California.
Eakins, David M.
 1966 "The Development of Corporate Liberal Policy Research in the United States 1885-1965." Madison. Univ. of Wisconsin Ph.D. Dissertation (history).
 1969 "Business Planners and America's Postwar Expansion," in *Corporations and the Cold War,* David Horowitz (ed.), 143-172.
Eisenhower, Dwight D.
 1963 *Mandate for Change, 1953-1956.* Garden City, New York.
Ellis, Howard S.
 1950 *The Economics of Freedom.* New York.
Ellsberg, Daniel
 1972 *Papers on the War.* New York.
Esthus, Raymond
 1971 "President Roosevelt's Commitment to Britain to Intervene in a Pacific War" in *America and the Origins of World War II, 1933-1941,* Arnold A. Offner (comp.).
Falk, Richard
 1975 "A New Paradigm for International Legal Studies: Prospects and Proposals," *The Yale Law Journal* 84 (April):969-1021.
Fehrenback, T. R.
 1967 *FDR's Undeclared War 1939-1941.* New York.
Feis, Herbert
 1930 *Europe the World's Banker.* New York.
 1942 "Restoring Trade After the War," *Foreign Affairs* 20 (January):282-292.
 1960 *Between War and Peace: The Potsdam Conference.* Princeton, New Jersey.
Feuerlein, Willy and Elizabeth Hannan
 1941 *Dollars in Latin America.* New York.
Fifield, Russell H.
 1963 *Southeast Asia in United States Policy.* New York.
Fitzgerald, Frances
 1972 *Fire in the Lake: The Vietnamese and the Americans in Vietnam.* New York.
Forbes
 1973 "Who Gets the Most Pay?" *Forbes* (May 15):225-262.

Foreign Affairs
  1922 *Foreign Affairs* 1:1.
Fortune
  1970 "Fortune's Directory," *Fortune* 81 (May):182-222.
Frank, Andre Gunder
  1967 *Capitalism and Underdevelopment in Latin America: Historical Studies of Chile and Brazil.* New York.
Galbraith, John Kenneth
  1967 *The New Industrial State.* New York.
Gardner, Lloyd C.
  1964 *Economic Aspects of New Deal Diplomacy.* Madison, Wisconsin.
  1970 *Architects of Illusion.* Chicago.
Gardner, Lloyd C. (ed.)
  1974 *American Foreign Policy, Present to Past: A Narrative with Readings and Documents.* New York.
Gardner, Lloyd C., Walter F. LaFeber, and Thomas J. McCormick
  1973 *Creation of the American Empire: U.S. Diplomatic History.* Chicago.
Gardner, Richard N.
  1969 *Sterling-Dollar Diplomacy: The Origins and Prospects of Our International Economic Order.* New York.
Garraty, John A. and Robert A. Divine
  1968 *Twentieth Century America: Contemporary Documents and Opinions.* Boston.
Gay, Edwin F.
  1932 "The Great Depression," *Foreign Affairs* 10 (July):529-540.
Geiger, Theodore
  1953 *Communism Versus Progress in Guatemala.* Washington.
Gelfand, Lawrence E.
  1963 *The Inquiry.* New Haven, Connecticut.
Gimbel, John
  1968 *The American Occupation of Germany.* Stanford, California.
Goulden, Joseph C.
  1971 *The Money Givers.* New York.
Gramsci, Antonio
  1971 *Prison Notebooks.* New York.
Granovetter, Mark S.
  1973 "The Strength of Weak Ties," *American Journal of Sociology* 78 (May):1360-1380.

Graubard, Stephen R.
 1973 *Kissinger: Portrait of a Mind.* New York.
Green, Mark J., James M. Fallows, and David R. Zwick
 1972 *Who Runs Congress?* New York.
Grew, Joseph C.
 1952 *Turbulent Era: A Diplomatic Record of Forty Years, 1904-1945.* 2 volumes. Boston.
Grundy, Kenneth W.
 1973 *Confrontation and Accommodation in Southern Africa.* Berkeley, California.
Halberstam, David
 1972 *The Best and the Brightest.* New York.
Halperin, Morton H.
 1974 *Bureaucratic Politics and Foreign Policy.* Washington, D.C.
Hamilton, Richard F.
 1972 *Class and Politics in the United States.* New York.
Hammond, Paul Y.
 1963 "Directives for the Occupation of Germany," in *American Civil-Military Decisions,* Harold Stein (ed.), 311-464.
Hance, William A.
 1958 *African Economic Development.* New York.
Hance, William A. (ed.)
 1968 *Southern Africa and the United States.* New York.
Harbaugh, William H.
 1973 *Lawyer's Lawyer: The Life of John W. Davis.* New York.
Harr, John Ensor
 1969 *The Professional Diplomat.* Princeton, New Jersey.
Hayter, Teresa
 1971 *Aid as Imperialism.* Harmondsworth, England.
Heaton, Herbert
 1952 *A Scholar in Action: Edwin F. Gay.* Cambridge, Mass.
Henderson, William
 1955 "New Nations of Southeast Asia," Headline Series #110, Foreign Policy Association. New York.
Henderson, William (ed.)
 1963 *Southeast Asia: Problems of United States Policy.* Cambridge, Mass.
Hodgson, Godfrey
 1973 "The Establishment," *Foreign Policy* 10 (Spring):3-40.
Hooker, Nancy H. (ed.)
 1956 *The Moffat Papers: Selections from the Diplomatic Journals of Jay Pierrepont Moffat.* Cambridge, Mass.

Hoopes, Townsend
　1969　*The Limits of Intervention.* New York.
Hoover, Calvin B.
　1965　*Memoirs of Capitalism, Communism, and Nazism.* Durham, North Carolina.
Horowitz, David
　1965　*The Free World Colossus.* New York.
　1969　"The Foundations," *Ramparts* (April, May):38ff., and 36ff.
　1971　"The Making of America's China Policy," *Ramparts* (October):41-47.
Huberman, Leo
　1936　*Man's Worldly Goods: The Story of the Wealth of Nations.* New York.
Hull, Cordell
　1948　*Memoirs.* London.
Hultman, Tami and Reed Kramer
　1975　"Secret Documents on Southern Africa Exposed," *Southern Africa* 8 (February):4-7.
Ike, Nobutaka
　1967　*Japan's Decision for War, Records of the 1941 Policy Conferences.* Stanford, California.
International Economic Relations
　1934　*Report of the Commission of Inquiry into Policy in International Economic Relations.* Minneapolis, Minn.
International Encyclopedia of the Social Sciences
　1968　"Stratification, Social," 15:288-337.
Iriye, Akira
　1967　*Across the Pacific: An Inner History of American-East Asian Relations.* New York.
Israel, Fred J. (ed.)
　1966　*The War Diary of Breckenridge Long.* Lincoln, Nebraska.
Jalée, Pierre
　1968　*Pillage of the Third World.* New York.
Jessup, Philip C.
　1938　*Elihu Root.* New York.
Jones, F. C.
　1954　*Japan's New Order in East Asia: Its Rise and Fall, 1937-45.* London.
Kadushin, Charles
　1974　*The American Intellectual Elite.* Boston.

Bibliography

Kalb, Marvin and Bernard Kalb
    1974 *Kissinger.* Boston.
Katona, George, et. al.
    1970 *Survey of Consumer Finances.* Ann Arbor, Michigan.
Keller, Suzanne
    1963 *Beyond the Ruling Class.* New York.
Kennan, George F.
    1947 "The Sources of Soviet Conduct," *Foreign Affairs* 25 (July): 566-582.
    1967 *Memoirs, 1925-1950.* Boston.
    1971 "Hazardous Courses in Southern Africa," *Foreign Affairs* 49 (January):218-236.
Kennedy, John F.
    1960 *The Strategy of Peace.* New York.
Kennedy, Robert F.
    1968 *Thirteen Days.* New York.
King, John Kerry
    1956 *Southeast Asia in Perspective.* New York.
Kirk, Grayson L.
    1947 *The Study of International Relations in American Colleges and Universities.* New York.
Kissinger, Henry A.
    1957 *Nuclear Weapons and Foreign Policy.* New York.
    1958 *Nuclear Weapons and Foreign Policy.* New York.
    1961 *The Necessity for Choice.* New York.
Koen, Ross Y.
    1974 *The China Lobby in American Politics.* New York.
Kolko, Gabriel
    1968 *The Politics of War.* New York.
    1969 *The Roots of American Foreign Policy.* Boston.
Kolko, Joyce and Gabriel Kolko
    1972 *The Limits of Power.* New York.
Kraft, Joseph
    1958 "School for Statesmen," *Harpers* (July):64ff.
Kuklick, Bruce
    1972 *American Policy and the Division of Germany.* Ithaca, New York.
LaFeber, Walter
    1972 *America, Russia and the Cold War, 1945-1971.* New York.
Langer, William L. and S. Everett Gleason
    1952 *The Challenge to Isolation, 1937-1940.* New York.
    1953 *The Undeclared War, 1940-1941.* New York.

Laumann, Edward O., Lois M. Verbrugge, and Franz V. Pappi
   1974 "A Causal Modelling Approach to the Study of a Community Elite's Influence Structure," *American Sociological Review* 39 (April):162-174.
Lenin, V. I.
   1932 *State and Revolution*. New York.
   1939 *Imperialism: The Highest Stage of Capitalism*. New York.
Leopold, Richard W.
   1962 *The Growth of American Foreign Policy*. New York.
Lerner, Michael P.
   1973 *The New Socialist Revolution*. New York.
Levin, N. Gordon, Jr.
   1968 *Woodrow Wilson and World Politics*. New York.
Lewellen, Wilbur G.
   1971 *The Ownership Income of Management*. New York.
Link, Arthur S.
   1963 *American Epoch: A History of the United States Since the 1890's*. 3 volumes. New York.
Lippmann, Walter
   1934 "Self-Sufficiency: Some Random Reflections," *Foreign Affairs* 12 (January):207-215.
Luce, Henry R.
   1941 "The American Century," *Life* 10 (February 17):61-65.
Lukas, J. Anthony
   1971 "The Council on Foreign Relations—Is It a Club? Seminar? Presidium? 'Invisible Government'?," *New York Times Magazine* (November 21):34ff.
Lundberg, Ferdinand
   1938 *America's 60 Families*. New York.
   1968 *The Rich and the Super-Rich*. New York.
Magdoff, Harry
   1969 *The Age of Imperialism*. New York.
Mandel, Ernest
   1968 *Marxist Economic Theory*. 2 volumes. New York.
Marchetti, Victor and John D. Marks
   1974 *The CIA and the Cult of Intelligence*. New York.
Marlowe, John
   1972 *Cecil Rhodes: The Anatomy of Empire*. London.
Marx, Karl
   1963 *The Eighteenth Brumaire of Louis Bonaparte*. New York.
   1964 *Class Struggles in France, 1848-1850*. New York.
   1967 *Capital, A Critique of Political Economy*. New York.

Matthews, Donald R.
  1954 *The Social Background of Political Decision-Makers.* Boston.
May, Ernest R.
  1968 *American Imperialism.* New York.
Mayer, Arno J.
  1959 *Political Origins of the New Diplomacy.* New York.
  1967 *Politics and Diplomacy of Peacemaking.* New York.
Mennis, Bernard
  1971 *American Foreign Policy Officials.* Columbus, Ohio.
Menshikov, S.
  1969 *Millionaires and Managers.* Moscow.
Merrill, John C.
  1968 *The Elite Press.* New York.
Miliband, Ralph
  1969 *The State in Capitalist Society.* New York.
Miller, Francis P.
  1971 *Man from the Valley.* Chapel Hill, North Carolina.
Minter, William
  1973a "The Council on Foreign Relations: A Case Study in the Societal Bases of Foreign Policy Formation." Univ. of Wisconsin Ph.D. Dissertation (sociology).
  1973b *Portuguese Africa and the West.* New York.
Mitchell, J. Clyde (ed.)
  1969 *Social Networks in Urban Situations.* Manchester.
Monroe, Elizabeth
  1970 "The Round Table and the Middle East Peace Settlement, 1917-22," *The Round Table* 60 (November):479-490.
Moodys
  1975a *Bank and Finance Manual.* New York.
  1975b *Industrial Manual.* Volume II. New York.
Moore, Stanley W.
  1957 *The Critique of Capitalist Democracy.* New York.
Morgenthau, Henry, Jr.
  1945 *Germany Is Our Problem.* New York.
Morris, George
  1967 *The CIA and American Labor.* New York.
Murphy, Robert
  1964 *Diplomat Among Warriors.* New York.
NACLA (North American Congress on Latin America)
  1969 *The University-Military Complex.* New York.
  1970 *Subliminal Warfare: The Role of Latin American Studies.* New York.

1971 *Yanqui Dollar: The Contribution of U.S. Private Investment to Underdevelopment in Latin America.* New York.
1972 "Secret Memos from ITT," *NACLA's Latin America & Empire Report* (April).
1974 "Argentina: AIFLD Losing Its Grip," *NACLA's Latin America & Empire Report* (November).

National Council of Churches
1973 Corporate Information Center, *Church Investments, Corporations and Southern Africa.* New York.

Network Project
1973 *Directory of the Networks.* New York.

Nicolson, Harold
1934 *Peacemaking 1919.* London.

Nielsen, Waldemar A.
1965 *African Battleline.* New York.
1969 *The Great Powers and Africa.* New York.
1972 *The Big Foundations.* New York.

Nimocks, Walter
1968 *Milner's Young Men: The "Kindergarten" in Edwardian Imperial Affairs.* Durham, North Carolina.

Nixon, Edgar B. (ed.)
1969 *Franklin D. Roosevelt and Foreign Affairs.* Cambridge, Mass.

Nixon, Richard M.
1967 "Asia After Viet-Nam," *Foreign Affairs* 46 (October): 111-125.

Notter, Harley
1949 *Postwar Foreign Policy Preparation, 1939-1945.* Washington, D.C.

O'Connor, James
1973 *The Fiscal Crisis of the State.* New York.

Offner, Arnold A. (comp.)
1971 *America and the Origins of World War Two, 1933-1941.* Boston.

Ossowski, Stanislaw
1963 *Class Structure in the Social Consciousness.* New York.

Parenti, Michael (ed.)
1971 *Trends and Tragedies in American Foreign Policy.* Boston.

Parrini, Carl P.
1969 *Heir to Empire: United States Economic Diplomacy 1916-1923.* Pittsburgh, Pennsylvania.

Pasymowki, Eugene and Carl Gilbert
1971 "Bilderberg: The Cold War Internationale," *Congressional Record* 117 (September 15):32051-32060.

Paterson, Thomas G.
    1973 *Soviet-American Confrontation: Postwar Reconstruction and the Origins of the Cold War.* Baltimore.
    1974 *The Origins of the Cold War* (2nd edition). Lexington, Mass.
Payer, Cheryl
    1974 *The Debt Trap: The IMF and the Third World.* New York.
Pentagon Papers
    1971-1972 *Defense Department History of United States Decision-Making of Vietnam.* The Senator Gravel edition. 5 volumes. Boston.
Perlo, Victor
    1957 *The Empire of High Finance.* New York.
Perrucci, Robert and Marc Pilisuk
    1970 "Leaders and Ruling Elites: The Interorganizational Bases of Community Power," *American Sociological Review* 35 (December):1040-1057.
Pierson, George W.
    1969 *The Education of American Leaders.* New York.
Politics and Society
    1974 Volume 4, no. 2 (Winter).
Poulantzas, Nicos
    1970 *Pouvoir politique et classes sociales de l'état capitaliste.* Paris.
Prewitt, Kenneth and Alan Stone
    1973 *The Ruling Elites: Elite Theory, Power and American Democracy.* New York.
Price, Hoyt and Carl E. Schorske
    1947 *The Problems of Germany.* New York.
Projector, Dorothy S. and Gertrude S. Weiss
    1966 *Survey of Financial Characteristics of Consumers.* Washington, D.C.
Quigley, Carroll
    1966 *Tragedy and Hope.* New York.
Radosh, Ronald
    1969 *American Labor and United States Foreign Policy.* New York.
Ratchford, B. U. and W. D. Ross
    1947 *Berlin Reparations Assignment.* Chapel Hill, North Carolina.
Reischauer, Edwin O.
    1973 *Toward the 21st Century: Education for a Changing World.* New York.
Roberts, Henry L. and Paul A. Wilson
    1953 *Britain and the United States: Problems in Cooperation.* New York.

Roberts, Henry L.
　1956　*Russia and America: Dangers and Prospects.* New York.
Rockefeller Brothers Fund
　1961　*Prospects for America.* Garden City, New York.
Roosevelt, Franklin D.
　1941　"Defense and the Far East," *Vital Speeches of the Day,* 7 (August 15):649-650.
　1972　*Complete Presidential Press Conferences.* 25 volumes. New York
Rothwell, Victor Howard
　1971　*British War Aims and Peace Diplomacy, 1914-1918.* Oxford, England.
Royal Institute of International Affairs
　1956　*Four-Power Control in Germany and Austria.* London.
Russell, Ruth B.
　1958　*A History of the United Nations Charter: The Role of the United States, 1940-1945.* Washington, D.C.
Russett, Bruce M.
　1972　*No Clear and Present Danger: A Skeptical View of the United States Entry into World War II.* New York.
Sanderson, John B.
　1969　*An Interpretation of the Political Ideas of Marx and Engels.* London.
Schlesinger, Arthur M., Jr.
　1965　*A Thousand Days.* Boston.
Schrag, Peter
　1974　*Test of Loyalty: Daniel Ellsberg and the Rituals of Secret Government.* New York.
Schriftgiesser, Karl
　1960　*Business Comes of Age.* New York.
　1967　*Business and Public Policy.* Englewood Cliffs, New Jersey.
Schroeder, Paul W.
　1958　*The Axis Alliance and Japanese-American Relations, 1941.* Ithaca, New York.
Schurmann, Franz
　1974　*The Logic of World Power: An Inquiry into the Origins, Currents, and Contradictions of World Politics.* New York.
Shepardson, Whitney H.
　1934　"Nationalism and American Trade," *Foreign Affairs* 12 (April):403-417.
　1942　*The Interests of the United States as a World Power.* Claremont, California.
　1960　*Early History of the Council on Foreign Relations.* Stanford, California.

Sherwood, Robert E.
   1948 *Roosevelt and Hopkins: An Intimate History.* New York.

Shoup, Laurence H.
   1974 "Shaping the National Interest: The Council on Foreign Relations, the Department of State, and the Origins of the Postwar World, 1939-1943." Evanston, Illinois. Northwestern University. Ph.D. Dissertation (history).

Skolnick, Jerome H. and Elliott Currie
   1973 *Crisis in American Institutions.* Boston.

Smith, David N.
   1974 *Who Rules the Universities? An Essay in Class Analysis.* New York.

Smith, Gaddis
   1965 *American Diplomacy During the Second World War, 1941-1945.* New York.

Smith, James, Stephen Franklin and Douglas Wion
   1973 *The Concentration of Financial Assets in the United States.*

Smoot, Dan
   1962 *The Invisible Government.* Boston.

Social Register Association
   1920 *Social Register Locator, 1920.* XIII. New York.

Sonquist, John and Thomas Koenig
   1975 "Interlocking Directorates in the Top U.S. Corporations: A Graph Theory Approach," *The Insurgent Sociologist* 5 (Spring special issue):196-230.

Staley, Eugene
   1937 *Raw Materials in Peace and War.* New York.

Stanley, David T., Dean E. Mann, and Jameson W. Doig
   1967 *Men Who Govern: A Biographical Profile of Federal Political Executives.* Washington.

Statistical Abstract of the United States
   1972 Washington, D.C.

Steele, A. T.
   1966 *The American People and China.* New York.

Stimson, Henry L.
   1936 *The Far Eastern Crisis.* New York.

Stimson, Henry L. and McGeorge Bundy
   1947 *On Active Service in Peace and War.* New York.

Talese, Gay
   1969 *The Kingdom and the Power.* New York.

Tanzer, Lester (ed.)
   1961 *The Kennedy Circle.* Washington, D.C.

Taylor, Maxwell D.
  1972 *Swords and Plowshares.* New York.
Temperly, H. W. V. (ed.)
  1920 *A History of the Peace Conference of Paris.* London.
Thomas, John N.
  1974 *The Institute of Pacific Relations: Asian Scholars and American Politics.* Seattle, Washington.
Thomson, James C., Jr.
  1967 "Dragon Under Glass: Time for a New China Policy," *Atlantic* 220 (October):55-61.
  1974 "Getting Out and Speaking Out," *Foreign Policy* 13 (Winter):49-70.
Toynbee, Arnold
  1970 "Was Britain's Abdication Folly?," *The Round Table* 60 (April):219-229.
Trilateral Commission, the
  1973a *The Trilateral Commission.* Memorandum, March 15, 1973. New York.
  1973b *The Crisis of International Cooperation.* Triangle Paper 2 (October). New York.
  1973c Memorandum from Zbigniew Brzezinski. September 18, 1973.
  1973d *The Trilateral Commission: A Private American-European-Japanese Initiative on Matters of Common Concern.* New York.
  1974a *Energy: A Strategy for International Action.* Triangle Paper 6 (December). New York.
  1974b *Energy: The Imperative for a Trilateral Approach.* Triangle Paper 5 (June). New York.
  1974c *A Turning Point in North-South Economic Relations.* Triangle Paper 3 (June). New York.
  1974d *Trialogue* 6 (Winter). New York.
  1974e *Trialogue* 5 (May-July). New York.
  1975a *Trialogue* 7 (Summer). New York.
  1975b *Trialogue* 8 (Fall). New York.
  1975c *OPEC, The Trilateral World, and the Developing Countries: New Arrangements for Cooperation, 1976-1980.* Triangle Paper 7. New York.
  1975d *Trialogue* 9 (Winter). New York.
  1976a *Trialogue* 10 (Spring). New York.
Truman, Harry S.
  1955 *Memoirs.* New York.

Tugendhat, Christopher
 1971 *The Multinationals.* London.
Tully, Andrew
 1962 *CIA: The Inside Story.* New York.
United States Steel
 1973 *Annual Report.* New York.
Vernon, Raymond
 1971 *Sovereignty at Bay.* New York.
Villarejo, Don
 1962 *Stock Ownership and the Control of Corporations.* Detroit.
Viner, Jacob, et al.
 1945 *The United States in a Multi-National Economy.* New York.
Watt, David
 1970 "The Foundation of the Round Table," *The Round Table* 60 (November):425-433.
Weinstein, James
 1968 *The Corporate Ideal in the Liberal State.* Boston.
Welles, Sumner
 1951 *Seven Decisions that Shaped History.* New York.
White, Theodore H.
 1965 *The Making of the President 1964.* New York.
Wilkins, Mira
 1974 *The Maturing of Multinational Enterprise: American Business Abroad from 1914-1970.* Cambridge, Mass.
Williams, William Appleman
 1972 *The Tragedy of American Diplomacy.* New York.
Wilson, Theodore A.
 1969 *The First Summit: Roosevelt and Churchill at Placentia Bay 1941.* Boston.
Wise, David and Thomas B. Ross
 1964 *The Invisible Government.* New York.
Wolfe, Alan
 1974 "New Directions in the Marxist Theory of Politics," *Politics and Society* 4 (Winter):131-160.
Wrigley, Gladys M.
 1951 "Isaiah Bowman," *Geographical Review* 41 (January):7-65.
Ydigoras Fuentes, Miguel
 1963 *My War with Communism.* Englewood Cliffs, New Jersey.
Young, John P.
 1950 "Developing Plans for an International Monetary Fund and a World Bank," *Department of State Bulletin* 23 (November): 778-790.

Zeitlin, Maurice
    1974 "Corporate Ownership and Control: The Large Corporation and the Capitalist Class," *American Journal of Sociology* 79 (March):1073-1119.

Zeitlin, Maurice (ed.)
    1970 *American Society, Inc.* Chicago.

Zeitlin, Maurice, Lynda Ann Ewen and Richard Earl Ratcliff
    1974 "New Princes for Old? The Large Corporation and the Capitalist Class in Chile," *American Journal of Sociology* 80 (July):87-123.

Zink, Harold
    1957 *The United States in Germany: 1944-1955.* Princeton, New Jersey.

Zimmerman, Mitch
    1972 *International Runaway Shop: Why U.S. Companies are Moving Their Plants Abroad.* San Francisco.

Index

Acheson, Dean, 44, 150-52, 169, 208, 234, 242-43, 246, 248
African-American Institute, 217
Agnelli, Giovanni, 262
Altshul, Frank, 37, 40, 91, 94, 108-9, 121, 197, 203
American Assembly, 71-72
Anderson, Robert O., 107
Angell, James W., 190, 194
Arbenz Guzman, Jacobo, 195-98
Armas, Castillo, 195
Armstrong, Hamilton Fish, 5, 17, 24, 32, 38, 45, 59, 91, 103, 119-20, 137, 149-52, 154-57, 159 61, 163, 190, 202, 226
Asia Society, 73
Atlantic Council, 73-74
Austin, Warren R., 154

Baldwin, Hanson W., 66, 120-21
Ball, George W., 64, 238-43, 246, 263-64, 275
Baran, Paul, 273
Barnet, Richard, 5, 46, 273
Barnett, Doak, 69, 209-11
Beard, Charles A., 24

Beebe, Frederick S., 67
Beer, George Louis, 13, 44
Bell, Elliott V., 107, 109
Bergsten, C. Fred, 69, 269-70
Berle, Adolph A., 145, 150-52, 169, 196
Bernard, Prince of the Netherlands, 80
Bilderberg Group, 80
Bingham, Jonathan, 66
Blum, Robert, 210-11
Blumenthal, W. Michael, 257
Bowles, Chester, 64, 227
Bowman, Isaiah, 22-23, 26-27, 32, 71, 118, 120, 122-23, 150-53, 155-61, 163, 169-71
Braden, Spruille, 196-97
Bradley, Omar, 242
Brandt, Willy, 43
Brinton, Crane, 121
Brookings Institution, 61, 69-70, 269
Brown, Harold, 269
Brown, Irving, 88
Brown, Jerry, 277
Brown, Seyom, 69

328 Index

Brzezinski, Zbigniew, 49, 107, 260-61, 263-64, 268, 270-71, 275
Bunche, Ralph, 64
Bundy, McGeorge, 40, 64, 79, 204-5, 237, 239, 242-43, 246
Bundy, William P., 45-46, 49, 239-41, 246
Burden, W. A. M., 67, 69, 108
Bush, George, 61
Business Council, 109-10
Byrnes, James, 192

Cabot, John Moors, 197-98
Campbell, John Franklin, 46, 68
Camps, Miriam, 264-66, 271-72
Canfield, Cass, 17
Carnegie Corporation, 30, 37, 63, 78-79, 95
Carnegie Endowment for International Peace, 16, 68, 71
Carter, Jimmy, iii, 275-76
Case, Clifford, 65
Case, Everett N., 208
Castro, Fidel, 42
Center for Inter-American Relations, 73-74
Century Association, 92, 103, 123
Century Group, 123-24
Chamber of Commerce of the U.S.A., 110
Chancellor, John, 68
Chiang Kai-shek, 207
Church, Frank, 44, 62, 65
Churchill, Winston, 143, 192
Clay, Lucius, 192, 194
Clayton, William L., 193
Clemenceau, Georges, 20
Cleveland, Harlan, 231
Clifford, Clark, 241-42, 246
Cohen, Benjamin, 121, 150-52, 157, 161, 165, 169-71
Colby, William, 61
Coleman, William T., 275

Committee for Economic Development, 92, 109-10, 257
Compton, Karl T., 33
Connally, Tom, 153
Coolidge, Archibald Cary, 14, 17, 19, 91
Coolidge, T. Jefferson, 198-99
Cooper, Chester L., 240
Cooper, Richard N., 257-58, 261, 264, 277
Cosmos Club, 87
Council on Foreign Relations
  Beginnings, 11-17
  and Capitalist Class, 85-111
  and China Policy (1969-1972), 207-12
  and Cold War, 31-35
  Committees on Foreign Relations, 30-31, 208, 232
  and Cuban Missile Crisis, 199-207
  Early Goals and Programs, 17-22
  and Elite Universities, 75-77
  Expansion after World War II, 35-45
  Financial Backing, 92-96
  and Foreign Policy Organizations, 68-75
  and Foundations, 77-80
  and German Policy (1944-1946), 189-95
  and Guatemala Intervention (1954), 195-99
  and Media, 66-68
  and Morgan Financial Interest Group, 103-8
  and Multinational Corporations, 96-100
  and 1980's Project, iii, 254-80
  and Post–World War II Planning, 28-31, 117-76
  Role between the Wars, 22-28
  and Trilateral Commission, iii, 254-80

and Rockefeller Financial Interest Group, 103-8
and Southern African Policy, 212-19
and U.S. Government, 58-66
and Vietnam War, 38, 45-50, 223-49
War-Peace Studies Project, 28-29, 32, 34, 117-76, 255-56
Cravath, Paul D., 16-17, 104-5
Cronkite, Walter, 44
Currie, Lauchlin, 121
Curtis, Lionel, 12-14

Davis, John W., 16, 31, 91, 104-6, 171, 193, 226
Davis, Norman H., 25-32, 104-6, 119-21, 124-25, 148-57, 161, 163-64, 166, 170-71
Dayan, Moshe, 43
Dean, Arthur H., 108, 209, 240, 242
Dean, Gordon E., 41, 200-201, 203
Dennett, Tyler, 132
Diaz-Alejandro, Carlos, 257
Diebold, John, 211
Diebold, William, Jr., 40, 156, 264
Dillon, Clarence, 86
Dillon, Douglas, 61, 63, 78, 86, 101, 108-9, 205, 242-43, 246
Doko, Toshio, 261
Donovan, Hedley, 67, 109
Douglas, Lewis W., 26, 67, 95, 123, 194, 226
Drew, Elizabeth, 49
Dukakis, Michael, 277
Dulles, Allen W., 5, 61-62, 91, 95, 107, 120-21, 190, 194, 196, 199, 210, 235, 237, 246
Dulles, John Foster, 5, 26, 95, 121, 197, 199, 201, 209, 235, 246, 248
Dunn, James C., 170-71
DuPuy, William G., 240

Eckstein, Alexander, 211
Eisenhower, Dwight D., 35, 37, 62, 71, 195-96, 235-37, 246
Eliot, George Fielding, 121
Elliott, Osborn, 67
Ellis, Howard, 35
Ellsberg, Daniel, 46
Emerson, Rupert, 226
Erhard, Ludwig, 43

Falk, Richard, 45-46, 49, 257-58
Feis, Herbert, 23, 26, 104, 150-52, 164, 169
Fifield, Russell H., 231-32
Finletter, Thomas K., 105, 121
Finley, John H., 66
Fishel, Wesley R., 240
Flanders, Ralph E., 121
Ford Foundation, 39, 41, 63, 77-79, 95-96, 210, 213, 217, 260
Ford, Gerald, 64, 275
Foreign Affairs, 4, 17-18, 20, 22, 24-27, 34, 37, 39, 44-45, 57, 63-65, 68, 91-94, 119, 194, 199-200, 202, 211, 217, 235
Foreign Policy, 68, 258, 263
Foreign Policy Association, 31, 70-72
Fortas, Abe, 242
Fosdick, Raymond B., 95, 208
Foster, William C., 109, 202
Frank, Andre Gunder, 273
Frankel, Max, 66
Franklin, George S., Jr., 37-38, 40, 106-7, 210, 227, 260
Fraser, Leon, 108, 121, 190
Fredericks, Wayne, 213-15
Frelinghuysen, Peter, 66
Fujino, Chujiro, 261
Fulbright, J. William, 44, 66, 233

Gaither Committee, 201-2
Gardner, Richard N., 275
Gavin, James, 203
Gay, Edwin F., 16-19, 25, 105-6, 110, 124, 174

Index

Gilpatric, Roswell, 204
Giscard d'Estaing, Valery, 276
Goldberg, Arthur J., 47, 242
Goldwater, Barry, 233
Graham, Katherine, 67
Green, Jerome D., 95
Green, Joseph C., 171
Griffith, William, 216
Griswold, A. Whitney, 121
Gunther, John, 121

Hackworth, Green H., 150-52, 170
Halaby, Najeeb, 107
Halberstam, David, 233, 239
Hamilton, Edward K., 257
Hamilton, Maxwell, 132
Hance, William, 215
Hansen, Alvin H., 120-21, 125, 167-69, 175
Harrar, George, 78
Harriman, Roland, 67
Harriman, W. Averell, 32-33, 62, 67, 108, 193, 214, 234, 239, 246
Hartke, Vance, 44
Hasegawa, Norishige, 261
Hauge, Gabriel, 101, 108-9, 240
Hawkins, Harry C., 145, 150-52
Heath, Edward, 43
Heinz, Howard, 93
Helms, Richard, 61
Hemphill, Alexander, 15
Henderson, William, 227, 230-31
Hepburn, Arthur, 171
Hill, Robert D., 198
Hochschild, Harold, 213
Hoffman, Stanley H., 257-58, 264
Holland, William L., 198, 225-26
Hoover, Calvin, 192-93
Hoover, Herbert, 23
Hopkins, Harry, 146
Hornbeck, Stanley K., 170-71
Hotta, Shoyo, 261
Hottelet, Richard C., 68

Houghton Family, 86
House, Edward M., 13, 120
Hudson Institute, 69-70
Hughes, Charles Evan, 171-72
Hughes, Thomas L., 68
Hull, Cordell, 26, 119, 125, 135, 142, 145-48, 150-53, 155, 157, 168, 170-71, 233, 246, 248
Humphrey, Hubert, 65
Huntington, Samuel P., 257-58, 261, 277

Inquiry, The, 13
Institute for Defense Analysis, 69-70
Institute of Pacific Relations, 208, 225
Interim Committee (on Atomic Bomb), 33
International Bank for Reconstruction and Development (World Bank), 139, 166-69
International Energy Agency, 276
International Monetary Fund (IMF), 139, 166-69, 274

Jackson, Henry, 44
Jalée, Pierre, 273
Javits, Jacob, 44, 65
Jessup, Philip C., 208, 227-28
Johnson, Joseph E., 71, 226, 230, 241
Johnson, Lyndon B., 43, 64, 213-16, 224, 232-33, 238-44, 247
Josephs, Devereux C., 38, 106

Kahn, Herman, 69, 240
Kahn, Otto H., 93, 108
Kalb, Bernard, 4
Kalb, Marvin, 4, 68
"Keidanren," 261
Kennan, George F., 34, 217
Kennedy, Edward, 44
Kennedy, John F., 40, 43, 62-64,

203-4, 213-15, 233, 237-38, 247
Kennedy, Robert, 205, 242
Keppel, Frederick P., 95
Kerr, Philip (Lord Lothian), 13
King, John Kerry, 229-31
Kirk, Grayson, 107, 156, 160
Kirkland, Joseph Lane, 88
Kissinger, Henry A., 5, 41-42, 65, 89, 200-201, 203, 210-12, 218, 239, 245, 247-48, 263-64, 269, 275
Knox, Frank, 146, 247
Kono, Kumihiko, 261
Kraft, Joseph, 35, 194

Lamont, Thomas W., 13, 17-18, 94, 105
Langer, William L., 121
Lattimore, Owen, 121, 132, 141
Lawrence, David, 67
Leffingwell, Russell C., 91, 94-95, 104-6
Lehman, Mrs. Herbert, 94
Lehman, Robert, 199
Leith, C. K., 27-28
Lindsay, John, 59
Links Club, 87, 92
Lippman, Walter, 26
Lodge, Henry Cabot, 198, 239-40
Loudon, John, 262
Lovestone, Jay, 88
Lovett, Robert, 60, 63-64
Luce, Henry, 67, 176
Lukas, J. Anthony, 61

MacDonald, Gordon J., 257
MacEachron, David, 64
MacLaury, Bruce K., 257, 261
Maddox, William P., 156
Mallory, Walter H., 28, 38, 40, 91, 119-20, 125
Manning, Bayless, 48, 108, 254-55
Marcy, Carl, 66
Marshall, George C., 35

Marshall Plan, The, 35, 165
Martin, Graham A., 240
May, George O., 94, 105
May, Stacy, 123
Mazrui, Ali, 257
McCarthy, Eugene J., 242
McCarthy, Joseph R., 208
McClintock, John, 196, 199
McCloy, John J., 39-40, 59, 63-64, 79, 95, 105, 107, 193-94, 200, 202, 205, 239-40, 242, 247
McCone, John A., 61, 237
McCormick, Anne O'Hare, 150-52
McCoy, Frank L., 121
McGee, Gale W., 65
McGovern, George, 65
McHenry, Donald F., 218
McNamara, Robert S., 60, 63-64, 203-5, 247
Mellon Foundation, 260
Messersmith, George S., 119-20
Metropolitan Club, 87, 92
Miller, Frances P., 30, 123
Miller, Nathan L., 171
Mills, Ogden L., 26
Milner (Lord), 12-13
Mitchell, Wesley, 110
Mondale, Walter F., iii, 275
Morgan, House of, 103-6
Morgenthau, Hans J., 241
Morgenthau, Henry, Jr. (Morgenthau Plan), 33-34, 168, 191-94
Morton, Rogers, 275
Morton, Thruston B., 240
Mosely, Philip E., 40, 156-60
Moyers, Bill, 64, 107
Müller, Ronald, 273
Münchmeyer, Alwin, 262
Murrow, Edward R., 68

Nakamura, Toshio, 261
National Association of Manufacturers, 110
National Bureau of Economic Research, 110

332 Index

National Civic Federation, i, iv
National Committee on U.S.-China Relations, 210-11
National Foreign Trade Council, 110
National Industrial Conference Board, 110
National Planning Association, 71-72, 197, 199
Neal, Alfred C., 109
Ngo Dinh Diem, 237
Nielsen, Waldemar, 215-19
Nitze, Paul, 202, 204, 275
Nixon, Richard M., 43, 64-65, 207-8, 210-12, 224, 245, 247
Notter, Harley A., 151, 157-60, 170
Nye, Joseph S., 257-58, 264

Organization for Economic Cooperation and Development (OECD), 276
Organization of Petroleum Exporting Countries (OPEC), 270
Owen, Henry D., 69

Pasvolsky, Leo, 124-25, 131, 135, 145, 148-53, 155-60, 164-65, 169-71
Pell, Claiborne, 44, 65
Perkins, James A., 107, 202
Peterson, Peter G., 49
Peurifoy, John E., 196
Polk, Frank L., 104-5
Pratt, Mrs. Harold, 93
Pratt, William V., 121
Pye, Lucien, 210-11, 244

RAND Corporation, 69, 70
Rather, Dan, 44
Reed, Philip C., 106, 109
Reid, Ogden, 66
Reischauer, Edwin O., 263-64
Reston, James, 66
Reuther, Walter, 88
Rhodes, Cecil, 12-13

Rhodes Trust, 12
Richardson, Elliot, 245, 275
Riefler, Winfield W., 121, 123, 138, 166-67, 175
Roberts, Henry L., 39-40
Rockefeller Brothers Fund, 78-79, 201-2, 217
Rockefeller, David, 5, 35, 37-38, 46, 61, 78, 80, 94, 96, 106-7, 202, 214, 217, 240, 260, 262-64, 275
Rockefeller Foundation, 63-64, 78-79, 95, 107, 119, 122, 208, 226, 260
Rockefeller, John D., II, 93-94, 106
Rockefeller, John D., III, 40, 73, 78, 106, 231
Rockefeller, Laurence, 202
Rockefeller, Nelson, 61, 78, 89, 106, 196, 248
Rockefeller, Rodman, 78
Roosa, Robert V., 107, 110, 211, 244, 261
Roosevelt, Franklin D., 25-27, 33, 118-23, 128, 133, 142, 146-47, 149-50, 153, 163, 167-68, 170-71, 175, 192-93, 225, 233, 247
Roosevelt, Theodore, 19
Root, Elihu, 15-16, 19, 23, 63, 88, 93, 95
Rostow, Walt W., 40, 64, 239, 247
Rothschild, Edmond de, 262
Round Table, The, 13-14
Round Table Groups, 12-13
Royal Institute of International Affairs (Chatham House), 14, 42, 226
Ruml, Beardsley, 27
Rusk, Dean, 40, 63-64, 209, 213, 237, 239, 247-48, 275
Russell, Lindsay, 15

Salisbury, Harrison, 66

Sasaki, Kunihiko, 261
Schlesinger, Arthur, Jr., 63-64, 237
Schmidt, Helmut, 43
Schorr, Daniel L., 68
Schrag, Peter, 4
Schuirmann, Roscoe E., 171
Scott, Hugh, 66
Scott, James Brown, 14
Scranton, William W., 275
Seligman, Eustace, 209
Senior Advisory Group on Vietnam, 240, 242-44
Sharp, Walter R., 156, 158-60
Shepardson, Whitney H., 13-15, 19, 26-27, 91, 120, 123, 198
Shotwell, James T., 14, 121, 151, 174
Shulman, Marshall D., 49, 257
Slater, Joseph, 210
Smith, Gerard C., 260
Smith, Walter Bedell, 198
Sohl, Hans-Gunther, 262
Solomon, Richard H., 212
Spofford, Charles M., 35, 41, 106
Staley, Eugene, 121, 174-75
Stames, Stephen, 257
Standley, William H., 121-22
Stanton, Edwin F., 228-29
Stead, William T., 12
Steel, Ronald, 46
Stettinius, Edward R., Jr., 170-71
Stevenson, Adlai, 37, 203
Stimson, Henry L., 16, 23, 26, 28, 33, 59, 63, 146-47, 154, 193, 233, 247
Strong, George V., 121, 154, 164, 171
Sulzberger Family, 66
Symington, Stuart, 65

Talbot, Philips, 73
Talese, Gay, 66
Taylor, Maxwell D., 201-2, 239
Taylor, Myron C., 106, 150-53, 170-71

"Third Window," 277
Thompson, Robert G. K., 240
Thomson, James, 60
Trialogue, 277
Trilateral Commission, iii, 80, 260-62, 267-72, 275-77, 280
Truman, Harry, 33, 62, 193, 234-35, 247
Tuke, A. F., 262

Uemura, Kogoro, 261
Ullman, Richard H., 46, 49, 265
United Nations Association, 71-72, 217
University Club, 87, 92
Upgren, Arthur R., 125

Vance, Cyrus, 59, 64, 242-45, 247, 275
Viner, Jacob, 120-21, 138, 168, 175

Wallace, Henry A., 26
Wallace, Martha R., 49
Warburg, Paul M., 108
Warner, Edward, 123
Warnke, Paul, 64, 275
Warren, Charles, 28
Watson Family, 86, 94
Weinstein, James, i, iv
Welles, Sumner, 119, 125, 142, 148-53, 155-56, 160, 163, 170, 233, 247
White, Harry Dexter, 154, 168-69
White, Theodore, 4
Whiting, Alan S., 257
Whitney, John Hay, 86
Wickersham, George W., 15, 19
Willauer, Whiting, 197
Willets, Joseph H., 119
Wilson, Carroll L., 41, 48, 73
Wilson, Harold, 43
Wilson, Woodrow, 13
Winant, John G., 121
Wisner, Frank, 196
Woodcock, Leonard, 88

334 *Index*

Woodrow Wilson Foundation, 73, 93
World Affairs Councils, 111
World Order Models Project, 258
World Peace Foundation, 71
Wriston, Henry M., 31, 38, 40, 71, 89-90, 108, 226
Wriston, Walter, 90, 108

Wurf, Jerry, 88

Ydigoras Fuentes, Miguel, 198
Yost, Charles, 275
Young, Owen D., 106, 190

Zaibatsu, 261

About the Authors

Laurence H. Shoup received his Ph.D. from Northwestern University in 1974. He has taught United States history at the university level. He continues writing books.

William Minter is the editor of AfricaFocus Bulletin. He is the author of several books and many articles on African issues and U.S. policy.

Since this work was published in 1977, the Council on Foreign Relations has continued to play a key role in the formulation of an imperial foreign policy for the United States. The Council's 1980s Project, discussed in the final chapter of this book, was a major source of the corporate globalization policies faithfully followed by both Democratic and Republican administrations since the Carter Presidency. More recently, the Council played a central role in developing the consensus for invading Iraq within the higher circles of the United States power structure.

0-595-32426-6